D1760681

READERS' GUID C8 000 000 8:

CONSULTANT EDITOR: NICOLAS TREDELL

BIRMINGHAM LIBRARY SERVICES

DISCARD

Published

Lucie Armitt	George Eliot: *Adam Bede – The Mill on the Floss – Middlemarch*
Simon Avery	Thomas Hardy: *The Mayor of Casterbridge – Jude the Obscure*
Paul Baines	Daniel Defoe: *Robinson Crusoe – Moll Flanders*
Annika Bautz	Jane Austen: *Sense and Sensibility – Pride and Prejudice – Emma*
Matthew Beedham	The Novels of Kazuo Ishiguro
Richard Beynon	D.H. Lawrence: *The Rainbow – Women in*
Peter Boxall	Samuel Beckett: *Waiting for Godot – Endgame*
Claire Brennan	The Poetry of Sylvia Plath
Susan Bruce	Shakespeare: *King Lear*
Sandie Byrne	Jane Austen: *Mansfield Park*
Alison Chapman	Elizabeth Gaskell: *Mary Barton – North and South*
Peter Childs	The Fiction of Ian McEwan
Christine Clegg	Vladimir Nabokov: *Lolita*
John Coyle	James Joyce: *Ulysses – A Portrait of the as a Young Man*
Martin Coyle	Shakespeare: *Richard II*
Justin D. Edwards	Postcolonial Literature
Michael Faherty	The Poetry of W.B. Yeats
Sarah Gamble	The Fiction of Angela Carter
Jodi-Anne George	*Beowulf*
Jodi-Anne George	Chaucer: The General Prologue to *The Canterbury Tales*
Jane Goldman	Virginia Woolf: *To the Lighthouse – The Waves*
Huw Griffiths	Shakespeare: *Hamlet*
Vanessa Guignery	The Fiction of Julian Barnes
Louisa Hadley	The Fiction of A.S. Byatt
Geoffrey Harvey	Thomas Hardy: *Tess of the d'Urbervilles*
Paul Hendon	The Poetry of W.H. Auden
Terry Hodgson	The Plays of Tom Stoppard for Stage, Radio
William Hughes	Bram Stoker: *Dracula*
Stuart Hutchinson	Mark Twain: *Tom Sawyer – Huckleberry Finn*
Stuart Hutchinson	Edith Wharton: *The House of Mirth – The Custom of the Country*
Betty Jay	E.M. Forster: *A Passage to India*
Aaron Kelly	Twentieth-Century Irish Literature
Elmer Kennedy-Andrews	The Poetry of Seamus Heaney
Elmer Kennedy-Andrews	Nathaniel Hawthorne: *The Scarlet Letter*
Daniel Lea	George Orwell: *Animal Farm – Nineteen Eighty-Four*
Sara Lodge	Charlotte Bronte: *Jane Eyre*
Philippa Lyon	Twentieth-Century War Poetry
Merja Makinen	The Novels of Jeanette Winterson

Matt McGuire	Contemporary Scottish Literature
Timothy Milnes	Wordsworth: *The Prelude*
Jago Morrison	The Fiction of Chinua Achebe
Carl Plasa	Tony Morrison: *Beloved*
Carl Plasa	Jean Rhys: *Wide Sargasso Sea*
Nicholas Potter	Shakespeare: *Antony and Cleopatra*
Nicholas Potter	Shakespeare: *Othello*
Nicholas Potter	Shakespeare's Late Plays: *Pericles, Cymbeline, The Winter's Tale, The Tempest*
Steven Price	The Plays, Screenplays and Films of David Mamet
Andrew Radford	Victorian Sensation Fiction
Berthold Schoene-Harwood	Mary Shelley: *Frankenstein*
Nick Selby	T.S. Eliot: *The Waste Land*
Nick Selby	Herman Melville: *Moby Dick*
Nick Selby	The Poetry of Walt Whitman
David Smale	Salman Rushdie: *Midnight's Chidren – The Satanic Verses*
Patsy Stoneman	Emily Bronte: *Wuthering Heights*
Susie Thomas	Hanif Kureishi
Nicolas Tredell	F. Scott Fitzgerald: *The Great Gatsby*
Nicolas Tredell	Joseph Conrad: *Heart of Darkness*
Nicolas Tredell	Charles Dickens: *Great Expectations*
Nicolas Tredell	William Faulkner: *The Sound and the Fury – As I Lay Dying*
Nicolas Tredell	Shakespeare: *Macbeth*
Nicolas Tredell	The Fiction of Martin Amis
Matthew Woodcock	Shakespeare: *Henry V*
Angela Wright	Gothic Fiction

Forthcoming

Thomas P. Adler	Tennessee Williams: *A Streetcar Named Desire – Cat on a Hot Tin Roof*
Pascale Aebischer	Jacobean Drama
Brian Baker	Science Fiction
Stephen J. Burn:	Postmodern American Fiction
Sarah Haggarty and Jon Mee	William Blake: *Songs of Innocence and Experience*
Mardi Stewart	Victorian Women's Poetry
Nicholas Tredell	Shakespeare: *A Midsummer Night's Dream*
Michael Whitworth	Virginia Woolf: *Mrs Dalloway*
Gina Wisker	The Fiction of Margaret Atwood
Gillian Woods	Shakespeare: *Romeo and Juliet*

Readers' Guides to Essential Criticism
Series Standing Order
ISBN 1–4039–0108–2
(outside North America only)

You can receive future titles in this series as they are published by placing a standing order. Please contact your bookseller or, in the case of difficulty, write to us at the address below with your name and address, the title of the series and the ISBN quoted above.

Customer Services Department, Macmillan Distribution Ltd
Houndmills, Basingstoke, Hampshire RG21 6XS, England

Beowulf

JODI-ANNE GEORGE

Consultant editor: Nicolas Tredell

© Jodi-Anne George 2010

All rights reserved. No reproduction, copy or transmission of this publication may be made without written permission.

No portion of this publication may be reproduced, copied or transmitted save with written permission or in accordance with the provisions of the Copyright, Designs and Patents Act 1988, or under the terms of any licence permitting limited copying issued by the Copyright Licensing Agency, Saffron House, 6-10 Kirby Street, London EC1N 8TS.

Any person who does any unauthorized act in relation to this publication may be liable to criminal prosecution and civil claims for damages.

The author has asserted her right to be identified as the author of this work in accordance with the Copyright, Designs and Patents Act 1988.

First published 2010 by
PALGRAVE MACMILLAN

Palgrave Macmillan in the UK is an imprint of Macmillan Publishers Limited, registered in England, company number 785998, of Houndmills, Basingstoke, Hampshire RG21 6XS.

Palgrave Macmillan in the US is a division of St Martin's Press LLC, 175 Fifth Avenue, New York, NY 10010.

Palgrave Macmillan is the global academic imprint of the above companies and has companies and representatives throughout the world.

Palgrave® and Macmillan® are registered trademarks in the United States, the United Kingdom, Europe and other countries.

ISBN: 978–1–4039–9128–7 hardback
ISBN: 978–1–4039–9129–4 paperback

This book is printed on paper suitable for recycling and made from fully managed and sustained forest sources. Logging, pulping and manufacturing processes are expected to conform to the environmental regulations of the country of origin.

A catalogue record for this book is available from the British Library.

A catalog record for this book is available from the Library of Congress.

10 9 8 7 6 5 4 3 2 1
19 18 17 16 15 14 13 12 11 10

Printed and bound in Great Britain by
CPI Antony Rowe, Chippenham and Eastbourne

Contents

This section provides an overview of some of the most important critical debates surrounding the poem. Critics mentioned here include James Earle, R.D. Fulk and Christopher M. Cain, J.R.R. Tolkien, William Witherle Lawrence and Andrew Prescott.

This chapter begins by exploring the significance of 1705 to the history of the reception of *Beowulf*, and the significance of the librarian and antiquary Humphrey Wanley's Catalogue. Other topics include early editions and translations of the poem and critics' attempts to find possible analogues to it.

This chapter examines the types of interpretative approaches that began to replace the musings of the early philologists and editors of *Beowulf*. A great deal of the scholarship produced in the three decades covered here focuses on the possible sources of the Old English poem (both Classical and Scandinavian). During this period there were also ongoing discussions of the genre of *Beowulf* and attempts to establish the exact relationship between the text's Christian and pagan elements.

This chapter focuses on J.R.R. Tolkien's groundbreaking essay 'The Monsters and the Critics' and early attempts to read *Beowulf* as a *poem*. Critical approaches to the 'monsters' are also discussed, along with the question of whether *Beowulf* is divided into two or three sections.

The two decades under consideration in this chapter were important years for *Beowulf* criticism. A wide variety of new approaches to the poem emerged and familiar themes and subjects were revisited in fresh and interesting ways. In the light of Tolkien's earlier study, more criticism on the 'monsters' in *Beowulf* was being produced and the historicity of Beowulf himself was debated. The composition and role of the poem's original audience also came under the critical spotlight. And, by the mid-1960s, the New Criticism even began to assert its influence in the field.

CHAPTER FIVE   66

Stock-taking: the 1970s

This chapter covers a time when the landscape of *Beowulf* scholarship was rapidly changing. Feminist criticism of the poem began to emerge, and there were ongoing attempts to define what, exactly, *Beowulf* was about. Critical approaches to the Christian–pagan tension in the poem are also examined, as well as opinions concerning the poet's attitude towards his hero.

CHAPTER SIX   84

Critics on the Crest of a Wave: the 1980s

This chapter foregrounds approaches to the poem drawn from deconstruction, semiotics, cultural studies, feminism, masculinity studies and psychoanalysis in an attempt, as Seth Lerer puts it, 'to relocate *Beowulf* in the shifting canons of contemporary academic debate'.

CHAPTER SEVEN   97

An Embarrassment of Critical Riches: the 1990s to the present

Scholars during this period were especially prolific, as this chapter sets out to show. Historicist, anthropological, sociological and post-colonial readings of *Beowulf* are examined here. Also included are discussions of humour in the poem and its relationship to orality and the genre of *Beowulf*.

CHAPTER EIGHT   115

Beowulf in Popular Culture

This chapter provides a brief survey of some of the novels, films, animations, musical pieces, retellings for children, comic books and graphic novels based (faithfully or otherwise) on *Beowulf*.

Acknowledgements

I should like to thank the following: the Carnegie Trust for the Universities of Scotland for the generous support they gave me for this project, and Dr Chris Murray for sharing his encyclopaedic knowledge of graphic novels and comics. My greatest debt of gratitude, however, goes to Dr Brian Hoyle. Without his help and kindness this book would never have been completed. Thanks also to Dr Jim Stewart for the index.

The author and publisher wish to thank the following for use of copyright material:

HarperCollins Publishers Ltd, for excerpts from '*Beowulf*: The Monsters and the Critics', from *The Monsters and the Critics* by J.R.R. Tolkien. Reprinted by permission of HarperCollins Publishers Ltd. © J.R.R. Tolkien, 1936.

Houghton Mifflin Harcourt, for excerpts from '*Beowulf*: The Monsters and the Critics', from *The Monsters and the Critics* by J.R.R. Tolkien. Copyright © 1983 by Frank Richard Williamson and Christopher Reuel Tolkien as executors of the estate of J.R.R. Tolkien. Reprinted by permission of Houghton Mifflin Company. All rights reserved.

Every effort has been made to trace the copyright holders but if any have been inadvertently overlooked the publishers will be pleased to make the necessary arrangements at the first opportunity.

A Note about Dates

Wherever possible, dates have been given for authors and other significant figures, and for titles when they are first mentioned in the guide. In some cases, however, dates were unavailable.

INTRODUCTION

Hwæt!

In his *Thinking about Beowulf* (1994), James W. Earl confesses that:

■ I no longer trust those who say they know what *Beowulf* means, or even what it is about. The poem is hedged about with so many uncertainties – historical, textual, linguistic, hermeneutic [interpretive or explanatory] – that even the simplest and most straightforward statements can provoke a battle royal among scholars [...] Thus the analysis of the poem is endless.[1] □

Whilst in the opening remarks of this guide it is clearly too early to suggest whether or not Earl's statement represents the last word on *Beowulf*, it does establish a number of important facts about the Old English poem: it is enigmatic, incites contentious debate and is endlessly interpreted. These very characteristics more than explain why the body of criticism devoted to *Beowulf* is so large, and why it appears to grow almost daily. It goes without saying that '*Beowulf* is the work of Old English literature that has prompted, by far, the most intensive study.'[2] Because of this, the selection process for this guide has been long and painstaking. Part of the reason for the Old English poem's lasting popularity has to do, of course, with the very 'uncertainties' enumerated above (ones to which we will return throughout the course of this guide). To Earl's list we must also add a number of other questions surrounding the poem, ones that have been perpetually addressed by scholars throughout the history of *Beowulf* criticism. How, for example, do we define the genre of the poem? Many have predictably classified it as a heroic epic, whilst others argue, at least in part, for its status as a romance or even a heroic elegy. And, as we shall see, the debate does not stop there. As a tantalising taster of things to come, here is what Bertha S. Philpotts had to say in 1928 on the subject in her article 'Wyrd and Providence in Anglo-Saxon Thought':

■ for amid the multiplicity of theories about that poem there is unanimity on one point, and that is that the subject-matter of the poem is an anomaly. We certainly know of no other heroic poem which turns wholly on the slaying of monsters.[3] □

In addition, as R.D. Fulk and Christopher M. Cain point out in *A History of Old English Literature* (2003), *Beowulf* is also unique because:

■ The body of material in Old English verse devoted to native heroic legend is small – a mere speck in the corpus, actually, if *Beowulf* is removed from consideration. It could hardly be otherwise, since books were precious objects, the products of intense labor, and it is hardly to be expected that they should have been filled with matter unrelated to the sacred duties of the religious houses in which they were exclusively made. Germanic oral legend was in fact regarded by some as inimical [hostile] to religious devotion, as witnessed by the much-cited remark of Alcuin [Anglo-Latin cleric, scholar and poet] in regard to the practice of listening to heroic songs at the dinner table, *Quid Hinieldus cum Christo*? 'What has Ingeld to do with Christ?' This is in apparent reference to the Heothobard hero named at *Beowulf* 2064 and *Widsith* 48. The remark also reveals that some apparently saw no harm in such entertainments, and this doubtless explains why the few surviving scraps of Germanic legend found their way into manuscripts at all.[4] □

Another major talking point amongst critics concerns the relationship between the Christian and pagan beliefs simultaneously articulated in the poem. Theories abound here, though some were discredited rather early on. In 1928, for example, William Witherle Lawrence (1876–1958), in his oft reprinted volume *Beowulf and Epic Tradition*, argued that:

■ The older idea, that the Christian elements in *Beowulf* are interpolations [material inserted into a text] in an originally heathen poem, is now, as has already been suggested, generally abandoned. Careful study has shown no differences in style, metre, or dialect, such as would be likely to arise in the inserted sections. There is a possibility that some of the longer moralizing speeches are interpolated, but there is no direct proof of this.[5] □

There has also been endless speculation as to the exact nature of the 'monsters' in *Beowulf*. A major turning point in the history of scholarship devoted to this subject came with the publication of the now famous '*Beowulf*: The Monsters and the Critics' by John Roland Reuel (more commonly known as J.R.R.) Tolkien (1892–1973). This essay began life as a lecture and was, according to the poet Seamus Heaney (born 1939), the first critical account of the poem to argue that 'the *Beowulf* poet was an imaginative writer rather than some kind of backformation derived from nineteenth-century folklore and philology.'[6] Tolkien's piece was also the first contribution to *Beowulf* criticism that placed the monsters centre stage and argued for their symbolic significance. Tolkien stated, for example, that 'if the hero falls before a

dragon, then certainly he should achieve his early glory by vanquishing a foe of similar order [i.e. Grendel].'[7] Aside from identifying the
perfect symmetry at the heart of the poet's deployment of the monsters
in *Beowulf*, however, Tolkien also covers the same ground as James W.
Earl above when he notes the bewildering array of critical readings
of the poem. Tolkien speaks of *Beowulf* scholarship as a 'conflicting
babel',[8] and then wittily summarizes some of the divergent theories
advanced about the poem prior to 1936:

■ *Beowulf* is a half-baked native epic the development of which was killed
by Latin learning; it was inspired by emulation of Virgil [(70–19 BC), ancient
Roman poet, author of the *Aeneid*], and is a product of the education
that came in with Christianity; it is feeble and incompetent as narrative;
the rules of narrative are cleverly observed in the manner of the learned
epic; it is the confused product of a committee of muddle-headed and
probably beer-bemused Anglo-Saxons (this is a Gallic voice); it is a string
of pagan lays edited by monks; it is the work of a learned but inaccurate Christian antiquarian; it is a work of genius, rare and surprising in the
period, though the genius seems to have been shown principally in doing
something much better left undone (this is a very recent voice); it is a wild
folk-tale (general chorus); it is a poem of aristocratic and courtly tradition
(same voices); it is a hotchpotch; it is a sociological, anthropological, archaeological document; it is a mythical allegory (very old voices these and
generally shouted down, but not so far out as some of the newer cries); it
is rude and rough; it is a masterpiece of metrical art; it has no shape at all;
it is singularly weak in construction; it is a clever allegory of contemporary politics (old John Earle with some slight support from Mr. Girvan, only
they look to different periods); its architecture is solid; it is thin and cheap
(a solemn voice); it is undeniably weighty (the same voice); it is a national
epic; it is a translation from the Danish; it was imported by Frisian traders;
it is a burden to English syllabuses; and (final universal chorus of all voices)
it is worth studying.[9] □

Tolkien's somewhat tongue-in-cheek overview is particularly helpful
to readers coming to *Beowulf* criticism for the first time. It would be
difficult to find a more informed summary of the 'conflicting babel'
that was the scholarship of the poem in the early part of the twentieth
century. As such, many of the scholarly approaches that Tolkien alludes
to will be returned to throughout the course of this guide. Tolkien's
mention of 'old John Earle', for example, anticipates our discussion
in Chapter One of *The Deeds of Beowulf: An English Epic of the Eighth
Century, Done into Modern Prose* (1892, by John Earle (1824–1902)), and
the significance of the above reference to 'Mr. Girvan' will become
clear in Chapter Three when Ritchie Girvan's *Beowulf and the Seventh
Century: Language and Content* (1935) is examined. Tolkien's own essay

will also be revisited in Chapter Three, as this is where the major *Beowulf* criticism of the 1930s and 1940s will be addressed.

Before we can properly move on to our chronological examination of essential *Beowulf* criticism, however, a few things need to be remembered about the Old English poem. For example, like the majority of literary texts from the Anglo-Saxon age – a historical period lasting from approximately the fifth century until the Norman Conquest of 1066 – *Beowulf* is undatable and anonymous. In relation to this, S.A.J. Bradley in *Anglo-Saxon Poetry* (1982) points out that:

> ■ Only Cynewulf, as far as is known, took care to build into his poems an explicit identification of the 'I'-speaker of the narrative with himself, the author, by incorporating a signature in runes – and even of Cynewulf no certain historical documentation exists, so we can give him no sure dates. Otherwise, there is no named poet to whom a corpus of extant poetry in Old English can be assigned – neither Aldhelm, Bishop of Sherborne (died 709), nor Cædmon, recipient according to Bede [author of the *Ecclesiastical History of the English Nation*, 731], of a miraculous faculty for composing Christian poetry at Whitby between 657 and 680, both of whom have claims to be the first poet to treat Christian subject-matter in the English language.[10] □

Though Cynewulf is, as Bradley says, the only 'named poet to whom a corpus of extant poetry in Old English can be assigned', scholars have still repeatedly attempted to build up a plausible picture of the poet behind *Beowulf*. One such example is found in Signe M. Carlson's 'The Monsters of *Beowulf*: Creations of Literary Scholars' (1967). Carlson writes:

> ■ The Christian references in the poem have led scholars to believe that the *Beowulf* poet must have been a Christian. Since Grendel, his mother, and the dragon admittedly antedate both the poet and Christianity [Carlson argues elsewhere that these figures have their origins in folklore], Christian references to them are literary accretions [...] Except for a conscious effort to work Christianity into his poem, the *Beowulf* poet retold the history and folklore of his people as accurately as he could without the assistance of twentieth-century transcription techniques and devices.[11] □

Of course, any number of 'transcription techniques and devices' are used by scholars when studying Anglo-Saxon manuscripts. Extra help, however, is needed when it comes to the *Beowulf* manuscript (or, to give it its official name, Cotton MS. Vitellius A. xv) as sections of it were destroyed in a fire in 1731. The history of this manuscript is indeed an intriguing one, and Andrew Prescott, in his essay ' "Their Present Miserable State of Cremation": the Restoration of the Cotton

Library' (1997), offers one of the clearest and most interesting accounts of it. For readers of this guide, Prescott's discussion is invaluable and, as such, is worth quoting at some length:

> ■ In the British Library there is a manuscript, its edges scorched and brittle, of *Beowulf*, one of the very earliest poems in English and its first great literary masterpiece. It exists only in this one vellum codex [an ancient manuscript text in book form] and has survived for a thousand years, telling of an even earlier time, when the heroic age still was remembered by a Christian audience. □

As Prescott points out, the manuscript's origin was a mystery. It is first mentioned in 1563, and may have belonged to one of the monasteries that had recently been dissolved by Henry VIII. In due course it came into the possession of the antiquarian Sir Robert Cotton (1571–1631), forming part of a library that, augmented by his son and grandson, became the richest contemporary collection of Anglo-Saxon literary and historical documents. It comprised 14 bookcases of leather-bound volumes, 12 capped by a bust of one of the 12 Caesars, and the other two by Cleopatra and Faustina. The Beowulf manuscript was the 15th volume on the first shelf under the bust of Vitellius, and hence designated Vitellius A. xv.

The Cottonian library was willed to the British nation in 1700 and in the 1720s was re-housed in a supposedly safer home in Ashburnham House at Westminster. Within two years however, on 23 October 1731, a fire broke out. Despite the efforts of the trustees to carry the 958 manuscripts from the blazing building, throwing many out through the windows, 13 were destroyed and several hundred severely damaged by fire or water. Among those lost were a unique copy of *The Battle of Maldon* and Asser's *Life of Alfred* (Asser (died 909 or 910) was a monk of St David's who entered the household of King Alfred the Great (849–99; King of Wessex 871–99)). The leather cover of the *Beowulf* manuscript protected it, but it was burnt along its exposed edges (though, curiously, this damage was not mentioned at the time in the collection's catalogue).

When the British Museum was founded in 1753 it took over the collection. However, the *Beowulf* manuscript was left in its singed binding and the brittle pages gradually crumbled until the margins, and even some of the text itself, were lost forever. Prescott continues:

> ■ In 1786, some fifty years after the disastrous fire, G[rímur]. J[ónsson]. Thorkelin [1752–1829], an Icelandic scholar, came to the Museum, looking for documents relating to Denmark, where the first part of *Beowulf* takes place. He made two complete copies of the manuscript, the first time this

had been done, one by a professional copyist and the other, himself, and returned to Copenhagen to study them.

But then: calamity. Denmark was occupied during the Napoleonic Wars [1792–1815] and, in 1807, the English bombarded Copenhagen. Thorkelin's house burned and his manuscript for an edition of *Beowulf*, which just had been completed, was destroyed. The two transcripts were saved, however, and Thorkelin began his work over again, publishing the first printed edition of *Beowulf* in 1815.

The first English edition of *Beowulf* appeared in 1833, and, in its preparation, the manuscript was re-examined. It was discovered that the neglected volume had deteriorated even more and that many of the words Thorkelin had been able to decipher after the fire now were lost. Finally, in 1845, the British Museum took steps to preserve what remained. Each leaf was mounted on a paper frame and the manuscript rebound. Although this preserved the fragile edges, the paper and tape obscured some of the letters. Beginning in 1993, the manuscript has been re-examined and digitized as part of the Electronic Beowulf project and now is available on CD-ROM.

Almost two thousand letters have disappeared along the brittle edges. Were it not for Thorkelin's transcripts, which are in the Royal Library of Denmark, many of these lost words and letters could not have been restored. There are only three other major manuscript collections of Old English poetry that survive. One can imagine the thousands of pages that did not: the heroic epics, the chronicles, the religious and devotional works, the songs and tales of the Anglo-Saxon *scop* [poet].[12] □

Prescott takes us on a journey of a thousand years and more, chronicling along the way the hazardous history of the *Beowulf* manuscript from its inception (under still unknown circumstances) to its reincarnation in the shape of a CD-ROM. The vellum codex, which houses perhaps the greatest of Old English poems, has survived Viking raids, the Reformation, a fire and other, less violent, ravages of time. Looked at in this way, its survival seems nothing short of miraculous. But what of its preservation? Why, at some point around the year 1000, did someone believe that *Beowulf* was worth writing down in the first place? Karl Brunner, in 'Why was *Beowulf* Preserved?' (1954), argues that the Old English epic's 'Christian bent' is largely responsible for this longevity. He states that 'It is very likely due to this [...] and perhaps even to those Christian passages that the epic was long preserved and even alluded to in the *Blickling Homilies* [a large and incomplete collection of homilies written in Old English].'[13]

While this may have been partly true during the poem's early history, Brunner's theory does not go far enough to explain why *Beowulf* is still read and endlessly written about today. John D. Niles offers, I think, a more complex and wide-ranging answer in his essay 'Locating

Beowulf in Literary History' (1993). Niles summarizes here the various critical approaches down the ages that have been applied to the poem, invoking the concept of 'discourse' developed by the French thinker Michel Foucault (1926–84):

■ What I propose to ask is, 'What are the cultural questions to which *Beowulf* is an answer?' This perspective involves, among other things, looking upon Anglo-Saxon heroic poetry as a discourse, in Foucault's sense of a corporate means for dealing with a subject and authorizing views of it. Adopting this stance, we can inquire how the poetic tradition of which *Beowulf* is an example served as one important means by which culture defined itself, validated itself, and maintained its equilibrium through strategic adaptations during a period of major change.[14] □

Thanks in part to the impressive formalist scholarship of the past 50 years, we are accustomed to reading *Beowulf* as a superb work of art. The achievement of the broadly philological scholarship that has dominated the academies within living memory has been to create this poem as an aesthetic object worthy of minute critical inquiry. Structuralist rage for order, patristic [relating to the early Christian theologians or their writing] source hunting, and oral-formulaic analyses of patterned phrasing have indeed extended our knowledge of the text, its filiations and its internal systems of order. Paradoxically, the success of these forms of criticism may also have served to occlude our understanding of *Beowulf* as a socially embedded poetic act. As John Hermann has remarked: 'The problem is that it [the philological heritage] has been too successful; its very dominance keeps Old English studies from developing in new directions.'[15]

Like Hermann and some other youngish scholars, as well as some old-school scholars of a historical bent, I suspect that the issue of understanding a poem of this kind cannot be resolved by philological or aesthetic investigations alone. That is not to say that such inquiries, if well conducted, will not form the basis of our understanding. They will. But the underlying issue is ontological, not aesthetic. To paraphrase Leo Spitzer (1887–1960), what one wants to know is 'Why did the phenomenon of *Beowulf* happen at all?'[16]

This passage concludes by reiterating a compelling question, and one to which Niles provides something of an answer when he states that *Beowulf* and other poems of the same ilk 'served as one important means by which culture defined itself, validated itself, and maintained its equilibrium through strategic adaptations during a period of major change'. As it so happens, it is also the purpose of this guide, through a discussion of the essential criticism of the only extant epic in the vernacular from Anglo-Saxon England, to explore why *Beowulf* remains a literary and cultural 'phenomenon'.

In the following chapters of this guide, the history of *Beowulf* criticism will be charted chronologically, from its 'beginnings' in 1705 up until the present day. This unique history, however, is inextricably bound up with that of English literature in general. As Chris Jones reminds us, when the poet Ezra Pound (1885–1972) was taking courses in Old English at Hamilton College in upstate New York in the early years of the twentieth century, the majority of the syllabi would have been devoted to the study of grammar and the activity of translation.[17] This is largely due to the fact that, for a very long time, a debate raged over whether English (especially the study of English *literature*) was a legitimate subject for study at university level. A fascinating insight into the educational conditions of the time is found in William Benzie's *F.J. Furnivall, Victorian Scholar Adventurer* (1983):

■ The academic study of English as it is now pursued in schools, colleges, and universities has developed within only the last one hundred years. The Oxford English School, for instance, was not founded until 1893, and a chair of English language and literature was established in Cambridge only as recently as 1911. During much of the Victorian period, while Cambridge dons squabbled about the respectability of English studies and Oxford tangled with John Churton Collins [1848–1908], the fierce advocate of an English school there, the serious business of advancing and promoting English scholarship was in the hands of foreign scholars abroad, and private or professional scholars at home, working outside the university walls.[18] □

It was partly the study of philology – where an examination of the structure, historical development and relationships of a language or languages is paramount – which invested English studies with credibility. This is where Old and Middle English literature came into its own and (rather radically) crept onto university reading lists. Thus, the scholarly focus of a text like *Beowulf* was at first predominantly philological in nature. It goes without saying, however, that not everyone was pleased with this approach; John Churton Collins, for example, in his volume *The Study of English Literature: A Plea for its Recognition and Organization at the Universities* (1891) argued passionately against it:

■ Since its [English literature's] recognition as a subject of teaching it has been taught wherever it has been seriously taught on the same principle as the Classics. It has been regarded not as the expression of art and genius, but as mere material for the study of words, as mere pabulum [bland intellectual fodder] for philology. All that constitutes its intrinsic value as a liberal study has been ignored. Its masterpieces have been resolved into exercises in grammar, syntax, and etymology. Its history has been resolved into a barren catalogue of names, works, and dates. No faculty but the faculty of memory has been called into play in studying it.[19] □

The beginnings of *Beowulf* 'criticism' (if it can even be referred to as such in its early days) had its roots, as we shall see, in the 'barren catalogue' of philology and related fields. By the 1930s, however, the poem began to be read as an 'expression of art and genius'. From this stage onwards, a variety of approaches began to be applied to the poem. These ranged from formalist, structuralist, feminist, post-colonial and post-modern, to name but a few. In many ways, then, the history of *Beowulf* studies reflects the history of literary scholarship more generally, as this guide will implicitly demonstrate. The final chapter, however, will discuss the poem's equally vivid life outside the academy – its life in popular culture.

CHAPTER ONE

'Rude Beginning': 1705–1899

■ Poetry has been always classed among the most interesting productions of the human mind; and few topics of human research are more
curious than the history of this elegant art, from its rude beginning to that
degree of excellence to which it has long been raised by our ingenious
countrymen.[1] □

Signe M. Carlson, in 'The Monsters of *Beowulf*: Creations of Literary
Scholars' (1967), rather mischievously quipped that 'Since the *Beowulf*
poet is the earliest acknowledged scholar connected with the poem, we
should review his work first.'[2] As we have seen in the introduction to
this guide, however, there are no concrete facts about the *Beowulf* poet
and, as such, little can be said about the possible overall corpus of his
work. Readers, therefore, must be content to assign the 'rude beginning'
of *Beowulf* scholarship to the year 1705 (though some have argued for
1815 as the year in which the poem was rescued from obscurity).

JOHN EARLE

The significance of 1705 to the history of the reception of the Anglo-
Saxon epic was identified in the nineteenth century, for example by John
Earle in *The Deeds of Beowulf: An English Epic of the Eighth Century Done Into
Modern Prose* (1892). Douglas D. Short, in *Beowulf Scholarship: An Annotated
Bibliography* (1980), describes this volume as including 'an introduction
which features a detailed history of previous scholarship, a summary of
the poem, and [Earle's] own interpretation; *Beowulf* is a political allegory
written in the last quarter of the eighth century for the benefit of Ecgferth,
son of Offa [King of Mercia from 757–796].'[3] As stated above, Earle's summary of previous *Beowulf* scholarship included remarks concerning the
poem's re-emergence into the public consciousness (albeit of a fairly rar-
efied group) after years of obscurity; Earle discusses the significance in this
process of the librarian and antiquary Humphrey Wanley (1672–1726):

■ The existence of this poem [*Beowulf*] was unknown to the learned
world until the year 1705, when it was for the first time noticed in Wanley's

Catalogue of Anglo-Saxon Manuscripts. It is a good illustration of the wide differences between the poetry and the prose of our early period, that Wanley, who was able to give a very good account of a prose manuscript, was quite at a loss when examining the Beowulf [sic] [...] [H]e was very wide of the mark in supposing it to be a description of wars between Denmark and Sweden. It is the more to be deplored that his discovery should have been so imperfect, and his description so uninviting, as the Manuscript was at that time still entire, and so continued to be for twenty-six years after the appearance of Wanley's Catalogue. During this period a complete copy might have been taken, had Wanley's notice afforded any hint of the importance of the poem.[4] □

In the midst of his account of Humphrey Wanley's central role in the very earliest studies of *Beowulf*, Earle alerts us to a serious error contained in the Catalogue: it states that the poem was essentially 'a description of wars between Denmark and Sweden'. This does not say much for Wanley's ability to read Anglo-Saxon, though, in all fairness, not many people in the eighteenth century understood the language. Careful readers may also have noticed that Earle refers to '*the* Beowulf' (my italics). This was the title originally adopted for the poem, and it was in common usage until well into the twentieth century. J.R.R. Tolkien, for instance, in his '*Beowulf*: The Monsters and the Critics' of 1936 (see Chapter Three of this guide for a detailed discussion of this groundbreaking essay), makes implicit mention of this fact. For his own part, Tolkien referred to the epic simply as *Beowulf* and by so doing contributed to the emerging trend to drop the extraneous 'the'. Earle also alludes to something perhaps even more significant to *Beowulf* scholars, however, when he states that 'It is the more to be deplored that his discovery should have been so imperfect, and his description so uninviting, as the Manuscript was at that time still entire, and so continued to be for twenty-six years after the appearance of Wanley's Catalogue.'[5] What Earle is making reference to here is, of course, the fire of 1731 which partially damaged the unique copy of the poem and other texts collated within the same manuscript (see the introduction to this guide for a detailed discussion of the history of the *Beowulf* manuscript). To make matters worse, as Earle makes clear, no transcription of *Beowulf* in its entirety was made before this disaster struck.

GRÍMUR JÓNSSON THORKELIN

As stated above, 1815 marked another significant beginning in the study of *Beowulf*. In that year, Grímur Jónsson Thorkelin published the first edition of the poem (for a fuller discussion of Thorkelin and the *Beowulf* manuscript, see the introduction to this guide). Several years previously, in 1787, Thorkelin had commissioned a transcript of *Beowulf*. At a later date, he also transcribed the manuscript himself. On the basis of this edition *Beowulf* became much more widely known, especially as Thorkelin's text was written about by English and foreign reviewers alike. As time went on, however, the 1815 edition was predictably eclipsed by the work of other scholars in the field. Illustrative of its decline in popularity is Earle's remark of 1892 that 'it is enough now for us to say that in the present state of our knowledge, this first edition is chiefly valuable as a historical monument and a literary curiosity.'[6]

In the introduction to his edition, Thorkelin advances some theories about *Beowulf* that have long since been discredited; one such assertion is that the original author and audience of the poem were Danish. The propagandistic nature of this assertion seems clear in the light of Frank Cooley's observations in his article 'Early Danish Criticism of *Beowulf*' (1940):

■ As a result, then, of a growing interest in the national past and of the desire to examine a piece of literature [*Beowulf*] which seemed to offer unique information about that past, Thorkelin, aided by the Danish government, came to England in 1785 for the express purpose of seeking out documents that would cast light on the history of Denmark.[7] □

Turning to Earle again, we get a useful summary of Thorkelin's nationalistic argument:

■ According to the theory which he [Thorkelin] had formed in the course of his labours, this poem [*Beowulf*] was supposed to be a translation from a Danish original which had been written by an author contemporary with his heroes and personally acquainted with them; and he thought this Anglo-Saxon translation might have been executed by or at the command of King Alfred.[8] □

Other scholars, largely Scandinavian, weighed in to support Thorkelin. Indeed, questions of *Beowulf*'s authorship and provenance loomed large and became tied to a broadly nationalist agenda. P.E. Müller, for example, whilst refuting the theory of Danish authorship in his review of Thorkelin, speculated that *Beowulf* might very well have been of Icelandic origin. And, not surprisingly under the circumstances, many English scholars believed the poem to have *English* roots.

STOPFORD A. BROOKE

Perhaps the most lyrical defence of this view was voiced by Stopford A. Brooke (1832–1916) in his *The History of Early English Literature, being the History of English Poetry from its Beginnings to the Accession of King Ælfred* (1892):

■ The last thing to say with regard to these questions of date, origin, and place is that we may fairly claim the poem as English. It is in our tongue, and in our country alone that it is preserved. The memory of it seems to have died out of South Sweden and the Danish isles. It was kept alive by the Angles, and those who preserved it and the country that sheltered it may claim the honour of its possession. In its pages are our folk, their ways of life and fashion of thought.[9] □

Brooke ultimately brings this stage of his argument to a rousing, not to say jingoistic, climax:

■ Gentle like [Viscount Horatio] Nelson [(1758–1805) British naval hero who died in 1805 at the Battle of Trafalgar], he [Beowulf] had Nelson's iron resoluteness. What he undertook to do, he went through without a thought save of getting to the end of it. His very words when he spoke made those who heard him conscious of his firm-set purpose (line 611). 'Firm-minded Prince' is one of his names. The heights his character gained he was able to keep; and a similar phrase to that is twice used of the hero. Fear is wholly unknown to him and he seems, like Nelson, to have inspired his captains with his own courage. It is a notable touch that when his thegns go to bed in the hall that Grendel haunts, it is said of them 'that none of them thought that he should ever again seek his well-loved home, the folk in the free burg where he was brought up' – and with this thought they all fell asleep. It is a trait worthy of the crew of the *Victory* [Nelson's flagship].[10] □

The above extract is a very good example of Marijane Osborn's comment that *Beowulf* was 'nationalized according to the politics of the translator [or critic]'.[11] Perhaps Chris Jones, in *Strange Likeness: the Use of Old English in Twentieth-Century Poetry* (2006), does the best job of putting this 'nationalizing' tendency into its proper historical perspective:

■ This is not to say that it [*Beowulf*] may not have been used politically by the inhabitants of Anglo-Saxon England [...] [T]he description of Offa, king of the continental Angles, at lines 1975b-1960 may have been intended to flatter the royal line of Mercia [one of the Anglo-Saxon kingdoms], whose own Offa [King of Mercia 757–96] claimed descent from Offa the Angle [...] [*Beowulf*] was (at some stage of its uncertain genesis) an Englishing of southern Scandinavian stories and materials.[12] □

We must not, however, lose sight of the potentially darker political significance of these repeated attempts to appropriate *Beowulf* for one country or another. Conor McCarthy defines it somewhat controversially in his article 'Language and History in Seamus Heaney's *Beowulf*' (2001) as: 'This prejudice in favour of a notion of linguistic purity [in *Beowulf*] is bound up with some of the explicitly racist ideologies which have historically underpinned Anglo-Saxon studies.'[13]

R.D. FULK AND CHRISTOPHER M. CAIN

In addition, R.D. Fulk and Christopher M. Cain point out that the treasure hunt to find possible analogues to *Beowulf* was mostly finished by the close of the nineteenth century, a period when tracing the (alleged) 'cultural roots' of a literary text was very much in vogue. They then get to the heart of the matter:

■ Because the *Liedertheorie* [a theory of composite authorship often associated with epic poetry] promoted the dissection of the poem into so many disparate accretions on the central narrative of the monster fights, it also suggested that there was nothing untoward in the practice of identifying the poem's religious sentiments as later intrusions on an original 'pagan' composition. 'Paganism' in such a context almost never refers to a body of religious belief, and so in denoting all that is not Christian it becomes a thinly veiled reference to a notion of cultural purity, exposing a program to recover an imagined era in which Germanic peoples lived in noble simplicity, uncorrupted by foreign influences. Naturally, the xenophobic implications of such a critical practice were in tune with the social conditions that gave rise to Nazism (a movement supported by a great many philologists, not all of them German [...]), and the turn away from the study of *Beowulf* in comparative Germanic contexts in the twentieth century was certainly in part a consequence of the ongoing critical reaction to German nationalism [...] In at least equal part, though, it was a product of English nationalism, which prompted a 'reclaiming' of early texts from German textual methods and even a renaming of the language, from 'Anglo-Saxon' (Germ, *Angelsächsisch*) to 'Old English'.[14] □

All of these examples of *Beowulf* being made to fit a specific national dress are also, equally, instances of readers looking for 'relevance' in an ancient text; and this way of reading still has, of course, tremendous resonance today. As John D. Niles writes in the Introduction to *A Beowulf Handbook* (a volume published in 1972 to be discussed at greater length in the final chapter of this guide):

■ The future of *Beowulf* studies, I suspect, will not belong to those who just read the text, in the narrow sense of interpreting. It will lie with those who also use and take pleasure in it, adapting it to their own purposes in the world in which they live, as the poet's own listeners and readers surely did.[15] □

Beowulf was not just edited in the eighteenth and nineteenth centuries, however. It was also beginning to be appraised as *literature* rather than analysed merely for its philological content (though many critics still argue that this type of literary appreciation of the poem did not come into its own until 1936, with the publication of Tolkien's famous essay). If this seems to be stating the obvious, it must be remembered that in the 1930s J.R.R. Tolkien was still troubled by the lack of critical engagement with the poem:

> ■ I have read enough, I think, to venture the opinion that *Beowulfiana* is, while rich in many departments, especially poor in one. It is poor in criticism, criticism that is directed to the understanding of a poem as a poem. It has been said of *Beowulf* itself that its weakness lies in placing the unimportant things at the centre and the important on the outer edges. This is one of the opinions that I wish specially to consider. I think it profoundly untrue of the poem, but strikingly true of the literature about it. *Beowulf* has been used as a quarry of fact and fancy far more assiduously than it has been studied as a work of art.[16] □

SHARON TURNER

One tentative nineteenth-century engagement with Beowulf as art is found in *The History of the Manners, Landed Property, Government, Laws, Poetry, Literature, Religion, and Language, of the Anglo-Saxons* by Sharon Turner (1768–1847). This work, comprising three volumes, was written between 1799 and 1805 and is the first serious piece of scholarship to examine the migrations of the Anglo-Saxon peoples. Turner, a historian of some renown, was possibly influenced in his choice of this unusual subject matter by *Reliques of Ancient English Poetry* (1765), the first of the great English ballad collections, which was compiled by Sir Thomas Percy (1729–1811). In Turner's *History*, the roughly one dozen references to *Beowulf* are somewhat eclectic in nature. Turner's attention initially focuses on Beowulf's 'surname', for example:

> ■ No peculiar titles, as with us, seem to have distinguished the nobly born; they were rather marked out to their fellows by the name of the family which had become illustrious [...] Their title was formed by the addition of ing to the name of the ancestor whose fame produced their glory [...] So Beowulf, the hero of an Anglo-Saxon poem, was one of the Scyldingas.[17] □

As interesting as this fact no doubt is, perhaps the most important observations that Turner makes about the poem are the following:

■ The most interesting remains of the Anglo-Saxon poetry which time has suffered to reach us, are contained in the Anglo-Saxon poem in the Cotton library, Vitellius, A. 15. [Humphrey] Wanley mentions it as a poem 'in which seem to be described the wars which one Beowulf, a Dane of the royal race of the Scyldingi, waged against the reguli of Sweden'. But this account of the contents of the MS is incorrect. It is a composition more curious and important. It is the narration of the attempt of Beowulf to wreak the fæhthe or deadly feud on Hrothgar, for a homicide which he had committed. It may be called an Anglo-Saxon epic poem. It abounds in speeches which Beowulf and Hrothgar and their partisans make to each other, with much occasional description and sentiment.[18] □

The irony, of course, is that Wanley was not the only early reader (if we can call him that, seeing as neither he nor Turner knew any Old English) of the poem to get it wrong. It is clear that Turner's summary of the plot of *Beowulf* is glaringly incorrect; Hrothgar is emphatically not a murderer upon whom the hero seeks to avenge himself. However, though Turner fundamentally failed to understand the poem, he still recognized its value. This is seen towards the end of his book when he writes that 'It would occupy too much room in the present volume to give a further account of this interesting poem, which well deserves to be submitted to the public, with a translation and with ample notes.'[19]

Interestingly, Knut Stjerna (1874–1909), another early champion of *Beowulf*, also provided a flawed reading of an important moment in the poem. Of the woman who appears to prophesy doom at Beowulf's funeral, Stjerna wrote: 'The bale-fire is kindled, and whilst the flames blaze up and the smoke ascends to the skies, a woman (the widowed queen?) with her hair bound up in token of grief, gives voice to a series of dirges, and the bystanders burst into wailing.'[20] As we know, one of the most puzzling aspects of the hero's biography is that he has no wife. Stjerna, however, was not the only one to invent a mate for Beowulf. William Morris (1834–1896), among others, also included this female figure in his translation of the poem. In section XLIII, titled 'The Burial of Beowulf', Morris's rendering reads:

■ Likewise a sad lay the wife of aforetime
For Beowulf the King, with her hair all upbounden,
Sang sorrow-careful; said oft and over
That harm-days for herself in hard wise she dreaded,
The slaughter-falls many, much fear of the warrior,
The shaming and bondage. Heaven swallow'd the reek.[21] □

THOMAS ARNOLD

The thorny issues of dating and authorship (which recur periodically throughout the course of this guide) were addressed by Thomas Arnold (1823–1900). In his *Beowulf A Heroic Poem of the Eighth Century* (1876), he speaks to both topics. As for the time at which the epic was written, Arnold has this to say:

■ If evidence of similarity of diction which we have adduced have any value, it tends to show that *Beowulf* belongs to the same age with *Guðlac*, *Elene*, and *Christ*. Therefore, whatever independent evidence we have, tending to fix the age of these poems, tends also to fix the date of *Beowulf* [...] [T]he poem must therefore have been written in the first half of the eighth century [part of Arnold's argument here is based on the fact that St Guðlac died in 714].[22] □

Arnold also poses a series of questions to which we will return throughout the course of this guide:

■ With regard to the composition of *Beowulf*, several questions suggest themselves. Is it a single poem, preserved to us as it was originally written – or is it a single poem, more or less interpolated? – or an amalgam of two or more distinct poems, which criticism is competent to distinguish and recover? – or, lastly, is it such an amalgam padded and stuffed out by later interpolations?[23] □

And of the *Beowulf* poet, Arnold muses that 'it is more probable that the author was a Churchman than a layman; but if so, he was a Churchman *in a lay mood*. He delights in the concrete; loves persons, places, things, passions, adventures.'[24] A statement such as this ties in rather neatly with another important question about the poem, a question which critics (as we shall see) continue to revisit: what is the relationship between Christianity and paganism in *Beowulf*?

FRANCIS ADELBERT BLACKBURN

One important response to this was 'The Christian Coloring in the *Beowulf*' (1897) by Francis Adelbert Blackburn (1845–1923). Blackburn begins his article with a series of hypotheses:

■ It is admitted by all critics that the *Beowulf* is essentially a heathen poem; that its materials are drawn from tales composed before the conversion of the Angles and Saxons to Christianity, and that there was a time when these tales were repeated without the Christian reflections and allusions that are found in the poem that has reached us. But in what form this heathen material existed before it was put into its present shape is a question on which opinions are widely different. In the nature of the case we can look for no entire consensus of opinion and no exact answer to the question; the most that one can expect to establish is at the best only a probability.

The following hypotheses are possible:

- The poem was composed by a Christian, who had heard the stories and used them as the material for his work.
- The poem was composed by a Christian, who used old lays as his material. (This differs from the first supposition in assuming that the tales had already been versified and were in poetical forms before they were used by the author.)
- The poem was composed by a heathen, either from old stories or from old lays. At a later date it was revised by a Christian poet, to whom we owe the Christian allusions found in it. (This hypothesis differs from the others in assuming the existence of a complete poem without the Christian coloring.)[25] □

After 20 pages of close textual analysis, Blackburn presents his own findings:

■ The conclusions reached in this study of the Christian allusions in *Beowulf* are these:–

Of the passages in the *Beowulf* that show a Christian coloring, two are interpolated. The interpolation is proved in the case of one of these by the statements in it, which are contradicted by the evidence of the poem itself; in the case of the other by the dislocated arrangement, which shows an unskilful insertion of marginal matter. A small portion of this latter is repeated by interpolation farther on.

All the other passages in which any Christian tone can be detected have been made to suggest Christian ideas by slight changes such as a copyist could easily make. The evidence for this conclusion is found in the colorless character of the allusions, which appears in the entire lack of reference to anything distinctively Christian as contrasted with heathenism. Only on some such theory can we explain the entire lack of any reference to Christ, to New Testament narratives and teachings, and to Church doctrines and practices most in vogue at the time.

From these two conclusions there naturally springs a third; that the *Beowulf* once existed as a whole without the Christian allusions.[26] □

Any discussion of *Beowulf* scholarship published before the twentieth century must not fail to mention translations, as it can be argued that translation is in part a form of interpretation. It has been proposed that the first accessible translation of the poem into English was by

John Mitchell Kemble (1807–1857). Kemble, according to Marijane Osborn:

■ published an edition of the poem in 1833, improved it greatly in a second edition of 1835, and followed this with a prose translation in 1837 [...] With no pretensions whatever to artistry [...] Kemble translated the poem into an English prose as literal as he could make it while remaining comprehensible [...] Kemble's scholarly rendering is the first strictly literal translation to succeed, and the last in modern English that was needed in order for non-Anglo-Saxonists to have access to the poem, though of course other translations proliferated and improved as the text was better understood.[27] □

WILLIAM MORRIS

The translation of *Beowulf* by William Morris, already alluded to above, should also be mentioned here as it is an important, as well as truly interesting, example of an artist's response to the poem. Morris, the well-known Pre-Raphaelite artist and writer, began work on the Anglo-Saxon epic in August of 1892. Before he started his *Beowulf* project, however, Morris had had some success as a translator. Despite this, his rendering of *Beowulf* has been judged to be something of a flop. Fiona MacCarthy, in her acclaimed biography of Morris, sums up the situation well:

■ Simultaneously with *Chaucer*, Morris was working on his *Beowulf* translation. He was not in any sense an Anglo-Saxon scholar. He worked from the original but with a prose paraphrase supplied by the more expert A.J. Wyatt [whose own scholarly edition of the poem was critically admired] of Christ's College, Cambridge, which he used as a safety net [...] As he worked through the 3,182 lines of the original he took it week by week to read to Ned and Georgie [the Pre-Raphaelite painter Edward Burne-Jones (1833–1898) and his wife Georgina (1840–1920)] at the Sunday breakfasts at The Grange. Few people have a good word to say for Morris' *Beowulf* (least of all in Oxford). I will not attempt one. It is Morris at his most garrulous and loose. The translation is an unexpected failure *since Morris, with his taste for the heroic, might have been expected to respond to the starkness of the setting and the embattlements of giants* [my italics].[28] □

MacCarthy's final words here are especially significant, speaking as they do to the elegiac mood of the poem as well as to one of its central conflicts. They also demonstrate the highly personal ways in which people have responded, or have been expected to respond, to the Anglo-Saxon epic.

Though MacCarthy represents a school of thought which views Morris' *Beowulf* as 'an unexpected failure', it is important to note that not everyone has shared this opinion. The poet Ezra Pound, for one, held Morris and Wyatt's translation in very high regard. As an undergraduate, Pound proudly used Wyatt's 1894 edition – 'the most accurate and up-to-date in its scholarship'[29] – of *Beowulf* and, as Chris Jones has mused:

■ Indeed, given Pound's enthusiasm for both Old English and Morris, it is not unlikely that he had read Morris's 'The Tale of Beowulf', perhaps in the reading room of the British Library. While there is no evidence for this, the similarities in method between Morris's 'Beowulf' and Pound's 'Seafarer' [his poem, first published in 1911, based on the Old English elegy of the same name] are striking. Fred Robinson [in 'Ezra Pound and the Old English Tradition', in *The Tomb of Beowulf and Other Essays on Old English* (Oxford: Blackwell, 1993), p. 272] takes it for granted that 'Morris was certainly a great influence on Pound' in this respect.[30] □

Usefully, in relation to the more immediate concerns of this guide, Morris himself provided his own (clearly heartfelt) reading of *Beowulf*:

■ The great beauty, the real value, of Beowulf [sic] is in its dignity of style. In construction it is curiously weak, in a sense preposterous; for while the main story is simplicity itself, the merest commonplace of heroic legend, all about it, in the historic allusions, there are revelations of a whole world of tragedy, plots different in import from that of Beowulf [sic], more like the tragic themes of Iceland. Yet with this radical defect, a disproportion that puts the irrelevances in the centre and the serious things on the outer edges, the poem of Beowulf [sic] is unmistakably heroic and weighty. The thing itself is cheap; the moral and the spirit of it can only be matched among the noblest authors. It is not in the operations against Grendel, but in the humanities of the more leisurely interludes, the conversation of Beowulf and Hrothgar, and such things, that the poet truly asserts his power. It has often been pointed out how like the circumstances are in the welcome of Beowulf at Heorot and the reception of Ulysses [or Odysseus, the hero of Homer's *Odyssey*] in Phæcia [an island mentioned in Greek mythology]. Hrothgar and his queen are not less gentle than Alcinous [the king of Phæcia] and Arete [a minor Greek goddess of virtue]. There is nothing to compare with them in the Norse poems: it is not till the prose history of Iceland appears that one meets with the like temper there. It is not common in any age; it is notably wanting in Middle English literature, because it is an aristocratic temper, secure of itself, and not imitable by the poets of an uncourtly language composing for a simpleminded audience.[31] □

Morris' mention of the similarity between Beowulf and Ulysses leads us rather neatly to the next chapter of this guide where, amongst other things, the relationship between *Beowulf* and classical epic will be explored. As we leave the nineteenth century with more than a hundred years of *Beowulf* criticism ahead of us, the words of John Earle come to mind: 'The criticism of the text shows no sign of being exhausted.'[32] Little could he know, back in 1892, what an understatement this would prove to be. The situation was about to change rather dramatically, as more and more scholars and general readers gained access to the poem. Just how radical a transformation this would be is indicated in John D. Niles's account of *Beowulf*'s 600 years in the wilderness:

■ Not every period has taken part in the making of *Beowulf* [...] Unlike many other masterworks of literature, this poem has had no unbroken history of reading. No one seems to have read it – or if anyone did, then no one left a record of any mental glosses on it – during a period of time extending from the twelfth century, or thereabouts, until the late eighteenth century.[33] □

As the next chapter will show, by 1900, where *Beowulf* was concerned, critics began to make up for lost time.

CHAPTER TWO

'Conflicting Babel': 1900–1931

In this chapter we will look at the types of interpretative approaches that began to replace the musings of the early philologists and editors of *Beowulf*. A great deal of the scholarship produced in the three decades covered by this chapter focuses on the possible sources of the Old English poem (both Classical and Scandinavian). During this period there were also ongoing discussions of the genre of *Beowulf* and attempts to establish the exact relationship between the text's Christian and pagan elements. As the introduction to this guide showed, J.R.R. Tolkien identified the 'conflicting babel' that was *Beowulf* criticism in the early decades of the twentieth century. In his summary of theories about the poem, Tolkien mentions that some scholars believed *Beowulf* to have been 'inspired by emulation of Virgil'.[1] Virgil (or Vergil), it must be remembered, was the author of the *Aeneid*, a Latin epic composed in the first century BC. The hero of his poem is Aeneas, a Trojan who travels to Italy after the destruction of Troy and through the workings of fate becomes the founder of Rome.

TOM BURNS HABER

Our discussion of the (alleged) relationship between *Beowulf* and the *Aeneid* will begin with Tom Burns Haber's straightforwardly titled *A Comparative Study of the Beowulf and the Aeneid* (1931). Haber begins his work by pointing out something we already know, that 'It is not a new theory that Vergil's *Aeneid* may have had something to do in the composition of the Old English epic *Beowulf*.'[2]

In the 'Survey of Opinion' that follows, Haber presents various arguments concerning the possible connection between the two epics. One critic he cites here is W.P. Ker. William Paton Ker (1855–1931), to give him his full name, claims in *The Dark Ages* (first published in 1904) that:

■ There is too much education in *Beowulf*, and it may be that the larger kind of heroic poem was attained in England only through the example of Latin narrative. The English epic is possibly due to Virgil and Statius [Publius Papinius Statius, a Roman poet who lived from c. 45–96]; possibly to Juvencus [C. Vettius Aquilinus Juvencus, a Christian Latin poet of the fourth century] and other Christian poets, to the authors studied by [St] Aldhelm [639–709] and Bede [or Baeda, c. 673–735].

[...] Yet while there may be about the Anglo-Saxon epic this suspicion of foreign and learned influence, the Anglo-Saxon, or rather the West German type, was capable of growth, for all its slowness, as the Norse type of poetic story was not, for all its energy and curiosity.[3] □

Readers of this guide should note, however, that not everyone saw such a close connection between classical epic and the Old English poem. In a review of Haber's *A Comparative Study of the Beowulf and the Aeneid*, for example, R.B. (Richard Broxton) Onians begins by arguing that, firstly, Haber's thesis is not unique:

■ The general thought is not new, having occurred to [Georg] Zappert, [Alois] Brandl, [William Witherle] Lawrence, [Neil R.] Ker, [Raymond Wilson] Chambers and others. One who wrote, as the author of *Beowulf* appears to have done, in the first half of the eighth century might well have read Virgil if he belonged to the small circle of scholars like Aldhelm and Alcuin. Mr. Haber would pass from this possibility to his probability.[4] □

This movement from 'possibility' to 'probability' is what Onians clearly takes issue with. Onians also criticizes the fact that 'Mr. Haber adduces a good deal of evidence for what has long been recognized: that the writing of Anglo-Saxon was affected by the Christian use of Latin; but proves little or nothing for a direct knowledge of Virgil.'[5] Thus, all in all, Onians accuses Haber's work of lacking in originality and conclusive proof.

Haber's analysis of *Beowulf* and the *Aeneid* is perhaps the most exhaustive exploration of the ways in which classical source material manifests itself in the Old English epic, however. In this important study we find the author arguing that:

■ The most the present writer can hope for is that he may establish the strong probability that there is in the *Beowulf* evidence that the author did possess an acquaintance with the *Aeneid* and took from it various plot-motifs, stylistic devices, and turns of expression which appear in the Anglo-Saxon epic. It will be shown that the *Beowulf* in many details is out of harmony with the literature of which it is chronologically a part, and that not infrequently it leaves the impression of departing significantly from the traditions of the people among whom it arose. An attempt will be made to show that some of these broader inconsistencies may find explanation in references to the *Aeneid*.[6] □

Haber continues on an even more emphatic note:

■ Indeed, one would be much more inclined to believe that Vergil was known to the *Beowulf*-poet than to attempt to explain how the Old English writer could have failed to come into contact with and be impressed by the author of the *Aeneid*. This is posing a choice between probabilities; but in the light of the best evidence available, the weight of probability seems to point to Vergil as the chief extraneous influence on the Anglo-Saxon epos [early epic poetry from the oral tradition].[7] □

It is equally interesting to cite what Haber has to say about the like-lihood of the *Beowulf* poet mining Homer's *Odyssey* for inspiration as well:

■ Homer has been studied as a source nearer akin than Vergil to the *Beowulf*. [R.W.] Chambers remarks that 'It has been urged, as a *reductio ad absurdum* of the view which would connect *Beowulf* with Vergil, that the relation to the *Odyssey* is more obvious than that to the *Aeneid*.' There is no doubt that Greek was known in Britain at the time of the compos-ition of the *Beowulf*, and Irish scholars had known it long before; but in comparison with Latin manuscripts, Greek manuscripts must have been extremely rare.[8] □

Despite this assertion, we know (see Chapter One of this guide) that William Morris also reflected upon a possible link between *Beowulf* and the *Odyssey*: 'It has often been pointed out how like the circum-stances are in the welcome of Beowulf at Heorot and the reception of Ulysses in Phæcia. Hrothgar and his queen are not less gentle than Alcinous and Arete.'[9]

ALBERT STANBURROUGH COOK

Not everyone in the early decades of the twentieth century was, how-ever, as sceptical as Haber concerning the Anglo-Saxon's possible use of ancient Greek texts. For example, Albert Stanburrough Cook (1853–1927), one of the most respected and prolific mediaeval scholars and philologists of his generation, took the opposite view:

■ we ought not to be surprised if Homeric influence is discernable in *Beowulf* [...] Such clear traces I discern at the close of *Beowulf*, where the hero's funeral and monument are described, as compared with those near the end of the *Iliad* and *Odyssey* which depict the obsequies [funeral rites] of Patroclus [Achilles' best friend], Hector [a Trojan prince, and Troy's pre-eminent soldier, killed by Achilles] and Achilles [the central character, and greatest warrior, of the *Iliad*].[10] □

As one might expect, Cook then proceeds to enumerate these 'clear traces' of influence. Of the seven points he lists, number six is certainly the most provocative: 'The aged wife of Beowulf utters a lament for her husband [...], as does Andromache [Hector's widow] over Hector. That of Andromache is much longer, partly because of her concern for her child.' (339) As has already been mentioned above, there is no suggestion in the poem of the hero having ever taken a wife, nor is there any reference to him having children. Nevertheless, Cook was not alone is raising the possibility that Beowulf might have been married: recall, for example, Knut Stjerna's comment on this subject in Chapter One of this guide. Kemp Malone also tentatively remarks that: 'At Beowulf's funeral a female mourner (his wife?) appears, indeed, but only as a subordinate figure, while the ceremonies are in the hands of others.'[11]

Whilst the subject of Beowulf's marital status (as well as other aspects of his biography) is one to which we will return later in this guide, it might be useful here to have a brief look at the passage Cook, Stjerna and Malone all base their arguments on:

■ Swylce giomorgyd (s)io g(eo)meowle
(æfter Biowulfe b)undenheorde
(song) sorgcearig, sæde geneahhe,
þæt hio hyre (hearmda gas) hearde (ondre)de,
wælfylla worn, (wigen)des egesan,
hy[n]ðo (ond) h(æftny)d.

[ll. 3150–55ᵃ]

[Then the woman, wavy-haired, sang a mournful song about Beowulf. She said repeatedly that she sorely dreaded for herself invasions of armies, numerous slaughters, terror of warriors, oppression and captivity.] [Guide author's translation] □

The intensity of this anonymous woman's mourning for Beowulf has led some scholars, as we have seen, to view her as the hero's wife. Whilst we cannot, of course, dismiss this interpretation altogether, it is worth mentioning that the 'wavy-haired' female could just as easily be symbolic of the vulnerability of Beowulf's nation now that he is dead. This is in some way supported by Jane Chance in her essay 'The Structural Unity of *Beowulf*: The Problem of Grendel's Mother' (1990):

■ The nameless and unidentified Geat woman who appears, like the other female characters [in the poem], after a battle – this one between Beowulf and the dragon – mourns at the pyre. That is, the effort of the peacemaker, while valuable in worldly and social terms, ultimately must fail because of the nature of this world.[12] □

Chance offers us a transpersonal, gendered reading of the passage here, for in Anglo-Saxon literature and culture the role of peacemaker was traditionally reserved for women. Likewise, keening (a wailing lament for the dead) is also primarily done by women.

MARGARET SCHLAUCH

The question of how far back the ancient origins of *Beowulf* can be traced was also still being mulled over in the 1950s (the potential dangers of this type of approach were discussed in Chapter One of this guide). Margaret Schlauch, for example, effectively weighed in to support Haber's thesis in her book *English Medieval Literature and its Social Foundations* (1956). In this volume, Schlauch upholds the view that the *Aeneid* had 'possibly helped to shape the structure of *Beowulf* as a completed epic'.[13] Schlauch's main defence of this position is found in the following passage:

■ the missions of the two epic heroes [Aeneas and Beowulf] are comparable. Virgil, writing in the heyday of the Roman empire [which lasted from roughly 27 BC to 476 AD], was using epic narrative modelled after Homer's *Iliad* and *Odyssey*, in order to glorify the Emperor Augustus [63 BC–14 AD], and with him the dominating political role of Italy in the ancient world. To do so he borrowed the machinery of the pre-imperial tribal epic in which individual heroes are closely identified with the welfare of small tribal units. The *Beowulf* poet, himself living in such a tribal society, could easily have drawn upon the pseudo-tribal poem of the ancient Roman. Beowulf is a hero devoted to the welfare of his people, according to the theory if not the practice of the ruling-class tribal code, just as Aeneas pretends to be such a simple unselfish hero while revealing the historical traits of the world-ruling Augustus.[14] □

She opens up the argument further by adding that:

■ Most opinion is agreed [...] that *Beowulf* is a unified poem with aesthetic qualities of a higher order [than had previously been thought], composed more or less as we have it today. A single author shaped its materials (of whatever kind, however obtained) according to his ideology, and that ideology was the product of tribal history modified through recent conversion to Christianity. His aesthetic values are generally thought to have been affected by classical models, though scholars differ as to the extent of the influence.[15] □

At this stage, it might be beneficial to ask what else about *Beowulf*, aside from its possible indebtedness to classical sources, suggests 'too much education'? One answer to this question might be to say that there is an obvious knowledge of history, mythology, Northern literature and folklore displayed in the poem (we will return to the historicity of *Beowulf* later in this guide).

BEOWULF AND CAIN

The poet's familiarity with the Bible also clearly demonstrates an educated mind at work. Interestingly though, as many scholars have noted before now, all of the explicit biblical references in *Beowulf* are from the Old Testament. Perhaps the best known of these allusions concerns Grendel's genealogy. In lines 102–16 we are told that

■ wæs se grimma gæst Grendel haten,
mære mearcstapa, se þe moras heold,
fen ond fæsten; fifelcynnes eard
wonsæli wer weardode hwile,
siþðan him Scyppend forscrifen hæfde
in Caines cynne – þone cwealm gewræc
ece Drihten, þæs þe he Abel slog;
ne gefeah he þære fæhðe, ac he hine feor for wræc,
Metod for þy mane mancynne fram.
Þanon untydras ealle onwocon,
eotenas ond ylfe ond orcneas,
swylce gigantas, þa wið Gode wunnon
lange þrage; he him ðæs lean forgeald.

[The grim spirit was called Grendel, an infamous boundary-stepper, one who held the moors, fen and fastness. Unhappy man. He dwelt for a while in the country of the race of monsters, since God had condemned them as the kin of Cain. The Eternal Lord revenged the killing in which he slew Abel. Cain experienced no joy in that feud, but He, the Ruler, for that crime banished him far away from mankind. Then from him derived all abject things: trolls and elves and monstrous beings. Also the giants who fought with God for a long time. He gave them their reward for that.] [Guide author's translation] □

In this tremendously atmospheric passage the poet, as we can see, refers to Grendel as one of 'the kin of Cain' (107[a]). This is clearly a significant point; so much so, in fact, that it is brought up again a little later in the poem in relation both to Grendel and his mother:

■ Grendles modor,
ides aglæcwif yrmþe gemunde,

se þe wæteregesan wunian scolde,
cealde streamas, siþðan Cain wearð
to ecgbanan angan breþer,
fæderenmæge; he þa fag gewat,
morþre gemearcod mandream floen,
westen warode. Þanon woc fela
geosceaftgasta; wæs þæra Grendel sum,
heorowearh hetelic.

[ll.1258^b-1267^a]

[Grendel's mother, woman, female monster, remembered her misery, she who had to dwell in the water-terror, the cold streams, since Cain became the sword-slayer of his only brother, his own paternal kinsman. Then Cain went as an outlaw, a murderer marked out, to flee the joys of men. He kept to the wilderness. Then from him sprang many a doomed spirit. One of them was Grendel, a hostile outlaw.] [Guide author's translation] □

The story of Cain's murder of his brother Abel because of jealousy is found in Chapter 4 of the Old Testament book of Genesis which, in the King James Version of the Bible, reads as follows:

[1] And Adam knew Eve his wife; and she conceived, and bare Cain, and said, I have gotten a man from the LORD.
[2] And she again bare his brother Abel. And Abel was a keeper of sheep, but Cain was a tiller of the ground.
[3] And in process of time it came to pass, that Cain brought of the fruit of the ground an offering unto the LORD.
[4] And Abel, he also brought of the firstlings of his flock and of the fat thereof. And the LORD had respect unto Abel and to his offering.
[5] But unto Cain and to his offering he had not respect. And Cain was very wroth, and his countenance fell.
[6] And the LORD said unto Cain, Why art thou wroth? and why is thy countenance fallen?
[7] If thou doest well, shalt thou not be accepted? and if thou doest not well, sin lieth at the door. And unto thee shall be his desire, and thou shalt rule over him.
[8] And Cain talked with Abel his brother: and it came to pass, when they were in the field, that Cain rose up against Abel his brother, and slew him.
[9] And the LORD said unto Cain, Where is Abel thy brother? And he said, I know not: Am I my brother's keeper?
[10] And he said, What hast thou done? the voice of thy brother's blood crieth unto me from the ground.
[11] And now art thou cursed from the earth, which hath opened her mouth to receive thy brother's blood from thy hand;
[12] When thou tillest the ground, it shall not henceforth yield unto thee her strength; a fugitive and a vagabond shalt thou be in the earth.

[13] And Cain said unto the LORD, My punishment is greater than I can bear.

[14] Behold, thou hast driven me out this day from the face of the earth; and from thy face shall I be hid; and I shall be a fugitive and a vagabond in the earth; and it shall come to pass, that every one that findeth me shall slay me.

[15] And the LORD said unto him, Therefore whosoever slayeth Cain, vengeance shall be taken on him sevenfold. And the LORD set a mark upon Cain, lest any finding him should kill him.

Grendel is, therefore, a descendant of the first murderer; the one from whom all evil is said to spring. In the passage above describing Grendel's lineage, the poet also tells us that Beowulf's foe is a 'grim spirit' (grima gæst, 102[a]) and (literally and figuratively) a wanderer along the borders (mearcstapa, 103[a]) of the wastelands and moors. Clearly, this description is meant to emphasize the similarity between Grendel and Cain as both are exiles, figures on the margins of society. In Genesis 4: 13–14, Cain speaks of the overwhelming pain he feels at the thought of his future ostracism from the world he has come to know: 'My punishment is greater than I can bear. Behold, thou hast driven me out this day from the face of the earth; and from thy face shall I be hid; and I shall be a fugitive and a vagabond in the earth.' We should also keep in mind that, for the average Anglo-Saxon, the idea of exile was as terrifying as it was to the Cain of the Bible.

MICHAEL SWANTON

Michael Swanton, for example, in *English Literature before Chaucer* (1987) writes that:

■ The figure of the exile haunts the Anglo-Saxon imagination as a constant nagging fear of the possibility, even likelihood, of the dispersal of the comitatus [the warrior band] consequent on internal dissension or external attack. Since one's place in the hall is what gives one's life significance and meaning, to be deprived, for whatever reason, of a place in that society, is the ultimate catastrophe that might befall an individual. Outside those known bonds lay an alien and hostile world in which even the best men might well be incapable of establishing new relationships. The lonely man was not yet imbued with the romantic aura that a later age might ascribe to him. The solitary outsider was not just to be pitied, but distrusted: the wolf's head of the outlaw especially shunned. There were all sorts of reasons for being in the state of exile – not all of them the result of innocent misfortune. In real life a man might be exiled from society for all sorts of wickedness [...] In literature the list of wicked exiles is headed by Cain, his brother's slayer, condemned by God himself to be shunned [...], and from whom were descended a whole brood of outcast monsters, hobgoblins, and trolls, most notably Beowulf's opponent Grendel himself 'who bore God's anger'.[16] □

Swanton, in a related passage from this same volume, also offers a detailed reading of the character of Grendel (a topic to which we shall return throughout the course of this guide) in the light of the 'monster's' benighted ancestry:

■ The main outline of Grendel's function within the poem is plain: a creature of darkness and night, outcast from God by the society of men, together with hobgoblins and all other monstrous progenies hostile to human happiness. Associated by the poet with Cain, primordial kinslayer and therefore symbol of elemental social disunity [...], he stalks abroad, ravaging only by night when the sun, *Godes candel* [God's candle], is far from the sky. He has made his home with all that is antithetical to Heorot [Hrothgar's hall], inhabiting an unvisited land, solitary paths, perilous swamps, and the misty wastelands. His lair is a place very like hell, a dreadful region shunned by all that is good in nature like the noble hart, *heorot*, a major Germanic symbol of both regality and purity. Banished from the society of men, obliged to take the paths of an outcast, he treads the wilderness as an exile, a solitary figure. Such loneliness has none of the romantic aura that a later age might ascribe to it. For heroic society, the solitary figure is invariably suspect and probably vicious, an object of fear and distrust. Although this monster has been proscribed by God, Danish society seems still to be subject to his depredation. He is not effectively banished for ever. Haunting the borders of human society, he is always present, neither in nor fully out of it, the corporeal substance of fear, always ready to intrude given opportunity enough. Well known to both the people and the counsellors of the king, Grendel and his dam tread the wastelands in the likeness of men, but misshapen, a mockery of the form of human society, and a public enemy.[17] □

In a witty take on this matter, E.B. Irving, Jr., wrote in 1966 that 'Cain begat the race of Grendel, and Grendel begat the race of scholars who speculate as to what his significance might be.'[18] Suffice to say that throughout the course of this guide we will be revisiting this particular 'race of scholars' to see what more they have to say on the subject of Grendel's significance and meaning within the poem. Before leaving this topic, however, it is also worth noting here another piece of scholarship from the beginning of the twentieth century, Oliver F. Emerson's 'Legends of Cain, Especially in Old and Middle English' (1906). This article is one of the first critical explorations of the significance of Grendel's ancestral affinity with Cain. It also makes for interesting comparative reading with a piece written 50 years later, Robert L. Chapman's 'Alas, Poor Grendel' (1956).

Aside from providing a compelling commentary on Grendel's role as an exile, Swanton also alludes here to a significant aspect of the creature's lair: 'it is a place very like hell.' Swanton was not, however, the first critic to remark upon this similarity: Friedrich Klaeber, for example, made the same point in 1911 in his seminal study 'The Christian Elements in *Beowulf*': 'It is well known that Grendel, a creature derived from Nordic legend (originally folk–tales), underwent a thorough Christianizing; the common *scucca*, *scinna* [an evil spirit; ghost] was transformed into a demonic creature, a descendant of Cain. Likewise, the description of Grendel's dwelling brings to mind a Christian hell.'[19]

CARLETON BROWN

There is also Carleton Brown's article of 1938, '*Beowulf* and the *Blickling Homilies* and Some Textual Notes':

■ Richard Morris, in editing the *Blickling Homilies* [an incomplete collection of 18 Old English prose homilies and sermons] called attention to the XVIIth [17th] Homily which presents striking resemblances to the description of the mere of Grendel in *Beowulf* [...] Though almost sixty years have passed since this resemblance was pointed out, during this whole period it has received scant attention from students of Old English, being either ignored altogether or dismissed with only brief discussion.

Whatever relation may exist between this passage in the Blickling Homily and *Beowulf*, it is recognized that the Homily shows direct dependence upon the apocryphal [pertaining to biblical books whose credibility has been questioned] *Visio Pauli* [the fourth-century Apocalypse of Paul, part of the New Testament Apocrypha] [...] No doubt it was this fact which led [Friedrich] Klaeber, in commenting on the similarity between the *Beowulf* description and the Homily, to point to the *Visio Pauli* as one of the sources which influenced the Anglo-Saxon poet. 'Manifestly,' he remarks, 'conceptions of the Christian hell have entered into the picture' of Grendel's mere: 'The moors and wastes, mists and darkness, the cliffs, the bottomless deep, the loathsome *wyrmas* [worms, serpents, reptiles], can all be traced in early accounts of hell, including Anglo-Saxon religious literature.' From this he concludes: 'It is hardly going too far to attribute the remarkable agreement to the use of the same or a very similar source.'[20] □

An instance such as this is, in part, what has led some critics to view *Beowulf* as a Christian allegory. Indeed, as we have seen in the introduction to this guide, the exact nature of the relationship between Christianity and paganism in the poem is a major topic of academic inquiry and it is one to which we will return a little later in this chapter.

BEOWULF AND THE FLOOD

The other major Old Testament reference in *Beowulf* occurs during the celebrations at Heorot after the hero has killed Grendel's mother. Beowulf has returned from the mere with the hilt of the sword he used to kill his second adversary. The hilt is, in turn, given into the hand of Hrothgar and the poet describes the moment in the following manner:

> ■ Hroðgar maðelode – hylt sceawode,
> ealde lafe, on ðæm wæs or writen
> fyrngewinnes, syððan flod ofsloh,
> gifen geotende giganta cyn,
> frecne geferdon; þæt wæs fremde þeod
> ecean Dryhtne; him þæs endelean
> þurh wæteres wylm Waldend sealed.
>
> [ll. 1687–1693]

[Hrothgar spoke – he looked hard at the hilt, the old remnant, on which was engraved the origin of the ancient feud, when the flood, the flowing sea, slew the giants' race. They suffered mightily. That was a folk estranged from the Lord. The Ruler dealt them out a final reward through the water's raging.] [Guide author's translation] □

The flood is Noah's Flood, the story of which is found in Chapters 6–7 of the book of Genesis:

[5] And GOD saw that the wickedness of man was great in the earth, and that every imagination of the thoughts of his heart was only evil continually.

[6] And it repented the LORD that he had made man on the earth, and it grieved him at his heart.

[7] And the LORD said, I will destroy man whom I have created from the face of the earth; both man, and beast, and the creeping thing, and the fowls of the air; for it repenteth me that I have made them.

[8] But Noah found grace in the eyes of the LORD.

[13] And God said unto Noah, The end of all flesh is come before me; for the earth is filled with violence through them; and, behold, I will destroy them with the earth.

[14] Make thee an ark of gopher wood; rooms shalt thou make in the ark, and shalt pitch it within and without with pitch.

★ ★ ★

[Chapter 7]

[7] And Noah went in, and his sons, and his wife, and his sons' wives with him, into the ark, because of the waters of the flood.
[8] Of clean beasts, and of beasts that are not clean, and of fowls, and of every thing that creepeth upon the earth.
[9] There went in two and two unto Noah into the ark, the male and the female, as God had commanded Noah.
[10] And it came to pass after seven days, that the waters of the flood were upon the earth.

★ ★ ★

[15] And they went in unto Noah into the ark, two and two of all flesh, wherein is the breath of life.
[16] And they that went in, went in male and female of all flesh, as God had commanded him: and the LORD shut him in.
[17] And the flood was forty days upon the earth; and the waters increased, and bare up the ark, and it was lift up above the earth.
[18] And the waters prevailed, and were increased greatly upon the earth; and the ark went upon the face of the waters.
[19] And the waters prevailed exceedingly upon the earth; and all the high hills, that were under the whole heaven, were covered.
[20] Fifteen cubits upward did the waters prevail; and the mountains were covered.
[21] And all flesh died that moved upon the earth, both of fowl, and of cattle, and of beast, and of every creeping thing that creepeth upon the earth, and every man.
[22] All in whose nostrils was the breath of life, of all that was in the dry land, died.
[23] And every living substance was destroyed which was upon the face of the ground, both man, and cattle, and the creeping things, and the fowl of the heaven; and they were destroyed from the earth: and Noah only remained alive, and they that were with him in the ark.
[24] And the waters prevailed upon the earth an hundred and fifty days.

As with the story of Cain, the *Beowulf* poet has again drawn upon an example from the Bible where people are punished for their wicked-ness. The didactic function of this rather selective use of source material is not difficult to discern: the poem's audience is shown the terrible consequences of sin in the hopes that it will turn towards the path of righteousness like Abel and Noah.

R.W. CHAMBERS

In the previous chapter of this guide, a brief overview was provided of the various theories concerning both *Beowulf*'s authorship and provenance. As we have seen, scholars tussled with one another over these points, some arguing for the poem's Icelandic, Danish and even English origins. In the period covered by this present chapter, the question was, perhaps unsurprisingly, revisited. R.W. Chambers, for example, in his renowned edition of the poem (first published in 1921) saw the situation this way:

■ To deny that *Beowulf*, as we have it, is a translation from the Scandinavian does not, of course, involve any denial of the Scandinavian origin of the *story* of Beowulf's deeds. The fact that his achievements are framed in a Scandinavian setting, and that the closest parallels to them have to be sought in Scandinavian lands, makes it probable on *a priori* [deductive] grounds that the story had its origins there [...] Now linguistic evidence tends to show that *Beowulf* belongs to a time prior to the Viking settlement in England, and it is unlikely that the Scandinavian traditions embodied in *Beowulf* found their way to England just at time when communication with Scandinavian lands seems to have been suspended. We must conclude then that all this Scandinavian tradition probably spread to the Angles whilst they were still in their old continental home, was brought across to England by the settlers in the sixth century, was handed on by English bards from generation to generation, till the poem of *Beowulf* as we know it was formed in England.

Of course, if evidence can be produced that *Beowulf* is translated from some Scandinavian original, which was brought over in the seventh century or later, that is another matter. But the evidence produced so far is not merely inconclusive, but ludicrously inadequate.[21] □

Chambers' other noteworthy analysis of the poem is found in his '*Beowulf* and the Heroic Age' (1925), a piece which forms the Foreword to Archibald Strong's translation of the poem. '*Beowulf* and the Heroic Age' was judged by Tolkien to be 'the most significant single essay on the poem that I know'.[22] Tolkien's opinion was partly based, no doubt, on the fact that Chambers offers here a good old-fashioned historicist reading of the poem; he places *Beowulf* firmly within a historical context and dates it (as he does in the above extract from his edition) to the age of Bede. Bede, who flourished in the eighth century, is described by Chambers as 'the father of English History' and, as a consequence, 'we must reckon with him if we want to understand the origins of our own civilization.'[23] Chambers also returns us to a topic already considered in the present chapter of this guide, the relationship between *Beowulf* and earlier, classical poetry:

■ Yet it is difficult not to suspect the influence of the classical epic in *Beowulf*, when we notice how carefully the rules of the game are observed. The story begins *in medias res* [in the middle of things], but the hero recounts his earlier adventures at a banquet: the poet is not satisfied with telling us that there was minstrelsy at the banquet: he must give us a summary of the lay sung. And such classical influence is not, on *a priori* grounds, at all unlikely. Enthusiasm for Virgil was a possible thing enough in Northumbria at this date.[24] □

Despite this type of comparison, however, Chambers still believed that *Beowulf* was essentially inferior to its potential classical counterparts the *Æneid*, the *Iliad* and the *Odyssey*. This inferiority, Chambers argued, came largely from the fact that as he saw it, 'The main story of *Beowulf* is a wild folk-tale.'[25] This accusation troubled Tolkien, who addresses it at some length in his lecture '*Beowulf*: The Monsters and the Critics' (see especially pages 12–13). Chambers himself elaborates further upon this idea:

■ In the epoch of *Beowulf*, a Heroic Age more wild and primitive than that of Greece is brought into touch with Christendom, with the Sermon on the Mount, with Catholic theology and ideas of Heaven and Hell. We see the difference if we compare the wilder things – the folk-tale element – in *Beowulf* with the wilder things in Homer. Take for example the tale of Odysseus and the Cyclops – the No-Man trick. Odysseus is struggling with a monstrous and wicked foe, but he is not exactly thought of as struggling with the powers of darkness [...] But the gigantic foes whom Beowulf has to meet are identified with the foes of God. Grendel and the dragon are constantly referred to in language which is meant to recall the powers of darkness with which Christian men felt themselves to be encompassed. They are 'intimates of Hell,' 'adversaries of God,' 'offspring of Cain,' 'enemies of mankind.' Consequently, the matter of the main story of *Beowulf*, monstrous as it is, is not so far removed from common mediæval experience as it seems to us to be from our own [...] And so Beowulf, for all that he moves in the primitive Heroic Age of the Germans, nevertheless is almost a Christian knight.[26] □

Chambers concludes this part of his discussion by claiming that in *Beowulf* 'we find the character of the Christian hero, the mediæval knight, emerging from the turmoil of the Germanic Heroic Age.'[27] With this statement he is indirectly addressing the issue of the Christian–pagan tension in the poem, a topic of major importance. Chambers further argues that, when all is said and done, this Germanic Heroic inheritance is what accounts for the fact that 'In *Beowulf* all is aristocratic, and every-thing centres in the king.'[28] Despite this strain, however, Chambers insists that 'the whole spirit of *Beowulf* is Christian.'[29]

BERTHA PHILPOTTS

Another major exploration of the Christian–pagan tension (or perhaps 'balance' is a better way of putting this) found in *Beowulf* is Bertha Philpott's 'Wyrd and Providence in Anglo-Saxon Thought' (1928). Like Chambers before her, Philpotts argues that *Beowulf* is essentially a Christian poem: 'These ideas of Heaven, Hell and the justice of God, are the three ideas connected with the new faith which we find clearly indicated in *Beowulf*.'[30]

Her belief is also based partly on the fact that there are two anom-alies within the poem. These are:

■ that the great epic deals with monster-slaying instead of with heroic story, and that the hero does not quite belong to his environment [...] [These points] have led Professor Klæber to suggest that the author imported the figure of Beowulf into heroic story with a definitely Christian aim. He took him as his hero because a prince who delivered his people from a dragon would remind his audience of the Redeemer of their new faith. The story, in fact, lent itself to being made into a symbol or allegory of the central fact of the Christian faith.[31] □

And Philpotts concludes her thoughts on this topic with an observation similar to that of Chambers above:

■ What we can say here is that the Anglo-Saxons were the quickest of all the Nordic peoples to observe the discrepancy between their heroic stories and the new doctrines, and the most original in their efforts to create a new poetry on the lines of the old, yet in accord with the teachings of medieval Christianity.[32] □

In her essay Philpotts also addresses a topic of importance not just to *Beowulf* but to Anglo-Saxon poetry as a whole: the mood of melancholy and nostalgia which pervades much of the literature of the period:

■ It therefore seems more natural to explain the melancholy in Anglo-Saxon poems as a result of the clash between the pagan philosophy of life and the new doctrine, so readily accepted. On the one hand we have what W.P. Ker saw in the myth of Ragnarök [in Old Norse mythology a word meaning the final destiny of the gods], 'the assertion of the individual freedom [sic] against all the terrors and temptations of the world, [...] absolute resistance, perfect because without hope,' sometimes reaching an intensity of defiance which does not fear to arraign the gods. On the other hand, there is new knowledge that the world is ordered by a just Providence, so that resistance to what must be becomes no longer glorious but simply impious and foolish.[33] □

We shall return to some of these ideas in the following chapter of this guide, especially in relation to Beowulf's potential sources and the idea that it was already an 'antiquarian' poem at the time of its original composition.

CHAPTER THREE

The Monsters Meet the Critics: the 1930s and 1940s

In the introduction to this guide we saw how John Churton Collins bemoaned that, since its initial appearance on university syllabi, English literature had 'been regarded not as the expression of art and genius, but as mere material for the study of words, as mere pabulum for philology'. In relation to *Beowulf*, however, the appearance in 1936 of J.R.R. Tolkien's 'The Monsters and the Critics' changed things forever. This essay, initially given as the Sir Israel Gollancz Memorial Lecture to the British Academy on 25 November of that year, offered a reading of the poem distinct from those which had come before. For Tolkien, *Beowulf* was indeed a true 'expression of art and genius'. He did not, though, feel the same way about the existing scholarship on the Anglo-Saxon epic, as he believed that none of it addressed *Beowulf* as a *poem*. As a consequence, Tolkien himself set out to do just this in his British Academy lecture. Along the way he also provided a masterly, as well as occasionally humorous, overview of the history of *Beowulf* criticism up to 1935. And, as we will continue to see throughout the course of this guide, the cacophony of critical voices Tolkien identified back in 1936 still exists to this day where *Beowulf* is concerned.

J.R.R. TOLKIEN

In 'The Monsters and the Critics' Tolkien coupled a rather general and breathless summary of the history of *Beowulf* criticism with more detailed consideration of the work of W.P. Ker, R.W. Chambers and Ritchie Girvan – critics already familiar to readers of this guide. Ker's *The Dark Ages*, written approximately 30 years before Tolkien's lecture, comes under special scrutiny because of the reading of *Beowulf* offered within its pages. Ker wished to place *Beowulf* in the Anglo-Saxon epic tradition that had developed 'to its full proportions from earlier ruder experimental work, through a course of successive improvements like those that can be traced, for instance, in the growth of the Drama or the

Novel', but noted that much earlier work had been lost, and wished also that in *Beowulf* 'the process had gone a little further'. His chief criticism was that 'there is nothing much in the story': in contrast to Greek heroes like Theseus or Hercules, Beowulf's fame rests only on the slaying of monsters. With Grendel and his mother dead, he 'has nothing else to do' until the time comes for him, in old age, to face the Firedrake. Ker concedes, however, that the three episodes are well composed and by no means repetitive, and emphasizes the dignity of the poem's historic allusions and its descriptions of the conversations in the interludes between the battles that are unique in the Norse epic canon:

■ there is a change of temper between the wrestling with Grendel in the night at Heorot and the descent under the water to encounter Grendel's mother; while the sentiment of the Dragon is different again. But the great beauty, the real value, of *Beowulf* is in its dignity of style. In construction it is curiously weak, in a sense preposterous; for while the main story is simplicity itself, the merest commonplace of heroic legend, all about it, in the historic allusions, there are revelations of a whole world of tragedy, plots different in import from that of *Beowulf*, more like the tragic themes of Iceland. Yet with this radical defect, a disproportion that puts the irrelevances in the centre and the serious things on the outer edges, the poem of *Beowulf* is unmistakably heroic and weighty. The thing itself is cheap; the moral and the spirit of it can only be matched among the noblest authors. It is not in the operations against Grendel, but in the humanities of the more leisurely interludes, the conversation of Beowulf and Hrothgar, and such things, that the poet truly asserts his power. It has often been pointed out how like the circumstances are in the welcome of Beowulf at Heorot and the reception of Ulysses in Phæcia. Hrothgar and his queen are not less gentle than Alcinous and Arete. There is nothing to compare with them in the Norse poems: it is not till the prose histories of Iceland appear that one meets with the like temper there. It is not common in any age; it is notably wanting in Middle English literature, because it is an aristocratic temper, secure of itself, and not imitable by the poets of an uncourtly language composing for a simple-minded audience.[1] □

Whilst Tolkien acknowledged that, to British critics at any rate, the above passage remained 'a potent influence',[2] he did not concur with Ker's assessment that as a poem *Beowulf* was 'fundamentally flawed'.[3] Indeed, as Clare Lees has astutely argued in her essay 'Men and *Beowulf*' (2006), Tolkien felt the need to defend the poem against criticism such as Ker's on three fronts: aesthetically, structurally and thematically. The essay is grounded on, and framed by, an assertion of the poem's right to be read as poetry rather than as a poetic historical document: this is, in other words, an early and important example of New Criticism in Anglo-Saxon Studies.[4]

To put the reader more fully in the picture here, New Criticism 'advocated "close reading" and detailed textual analysis of poetry rather than an interest in the mind and personality of the poet, sources, the history of ideas and political and social implications. The application of semantics [a branch of linguistics dealing with the meanings of words] to this criticism was also important.'[5] R.D. Fulk and Christopher M. Cain, in *A History of Old English Literature*, lucidly explain how Tolkien's lecture on *Beowulf* exemplified the central tenets of the New Criticism. They also argue very convincingly that Tolkien's critique of existing *Beowulf* scholarship was as influential and groundbreaking as his actual reading of the poem 'since it is an explicit rejection of the prevailing critical interest in the poem primarily as a source for the comparative study of Germanic antiquities.'[6] Fulk and Cain further suggest that:

■ The poem may be like a tower built of old stones, but to call the tower a muddle, to knock it down and sift through the pieces for traces of earlier structures, is to misconstrue its purpose, since 'from the top of that tower' its builder 'had been able to look out upon the sea' (pp. 248–9) [Tolkien 2006, 8]. It is certainly not the case that no one had thought to examine *Beowulf* on such an aesthetic basis before this, but Tolkien managed to distill [sic] the critical mood of the day and mark in *Beowulf* studies a transition that was taking place on a much wider stage: the rise of 'literary criticism' in the modern sense as a respectable academic activity. The tenets of the New Criticism were formalist, and it is striking how many of those tenets are already implicit in Tolkien's essay: the rejection of historicism and other extraliterary considerations; the value placed on 'universal' literary virtues like balance (in the poem's structure), system (in the monsters' relation to that structure, paralleling the development of the hero), and organicism (in the iteration of balance at various levels of analysis, including the line, the episode, and the poem as a whole); the fetishization of the work as an autonomous and transcendent object, a work of assumed genius; and a fondness for irony. The thoroughness with which *Beowulf* scholarship was transformed by this change in critical fashion is reflected in anthologies of *Beowulf* criticism (Nicholson 1963, Fry 1968, Fulk 1991, Baker 1995), which uniformly include little or nothing written before 1936.[7] □

Another important observation made by Fulk and Cain here is that Tolkien's reading of *Beowulf* was the first to point out the true significance of Grendel, Grendel's mother and the dragon within the poem. The lecture's very title, 'The Monsters and the Critics', says it all. To give a critic such as Ker his due, however, the passage from *The Dark Ages* quoted above does give some consideration to these characters; Ker acknowledges, after all, that 'a correct and sober taste may have too contemptuously refused to attend to Grendel or the Firedrake.' Tolkien notes this and responds accordingly:

■ The chief virtue of the [Ker] passage (not the one for which it is usually esteemed) is that it does accord some attention to the monsters, despite correct and sober taste. But the contrast made between the radical defect of theme and structure, and at the same time the dignity, loftiness in converse, and well-wrought finish, has become a commonplace even in the best criticism, a paradox the strangeness of which has almost been forgotten in the process of swallowing it upon authority.[8] □

Tolkien's own, much more insistent, placing of the monsters at the centre of the poem was, however, groundbreaking – and perhaps even more so than he himself realized. This is in part because it was undoubtedly the cornerstone for the work of later critics such as Kenneth Sisam and Andy Orchard, both of whom argue that the entire *Beowulf* manuscript:

■ may have been compiled on the basis of an interest in monsters which is exhibited by at least four of the five texts it contains; he [Sisam in 1953] mused that a medieval cataloguer, seeking to sum up the contents of the manuscript, might well have described it as a 'book of various monsters, written in English'.[9] □

Orchard, in his *Pride and Prodigies: Studies in the Monsters of the Beowulf-Manuscript* (1995), sets out to explore the extent to which Sisam's theory is plausible. He also provides an excellent summary of the manuscript's contents and their potential unifying principles:

■ The six studies in this book seek to consider the motivation and background to the compilation of the *Beowulf*-manuscript, and in particular to address the question of the precise role and meaning both of the ancient monsters who stalk through the sources and of the heroes who battle against them. All five of the texts contained in that manuscript, namely *Judith*, *The Passion of Saint Christopher*, *The Wonders of the East*, *The Letter of Alexander to Aristotle*, and *Beowulf* itself, are examined in turn for the ways in which contrasting worlds and cultures, Latin and Germanic, Christian and secular, classical and biblical, are combined and reconciled in a manner so characteristic of the literature of Anglo-Saxon England. In addition, two other sources, the so-called *Liber monstrorum* [*The Book of Monsters*, a late seventh or early eighth-century Anglo-Latin catalogue of marvellous creatures] and the Icelandic *Grettis Saga* [an anonymous early fourteenth-century prose narrative], both of which have an established and important place in *Beowulf*-studies, are considered in detail for the further clues they offer to the twin themes of pride and prodigies which, I suggest, unite the text.[10] □

Monsters aside, the originality of Tolkien's reading of *Beowulf* also lay in the way it analysed the poem's structure. As T.M. Gang in his article 'Approaches to *Beowulf*' (1952) notes, Tolkien believed that the Anglo-Saxon epic was unified 'by its balance of contrasting halves and by the themes of man's struggle against the forces of evil'.[11] The relevant passage from 'The Monsters and the Critics' is as follows:

> ■ The general structure of the poem, so viewed, is not really difficult to perceive, if we look at the main points, the strategy, and neglect the many points of minor tactics. We must dismiss, of course, from mind the notion that *Beowulf* is a 'narrative poem', that it tells a tale or intends to tell a tale sequentially. The poem 'lacks steady advance': so Klaeber heads a critical section in his edition. But the poem was not meant to advance, steadily or unsteadily. It is essentially a balance, an opposition of ends and beginnings. In its simplest terms it is a contrasted description of two moments in a great life, rising and setting; an elaboration of the ancient and intensely moving contrast between youth and age, first achievement and final death. It is divided in consequence into two opposed portions, different in matter, manner and length: A from 1 to 2199 (including an exordium [an introductory section] of 52 lines); B from 2200 to 3182 (the end). There is no reason to cavil at this proportion; in any case, for the purpose and the production of the required effect, it proves in practice to be right.
>
>   This simple and *static* structure, solid and strong, is in each part much diversified, and capable of enduring this treatment. In the conduct of the presentation of Beowulf's rise to fame on the one hand, and of his kingship and death on the other, criticism can find things to question, especially if it is captious, but also much to praise, if it is attentive.[12] □

Tolkien, then, saw *Beowulf* as being essentially a poem of two halves and this is very much in keeping with the traditional way of viewing epic structure. In the first half of an epic we often see the hero in his youth departing from his homeland (on a *centrifugal* journey, in other words). The second half then portrays him as an old man returning home (this is known as *centripetal* movement). This is perfectly illustrated in Tolkien's comment above that '*Beowulf* is essentially a balance, an opposition of ends and beginnings. In its simplest terms it is a contrasted description of two moments in a great life, rising and setting; an elaboration of the ancient and intensely moving contrast between youth and age, first achievement and final death.' Many critics agree with Tolkien on this matter, but there are some dissenting voices. Seamus Heaney, for example, sees *Beowulf* as a poem of three parts and three peoples:

> ■ One way of reading *Beowulf* is to think of it as three agons in the hero's life, but another way would be to regard it as a poem that contemplates the

destinies of three peoples by tracing their interweaving histories in the story of the central character. First we meet the Danes – variously known as the Shieldings (after Shield Sheafson, the founder of their line), the Ingwins, the Spear-Danes, the Bright-Danes, the West-Danes, and so on – a people in the full summer of their power, symbolized by the high hall built by King Hrothgar, one 'meant to be a wonder of the world'. The threat to this superb people comes from within their own borders, from marshes beyond the pale, from the bottom of the haunted mere where 'Cain's clan', in the shape of Grendel and his troll-dam, trawl and scavenge and bide their time. But it also comes from without, from the Heathobards, for example, whom the Danes have defeated in battle and from whom they can therefore expect retaliatory war (see lines 2020–69).[13] □

Heaney of course touches upon much more here than just the structure of the poem. In his eloquent discussion of how the poem 'contemplates the destinies of three peoples' he also asks us to think about the poem's historicity. Once Grendel is brought into the equation, however, we seem to be back in the realm of story. How much of *Beowulf* was construed as fact, how much as fiction, by its original audience is almost impossible to say but it is a question that has, nevertheless, been of continued interest to critics working on the poem, Tolkien included. In 'The Monsters and the Critics' he writes, for example, that:

■ In *Beowulf* we have, then, a historical poem about the pagan past, or an attempt at one – literal historical fidelity founded on modern research was, of course, not attempted. It is a poem by a learned man writing of old times, who looking back on the heroism and sorrow feels in them something permanent and something symbolical. So far from being a confused semi-pagan – historically unlikely for a man of this sort in the period – he brought probably *first* to his task a knowledge of Christian poetry, especially that of the Cædmon school, and especially *Genesis*. He makes his minstrel sing in Heorot of the Creation of the earth and the lights of Heaven. So excellent is this choice as the theme of the harp that maddened Grendel lurking joyless in the dark without that it matters little whether this is anachronistic or not. *Secondly*, to his task the poet brought a considerable learning in native lays and traditions: only by learning and training could such things be acquired, they were no more born naturally into an Englishman of the seventh and eighth centuries, by simple virtue of being an 'Anglo-Saxon', than ready-made knowledge of poetry and history is inherited at birth by modern children.[14] □

It is relevant to mention here that the poem begins like a fairy tale with the words 'In geardagum'. We may translate this phrase as 'in days gone by', or even 'once upon a time'. This in turn brings us back to the question of genre, another subject explored by Tolkien:

■ *Beowulf* is not an 'epic', not even a magnified 'lay'. No terms borrowed from Greek or other literatures exactly fit: there is no reason why they should. Though if we must have a term, we should choose rather 'elegy'. It is an heroic-elegiac poem; and in a sense all its first 3,136 lines are the prelude to a dirge: *him þa gegiredan Geata/eode ad ofer eorðan unwaclicne* ['then the people of the Geats made ready for him a splendid pyre on the earth']: one of the most moving ever written.[15] □

We have another interesting departure from Ker here for, as we have seen, he was more than happy to call *Beowulf* the 'representative' Anglo-Saxon epic. On the other hand, E.M.W. Tillyard (1889–1962) in *The English Epic and its Background* (1954) argues that *Beowulf* sits largely outside the epic tradition:

■ Primarily *Beowulf* depicts the old Teutonic world, and the present question is whether it does so broadly enough and at the same time dramatically enough to reach epic height.

Intensity of a sort no one can deny to *Beowulf*. The descriptions of Beowulf's journey to Heorot, the watchman's challenge to him and his company when they land, and the journeys to and from the mere are brief and clear and exciting. Beowulf's own courage is cool and powerful to a degree, as when he tells Hrothgar before the fight with Grendel that he will need no burial if he loses, for Grendel will gnaw his bleeding body as he carries it to his lair. But one has only to think of the *Odyssey* on the one hand and of the Icelandic Sagas on the other to see that the world of *Beowulf* is comparatively narrow, that the poem does not truly fulfil the epic function of conveying the sense of what it was like to be alive at the time the author wrote. There are no touches of ordinary feeling or of homely quotidian [daily] life to supplement the grim exercises of heroic will-power or princely bounty: nothing like the sudden picture of the labourer returning home with the mist rising behind him which [John] Milton [1608–74] inserted in the last lines of *Paradise Lost* [1667; 1674]. The true epic amplitude is not here. The characters are powerful and adequate to the comparative narrowness of the world they inhabit. But there is no inner conflict, and they do nothing to widen by their own richness the setting in which they are placed. However evolved and sophisticated the art of *Beowulf* may be, that sophistication does not include the motivation of the actors.[16] □

Like Tolkein, Tillyard does not see *Beowulf* as an epic.

It is also worth considering here how Tolkien attempts to bring his lecture to some type of conclusion. As Lees points out, however, 'conclusion' is perhaps not the appropriate word for his notes to 'The

Monsters and the Critics' are long and preclude closure:

■ But, judging from the lengthy appendices attached to the essay, Tolkien's resolution was far from satisfactory; yet the article itself heralded a new generation of critics, all anxious to assign a role to Beowulf (the heroic warrior, the young man, the wise/old/proud king), to enlarge, as it were, Tolkien's preliminary analysis.[17] □

Here, however, is what Tolkien had to say:

■ And one last point, which those will feel who to-day preserve the ancient *pietas* towards the past: Beowulf is not a 'primitive' poem; it is a late one, using the materials (then still plentiful) preserved from a day already changing and passing, a time that has now for ever vanished, swallowed in oblivion; using them for a new purpose, with a wider sweep of imagination, if with a less bitter and concentrated force. When new Beowulf was already antiquarian, in a good sense, and it now produces a singular effect. For it is now to us itself ancient; and yet its maker was telling of things already old and weighted with regret, and he expended his art in making keen that touch upon the heart which sorrows have that are both poignant and remote.[18] □

Tolkien argues here that *Beowulf*'s original 'maker' (however we understand that term) had a similar relationship to the poem as that of its modern readers; both approach it, in effect, as antiquarians and see it as depicting a lost world.

The final word on Tolkien's lecture must go to the editors of *A Beowulf Handbook*, however, for they neatly summarize the lasting impact of 'The Monsters and the Critics': 'Tolkien's essay – actually more of a midlife crisis for *Beowulf* criticism than a beginning – soon became a point of departure for scholars approaching the poem as an aesthetic unity endowed with spiritual significance.'[19]

Tolkien also produced another scholarly essay on the poem after 'The Monsters and the Critics'. According to the writer's son, Christopher Tolkien, this piece, 'On Translating *Beowulf*', 'was contributed as "Prefatory Remarks on Prose Translation [sic] of *Beowulf*" to a new edition (1940) by Professor C.L. Wrenn of *Beowulf and the Finnesburg Fragment*, A Translation into *Modern English Prose*, by John R. Clark Hall (1911).'[20] The initial tone of this work is not dissimilar to that of 'The Monsters and the Critics', for Tolkien is as wary here of previous translators of *Beowulf* as he was in his famous lecture of its earlier critics. In 'On Translating *Beowulf*' Tolkien argues strongly against the rendering of the Anglo–Saxon poem into prose, largely due to the fact that metre and other poetic qualities are inevitably lost in the process. Furthermore, Tolkien believes that the only real use of a prose translation is to serve as an aid to study. He also warns here, however, that even a verse translation is no substitute for reading the original. The debates concerning the merits and pitfalls of literary translation continue up to the present day.

RITCHIE GIRVAN

Of course, many critics besides J.R.R. Tolkien were writing about *Beowulf* during the 1930s and 1940s, and we will now turn to these. Ritchie Girvan, for example, produced an important volume in 1935 entitled *Beowulf and the Seventh Century*, in which Girvan provides a somewhat traditional historicist reading of the poem and dates it to the Age of Bede (c. 680–700). In Chapter Three, 'Folk-Tale and History' (which is mentioned by Tolkien in 'The Monsters and the Critics'), Girvan also provides a very useful summary of the poem:

■ The subject of *Beowulf* is in conflict with two water-monsters who are in turn despatched, and after a long interval a conflict with a dragon laying waste the country-side. It too is killed by the hero who, however, gets his own death in the encounter. Both conflicts, for the first, though double, is to be regarded as one, are set amid an historical environment at a definite time, and real people are introduced in person or by allusion. There are numerous references to historical events or events which profess to be historical, but the history is the frame and the background, and the canvas is occupied by a couple of folk-tales seemingly as old as humanity. We need not doubt that such subjects were cultivated from the beginning by the Germanic poet, and it is certain that they lingered on in the people's memory. Tales of dragons together with a belief in dragons survived till recent times, and the popular mind is apt to accept with credulity stories of water-monsters. The stories, moreover, are often attached to real persons and localized precisely in time and place. The habit is so well known that examples are superfluous.[21] □

Girvan also anticipates Tolkien's labelling of *Beowulf* as 'an heroic–elegiac poem'[22] when he comes to address the overall mood of the poem:

■ One characteristic of *Beowulf* which cannot easily be separated from the English environment, and that precise time [the Age of Bede], is the atmosphere of pensive melancholy, a mood of sorrow excited by the decay of the splendours of the past, by the destruction which attends mortality and the works of man. Nowhere in England more than in Northumbria [the location of the famous monastery in Wearmouth-Jarrow where Bede resided] were men in the presence of an imposing greatness which had passed away. The ground was littered with the ruined fragments of a past which impressed the imagination as vividly as it provoked curiosity, but was only imperfectly understood, and remained mysterious, menacing – *eald enta geweorc* ['the old work of giants']. Deserted chambers rich in decoration, the empty temples of forgotten gods called forth an emotional response issuing in a sense of the transience of man's life and works, which poetry expressed itself in a melancholy characteristic of all Anglo-Saxon verse, and in life translated itself into a desire for escape from the burden of the world, an other-worldliness notable in Northumbria and not there alone.[23] □

Girvan's identification above of 'a melancholy characteristic of all Anglo-Saxon verse' raises an important point about the poetic corpus of which *Beowulf* is such a vital part – much of it is elegiac in nature. Indeed, there is even a small body of Old English poems know as The Elegies which oftentimes employ the *ubi sunt* technique. This can be explained as the dwelling on, or lamenting of, the transitory nature of life and beauty (*ubi sunt* is a Latin phrase meaning 'where are ...?'). And, in relation to *Beowulf* specifically, Frederick R. Rebsamen in *Beowulf Is My Name* (1971) finds another way of speaking about the poem as an elegy:

■ The puzzling things about Beowulf's life – his origin, the fact that he apparently never married and/or produced any children, his return alone from the battle that took the life of his lord, his apparent inactivity during the later Geat–Swede conflicts – these [...] cease to be bothersome when one accepts the idea that, after all, his creator was a major poet trying something big and new, involving the best standards of two different ways of life, and that his concentration upon theme and mood has made of Beowulf, in places, a puzzling character. If the reader further accepts, as I do, the idea that the poet was here presenting his personal elegy for the demise of an old and in many ways admirable tradition at the moment when it was giving into and merging its best qualities with a new one, then Beowulf as a character grows less and less puzzling and begins to make very good sense indeed.[24] □

These sentiments about the potentially flawed nature of 'Beowulf as a character' echo E.M.W. Tillyard's comment above that 'However evolved and sophisticated the art of *Beowulf* may be, that sophistication does not include the motivation of the actors.'[25] Rebsamen is, though, perhaps less negative in his assessment than Tillyard for he does suggest that the poet *intentionally* sacrificed character to theme and mood in his creation of a 'personal elegy'.

HENRY BOSLEY WOOLF

Not everyone, of course, sees Beowulf as a flawed character. In 1948, for example, Henry Bosley Woolf (1910–2004) refuted this very claim in 'On the Characterization of Beowulf'. Like many critics before and since, Woolf opens his article by mentioning the steady proliferation of *Beowulf* criticism or, to use his exact words, 'this mass of scholarly endeavour'.[26] For all this wealth of criticism, however, Woolf detects a gap in the scholarship: 'One aspect of the poet's artistry that has generally been passed over, and that to me seems increasingly effect-ive with each rereading of the poem, is his skill in characterization, especially of Beowulf.'[27] Woolf confines his analysis to the first part of the poem, and argues that the poet employed both direct and indirect ways of portraying Beowulf's character to his audience. Direct com-ments made in the poem tell us that the hero is strong, altruistic and highly regarded/esteemed. For our purposes, especially in the light of ongoing discussions in this guide of the Christian and pagan elements in the poem, the following statement is important:

> ■ Indeed, in these lines of direct characterization [lines 194–204, where Beowulf is initially introduced to the audience] one sees a combination of the two civilizations that are blended in the hero (and in the poem): the Germanic warrior renowned for his physical strength and the Christian knight revered for his spirit of helpfulness [and] as the action of the poem unfolds, [Beowulf] is portrayed as a man possessing various Christian virtues. Indeed, the moving lines with which the poem concludes may be looked upon as the logical outgrowth of what has been earlier revealed of the spiritual side of the Geatish champion, from the time of the prayer of thanksgiving for a safe voyage [lines 227b–228] on through the three fights.[28] □

By calling Beowulf a 'Christian knight', Woolf is placing him in the tradition of a Soldier of Christ, a character type that is often found in Anglo-Saxon religious poetry. Woolf's further remark that Beowulf is additionally characterized by a 'general spirit of helpfulness' only enhances the hero's spiritual status. Ultimately, along with critics like Tolkien, Woolf is formulating a case for *Beowulf* as a work of art. He calls the poem 'the greatest of Old English literary monuments'[29] and concludes that 'it seems worth noting that through his effective use of the various direct and indirect methods of characterization here pointed out, the author of *Beowulf* reveals another aspect of the art-istic skill which he lavished on the poem.'[30] At the heart of Woolf's argument is the belief that the poet's use of direct and indirect meth-ods of characterization is a strong indicator of his 'artistic skill.' This implicitly echoes Tolkien's belief (unique in its day) that there was a harmonious relationship between the theme and style of *Beowulf* and that, as a consequence, the poem was carefully plotted and structurally coherent.

ADRIEN BONJOUR

Like Tolkien, Adrien Bonjour was another critic who dominated *Beowulf* criticism for many years. Bonjour's reputation in the field, however, was not forged upon the strength of one groundbreaking lecture. Rather, he wrote a series of important essays on the poem throughout his career and these have been neatly distilled in his *Twelve Beowulf Papers, 1940–1960* (with additional comments) (1962). In the volume's preface, Bonjour remarks that all of the essays in the collection 'in fact involve questions more or less closely connected with the poet's artistry'. He returns us, then, to a by now familiar subject – that of the literary skill of *Beowulf*'s creator. Unlike in the days of Tolkien and Woolf, however, by 1962 (the publication date of *Twelve Beowulf Papers*) interest in this matter was much more widespread. For, as Bonjour notes (again in his preface), his decision to collect together his work on *Beowulf* was in response to 'the ever-increasing interest of *Beowulf* scholars and students in the various aspects of the poet's art'.

In his essay from 1940, 'The Use of Anticipation in *Beowulf*', Bonjour starts off by establishing the poem's genre. Unlike Tolkien or Tillyard (but similarly to Ker), Bonjour defines *Beowulf* as an epic. He then moves swiftly on to the main topic of his piece, the poet's use of anticipation and how it works in the poem. It is most obviously seen, as readers of this guide may have noted when reading the poem, in the fact that the outcomes of Beowulf's three great fights are given in advance of the actual action.

Defying normal expectations, however, Bonjour claims that the use of anticipation here implies a 'complete disregard for suspense'.[31] If this is indeed the case, why might the poet use this technique? Bonjour has a ready answer:

■ That the use of anticipations [...] give[s] the *Beowulf* poet a means of emphasizing the part played by fate and makes it the more pervasive [...] Decidedly, fate is given an important and pervasive part throughout the poem. The fact that it is used side by side with God, or even at times subordinated to Him, is merely evidence of the blending of the Christian and heathen elements so characteristic of *Beowulf*; but there it is, constantly present in our mind, lurking or striking, and the emphasis brought about by the repeated anticipations potently helps towards furthering the representation of fate, hovering above the whole drama. This not only justifies the way anticipation is used by the poet, but also makes it quite pertinent in the individual poem, and, above all, actually betrays the hand of the artist.[32] □

This passage clearly reminds us of another major theme running throughout the poem – *wyrd*, the Old English word for fate or destiny.

It is a much-discussed topic in *Beowulf* criticism and, as a consequence, makes an appearance throughout the course of the guide.

At the end of the decade, Bonjour turned to the mesmerizing subject of Grendel's mother in 'Grendel's Dam and the Composition of *Beowulf*' (1949). In the previous chapter of this guide we looked at Grendel and focused largely on his lineage as kin of Cain. Along with studies on the characterization of Beowulf, there is easily equal (if not surpassing in some quarters) interest in the figures of Grendel and his mother. As for the latter character, she is of especial interest to feminist critics, as we will see in the penultimate chapter of this guide. But in 1949 Bonjour also had something to say about her and her fight with Beowulf. He begins his study with a survey of some earlier criticism devoted to Grendel's mother – especially in relation to whether or not the *Beowulf* poet 'found the Grendel's dam motive in his story, together with Grendel'[33] or 'started from a single monster version and himself introduced the adventure with Grendel's dam as an epic elaboration.'[34] Again, we have cause to think back to Tolkien as he was adamant that *Beowulf* was structurally and stylistically unified. Bonjour makes us consider the contrast between the 'relative easiness of the victory over Grendel' and the 'deadly hardness of the fight with Grendel's dam.'[35] His argument in full is as follows:

■ Now the sudden and startling surprise at the deadly hardness of the fight with Grendel's dam, the awareness that the hero was practically vanquished before some kind of miracle saved him *in extremis*, such a narrow escape, all this gives us *a first intimation of his ultimate vulnerability* – though he is supreme among all men as a fighter of monsters. And here, the role of fate is particularly important. The hero is not yet doomed – therefore we have the magical apparition of the sword to save him at a moment when he seemed lost. This sword shows him, poetically, in the hands of fate (or God, for that matter). The poet introduced this motive to materialize divine intervention, to render it tangible in a striking way; had he merely referred to God's help, it would not have sounded much more than a formula. We thus feel vividly that by himself alone, in spite of his former victory and superior strength, the hero could hardly have overcome Grendel's dam. We have here, as it were, a real omen which is to get its full significance only in the first clear foreboding of his death (a consequence of inexorable doom) before the Dragon fight.[36] □

Bonjour suggests, then, that the real reason for the appearance of Grendel's mother in the poem is structural (other critics, as shall be seen, do not consign her to such a secondary role). In keeping with this belief, he states further that 'We suggest that such a conception of the structural role of the Grendel's dam section and all its implications cannot but help us to a better understanding of the organic unity of

Beowulf.'[37] Interestingly, Tolkien argued for *Beowulf* as a poem of two halves. Bonjour, however, makes us aware of another possibility: 'The conception of the structural role of Beowulf's fight with Grendel's dam [...] has been used as one of the arguments in favour of a fundamental division of the poem into three main parts instead of two.'[38]

In relation to Bonjour's comments above about Beowulf's battles with his supernatural foes, it might be useful to consider how Harold Bloom (born 1930) interprets these episodes in the poem. In his *Modern Critical Interpretations, Beowulf* (1987) he writes:

■ Rereading *Beowulf* gives one a fierce and somber sense of heroic loss, in a grim world, not wholly unlike the cosmos of Virgil's *Aeneid*. In spirit, the poem does seem to me more Virgilian than Christian. Though addressed to a Christian audience, it seems not to be addressed to them *as* Christians but as descendants of heroic warriors. Beowulf does not die so as to advance the truth but so as to maintain his own glory, the fame of a man who could slay a monster with only his own bare hands to do the heroic work. The bareness of those unfaltering hands counts much more than does the monster's descent from the wicked line of the accursed Cain.[39] □

Bloom returns us here to the idea of a possible link between *Beowulf* and classical epic, if in mood only. He also, however, reminds us of the heroic roots of the poem's original audience.

JOAN BLOMFIELD

Joan Blomfield, the first female critic to be discussed in this guide, is another major name in *Beowulf* criticism and the final scholar to be considered in this chapter. In her 1938 essay 'The Style and Structure of *Beowulf*' (the title is self-explanatory) she starts off by suggesting that an 'analysis of style is in this case a justifiable approach to analysis of structure.'[40] One of the stylistic features that Blomfield sees recurring in the poem is the use of contrast; for example the comparison of Beowulf's youth with Hrothgar's age. First impressions of Beowulf, after all, are that he is 'the all-powerful enterprise of untried youth'.[41] Blomfield continues:

■ Beowulf is connected with Hroðgar both by grateful allegiance, because of the favour shown to his father, and by his undertaking the trial of valour where others have failed. Complementing the knowledge that Hroðgar his *hold wine* ['gracious friend'] is in need is Beowulf's desire to crown his exploits by the supreme enterprise of *ðing wið þyrse* ['contest with the monster']. The duty of allegiance emerges in Hroðgar's recapitulation of Beowulf's *æþelu* ['nobility'] (457–72), the demands of Beowulf's career in his own account of his setting forth (405–41). Both are presaged in the greeting of Wulfgar (338–9), who recognizes in the bearing of Beowulf the *wlenco* ['pride'] and *higeþrymm* ['courage'] which have brought him to Heorot, as contrasted with *wræcsið* ['exile'] (which brought his father). The allusion is oblique – Wulfgar is challenging Beowulf as a stranger – and its application by so much the more pointed. The same alternation is at work throughout the poem. The suspension of the theme – the 'balance' of which Professor Tolkien speaks – demands a constant confrontation of the similar and dissimilar.[42] □

Blomfield also revisits subjects by now familiar to readers of this guide; she speaks of the artistry of the poet (with clear indebtedness to Tolkien) as well as the unity of the text, and argues that the digressions are integral to the story. Overall, Blomfield sees a tragic unity to *Beowulf* – again, an echo of Tolkien, this time of his reading of the poem as 'heroic-elegiac' – and she makes a strong case for the intellectual and artistic underpinnings of the poem:

■ The writer of *Beowulf* is in fact a true poet; he has created a tragic unity, he sees with the poet's eye which splits and recombines the elements of everyday perceptions. The signs and symbols that he uses are now unfamiliar, representations which need to be interpreted; we should not be misled into thinking them accidents. The ritual of language and exploitation of its metaphysical aspects which are the most outstanding features of this style have repeatedly won the attention of critics, and provide the best clues to the underlying structural unity.[43] □

As we shall see, this way of reading *Beowulf* would also be advocated by scholars writing in the decades to follow.

CHAPTER FOUR

The Debates Continue: the 1950s and 1960s

The two decades under consideration in this chapter were important years for *Beowulf* criticism. A wide variety of new approaches to the poem emerged and familiar themes and subjects were revisited in fresh and interesting ways. In the light of Tolkien's earlier study, more criticism on the 'monsters' in *Beowulf* was being produced and the historicity of Beowulf himself was debated. The composition and role of the poem's original audience also came under the critical spotlight. And, by the mid-1960s, the New Criticism even began to assert its influence in the field. When we turn to the beginning of the 1950s, however, a name which dominated Anglo-Saxon studies for many years suggests itself, C.L. Wrenn.

C.L. WRENN

Wrenn, in his famous edition of *Beowulf with the Finnesburg Fragment* (1953), presents the case for and against Beowulf as an actual historical figure:

■ The historicity of Beowulf himself must be, at best, but very shadowy. It is true that the mere attribution to him of supernatural feats of strength need not in itself imply that he had in fact no existence [...] But from the beginning the poet seems to assume that Beowulf is capable of more than human actions while at the same time remaining a very human hero; and that the fact that no clear allusions to this hero have so far been found outside the poem, and that the name Beowulf is only found once in OE [Old English] in ordinary use (in the Book of Life [sic] of the Lindisfarne monks of the early ninth century) and in two not very secure early place-names, tells against historical reality. True, we should expect the audience to look for a hero from the known or traditional Germanic past: but Beowulf may well have been known to them as a great hero from a kind of 'historicized folk mythology'.[1] □

Wrenn concludes, therefore, that 'The historicity of Beowulf himself, then, must remain for the present as "not proven," but by no means impossible.'[2] Wrenn here also provides us with another way of looking at the character of Beowulf when he describes him as 'a great hero from a kind of historicized folk mythology'. This description foregrounds the national importance of a character like Beowulf and suggests that he may have had a vital role to play in the collective psyche of the original audience of the poem.

Where the history of the actual poem was concerned, some type of consensus had been reached on its date if not its provenance. By 1967, *A Beowulf Reader* states, 'By and large Anglo-American scholarship has come to an agreement that it [the poem] is not earlier than about 700 and not much later than about 800. The agreement is impressive though it conceals two differing schools who would choose, the one Bede's Northumbria, and the other Offa's Mercia.'[3]

ROBERT L. CHAPMAN

In terms of a reappraisal of familiar themes, in 1955 H.L. Rogers revitalized the study of the inter-relationship between the structure of the poem and Beowulf's three famous fights, and from 1949 to 1951 Morton Bloomfield wrote '*Beowulf* and Christian Allegory: An Interpretation of Unferth'. In this article Unferth, Beowulf's nemesis, is read allegorically.

Some sympathetic studies of Grendel also emerged, one being Robert L. Chapman's 'Alas, Poor Grendel'. An excellent summary of this article is found in Douglas Short's *Beowulf Scholarship: An Annotated Bibliography* (1980), where its is stated that Chapman here '[f]inds a measure of sympathy in the poet's management of Grendel and his dam, both in certain features of his description of the two and the dramatic situations involving them'.[4] In 'Alas, Poor Grendel' Chapman identifies a 'curious ambivalence'[5] in the poet's attitude towards Beowulf's first adversary. He also explores the by now familiar Christian versus pagan debate generated by the poem and declares that, if the characterization of Grendel is anything to go by, the *Beowulf* poet 'was certainly not the mature and convinced orthodox believer that Klaeber and Miss Dorothy Whitelock would have him'.[6] This conclusion is rooted in Chapman's assertion that the poet's 'sympathy for Grendel [...] has its origin in a mistrust of election, in a rooted insistence on the unfettered and unsubmissive human will'.[7] To clarify this last statement a little, it might help to add here that Chapman sees Grendel as being portrayed as 'negatively elected' in the poem. This view is predicated on the fact that Grendel has no free will and was 'damned at birth' as a kinsman of Cain. He was, therefore, destined to suffer eternal damnation because of his nature, not his will. As a consequence, Chapman believes that the *Beowulf* poet saw Grendel's situation as being manifestly unfair and therefore tried to elicit some sympathy for him. Ultimately, Chapman's article is an excellent analysis of Grendel's possible metamorphosis from folktale troll to one of Beowulf's adversaries.

HENNING COHEN

During the period covered by this chapter of this guide, Henning Cohen also wrote an interesting article called simply '*Beowulf*, 86–92' (1958). Again, Short provides an expert summary, stating that Cohen:

> ■ asserts that Grendel is specifically motivated to attack Heorot by the singing of the *scop*, which the *Beowulf*-poet then illustrates. Similarly the dam is incited by her son's death, and the dragon by the theft of his cup. In providing motivation for each monster, the poet lends unity to the poem.'[8] □

What is particularly striking about this reading is how it sets the poem so firmly within its own cultural and historical contexts. Grendel is shown to be motivated by existential despair, a terrible by-product of his exile. As we know, exile was feared by the Anglo-Saxons and was something of a cultural preoccupation if the literature of the period is anything to judge by. We then see Grendel's mother's actions being incited by a desire to revenge her son's death; this revenge code was, as we know, an integral part of heroic warrior society. And even the dragon is operating within specific cultural parameters. When his hall is violated by the theft of his treasure, he suffers a violation of the hospitality code. As a consequence, he too has no choice but to seek revenge for this crime. This type of reading of the poem would no doubt have been approved of by J.C. Van Meurs, for in his article '*Beowulf* and Literary Criticism' (1955) he attacks critics such as Tolkien and Bonjour who, he asserts, view *Beowulf* from a modern literary perspective. According to Van Meurs, Tolkien's belief that *Beowulf* was a poem possessing artistic and structural unity is a direct consequence of this type of approach.

NORA K. CHADWICK

As attention is already focused on Grendel, Grendel's mother and the dragon, another relevant study should be mentioned at this juncture – Nora K. Chadwick's 'The Monsters and Beowulf' (1959). As might be expected, Chadwick begins her essay with a homage to Tolkien. She praises Tolkien's 'penetrating study' and suggests that its greatest strength was in 'emphasizing the value of the story to give scope to the hero and express the literary and spiritual ideals of the poet'.[9] Chadwick then goes on to ask a highly pertinent question: 'What is the nature of the monsters?'[10] She answers her own question in the following manner:

■ Grendel never speaks. A hideous light shines from his eyes, but we do not know what he looks like, or if, or how, he is clad, though he carries some kind of pouch or bag (*glof*). His claws are emphasized and the great strength of both him and his mother, as well as their invulnerability to ordinary weapons. The dragon is a fiery dragon, who guards the treasure of a race long dead in their ancestral barrow, and eventually, when robbed, flies about at night on errands of destruction to mankind.

Let us look for a moment at the words used to describe the monsters. Grendel is referred to as *eaten* (l. 761), a *þyrs* (l. 426), generally translated 'giant', 'demon', and *helle gast* (l. 1274), which, whether a compound [...] or not [...], probably means something like 'hellish spirit', or 'spirit of Hell'. His mother is referred to, not only as *grundwyrgen*, a *mere if mihtig* (l. 1518 f.), which may be translated 'she-wolf of the depths, a mighty sea-woman', or 'woman of the mere', but also, strangely enough, as *ides* (l. 1259) which is used apparently as a synonym with *aglæcwif*, a 'formidable' or 'terrifying woman', which follows it immediately in the context in l. 1259. *Ides* occurs again in line 1351 in an attempt to describe her as vaguely visualized 'in the form of a lady' (*ides onlicnes*). Elsewhere in the poem it is used only of a royal lady, or a lady of high degree. It is in fact a term of courtly epic diction, more dignified than *wif*. Mother and son are described as *helrunan* ['infernal spirits'].[11] □

In the light of Tolkien's earlier arguments against the reading of *Beowulf* in translation, a passage like the one above is very useful as it allows non-readers of Old English the opportunity to look at the original language of the poem. This, in turn, provides more insight into the mind of the *Beowulf* poet and his original intentions. What is particularly striking about the words used for Grendel's mother is how largely ambiguous they are: the multiple interpretations of *ides* is a good illustration of this.

The central core of Chadwick's essay, however, is a study of some potential Norse analogues and sources for *Beowulf*. Though the minutiae of this particular argument need not be of concern here, Chadwick's overall conclusion is of interest:

■ If the poet of *Beowulf* has found his story already fully developed in the ancient Scandinavian world; if again it is a story of the ancestors of the reigning house of East Anglia in his own day, when did the story come to England? Surely not as a contemporary Scandinavian theme, newly introduced. Although the personnel and the *mise-en-scène* [setting] are those of the Scandinavian world, the standards of conduct and the courtly diction and general tone have been completely Anglicized. The metre and form of the poem, the note of reflection and the 'elegiac' tone, the leisurely pageantry and the quiet dignity of the grand theme, are remote from early Norse and suggest that the tradition had long been known in the milieu in which the poet of *Beowulf* composed. These things suggest that the poet is composing a Scandinavian theme for a Scandinavian dynasty in a milieu in which both had become thoroughly English. Perhaps it was the East Anglian royal family, the Wuffingas, who introduced the original story relating to their ancestors from Gautland, and naturalized it among their own subjects in East Anglia.[12] □

Chadwick approaches the idea of *Beowulf* as a nationalistic text (a topic already broached in Chapter Two of this guide) from an unusual angle in that she associates the poem with the Wuffingas, the East Anglian royal family. This in turn also touches upon the knotty subject of the date and provenance of *Beowulf*, though no firm conclusions are reached by Chadwick on these matters.

SIGNE CARLSON

The 1950s and 1960s do very much seem to have been a time when the 'monsters' of *Beowulf* dominated the literary critical scene. Another valuable contribution to this field of study came in the form of Signe Carlson's 'The Monsters of *Beowulf*: Creations of Literary Scholars'. From the very outset Carlson's article packs quite a punch, opening as it does with the following sentiments:

■ 'History is the frame and the background, and the canvas is occupied by a couple of folktales seemingly as old as humanity,' wrote Ritchie Girvan of *Beowulf*, but literary scholars have had a hand in its delineation also. It is they who put the monsters in this greatest of Old English poems. Indeed, the word 'monster' does not appear in English until the fourteenth century; to get it into *Beowulf* along with the creatures represented by the word, they had to go to Latin for *monstrum* – and even there it originally meant 'a divine portent or warning'.[13] □

After asserting that the 'monsters' of *Beowulf* are largely a critical invention, Carlson then proceeds to investigate whether or not these creatures might have any basis in fact; it is also argued that this approach has never before been taken:

■ With hardly any exceptions, scholarship in regard to Grendel, his mother, and the dragon is based on Christian allusions made by the *Beowulf* poet, often debatable scholarly emendations to the text, and highly interpretative translations and adaptations. Therefore, a logical starting point in an examination of the text is the recognition of literary accretions that may be attributed to scholars who have altered folk tradition to suit themselves. Since the *Beowulf* poet is the earliest acknowledged scholar connected with the poem, we should review his work first. The efforts of scribes who copied the extant manuscript, scholars who translated the poem, and critics who based their theories on the labor of scribes and scholars will be discussed briefly. The result of this analysis, while not conclusive, may be the raising of serious doubts about present stereotyped thinking on the subject of the 'monsters' of *Beowulf*.[14] □

An overview of translations and adaptations of the poem follows, along with an extensive section on word studies. Carlson then continues:

■ Criticism regarding Grendel, his mother, and the dragon seems to fall into two main categories, the one treating of symbolic interpretation of these creatures and the other examining parallels and analogues in folklore. The ultimate origin of Grendel, his mother, and the dragon is not a matter of concern in either group. Symbolic interpretation is based on Christian allusions and the interpretative translations of key words of the type discussed above, while the comparison of episodes corresponding to those in which Grendel, his mother, and the dragon play their parts is limited primarily to the related folktales, although a few scholars have expressed an interest in a connection between the dragon's barrow and Stone Age treasure and burial mounds. Knut Stjerna's study of archeological counterparts for almost everything in *Beowulf* is in a class by itself and indicates his belief in a possible basis in fact for much of the folktale material of the poem.[15] □

Eschewing symbolic interpretations of the creatures, however, Carlson's article instead closes with an attempt to locate Grendel, Grendel's mother and the dragon within some type of historical reality:

■ A vague and arbitrary assignment of the origin of Grendel, his mother, and the dragon to 'remote antiquity' or the 'distant past', or conceding the existence of such creatures 'from time immemorial' seems out of place in this day when we can strike a target on the moon. A recognition of the likelihood that Germanic invaders encountered primitive indigenous inhabitants of Europe, just as European settlers later encountered the Indians of the Americas, can be a point of departure for further research along this line. A study of climatic changes and the rapidly declining numbers of many species of wildlife in Europe and elsewhere during the last two thousand years may lead to more insight into the existence and plight of the dragon.

There seems to be no reason for assuming that tales of such continuous and everyday occurrences as conflicts between the invaders and native inhabitants and between man and beast should be thought of as 'figments of imagination' with supernatural overtones, although the humanitarian sensibilities of the *Beowulf* poet and succeeding scholars may have been soothed by placing 'outside the normal order of things' what really belongs inside.[16] □

Carlson implicitly offers here a tantalizing, early post-colonial reading (with traces of eco-criticism thrown in) of the 'monsters' of *Beowulf*.

LARRY BENSON

In 1967, Larry Benson revisited the subject of religion in *Beowulf*. In an essay entitled 'The Pagan Coloring of *Beowulf*', he used an old-fashioned historical approach to argue that:

■ In the light of what we now know of attitudes towards the pagans in the late seventh and eighth centuries, it appears that the paganism of the poet's characters may have been a positive advantage to him rather than the insuperable difficulty that it seemed to early critics. Those crit-ics assumed that *Beowulf* was originally and essentially pagan, and what pagan elements the poem contains were therefore most easily explained as mere undigested lumps of primitive matter. We are still accustomed to think of the pagan elements as part of the original essence of the poem, the Christian elements as additions – beautifully integrated, but additions nevertheless, yet our reading of the poem does not accord with our the-ory. Christianity is part of the very fabric of *Beowulf*; the pagan elements are not. When we examine those elements that are actually pagan rather than secular, references to practices that ceased altogether or became criminal with the introduction of Christianity – augury, cremation, the wor-ship of idols – we find that they are few in number and easily isolable. Their removal would harm but not destroy the poem (which may explain why good critics have wanted to take some of them out), for one cannot imagine *Beowulf* in anything like its present state without its Christian basis, but one can easily conceive of it without its few touches of paganism [...] Probably it was the *Beowulf* poet who deepened the Christian meanings when he reshaped the inherited material; but probably it was also he who added the 'pagan coloring,' drawing on contemporary information about the Germanic pagans and on the prevalent attitude toward them to add both interest and a new dimension of meaning to his materials.[17] □

ADRIEN BONJOUR

Adrien Bonjour is also met again in this same collection, and this time, in his essay 'Jottings on *Beowulf* and the Aesthetic Approach' (1967), he explores the thorny topic of the poem's authorship:

■ The controversy that arose in the wake of the spectacular launching of the singer theory in Anglo-Saxon poetry shows no sign of abating. Indeed the gap between the supporters of unity of authorship in *Beowulf* and the neodisintegrators of the text of the poem is wider than ever [...] The positions of the two schools of *Beowulf* criticism are diametrically opposed mainly when it comes to over-all generalizations.[18] □

Bonjour also demonstrates that Francis P. Magoun, Jr. 'propounded in favor of a multiple authorship of the *Beowulf* poem',[19] and states that Magoun even went so far as to suggest 'that the *Beowulf* material in Cotton Vitellius A.XV is made up of originally independent songs by different singers, so that it is suitable to speak of a *Beowulf A* and a *Beowulf B*, soldered together by means of a *Beowulf A¹*.'[20] In the remainder of the essay, Bonjour attempts to refute Magoun's theory and present his own ideas concerning the unity of authorship. He also acknowledges an awareness of the fact that 'Such arguments [...] can best be applied when the pre-eminence of the poetic perception us fully recognized.'[21] This is something that, to Bonjour's mind at least, Magoun failed to do:

■ For, in the last resort, it is the poetry that counts. And it so happens that we might read on end most of the numerous interesting and valuable *Beowulf* articles written by Magoun and his followers without being aware that what they deal with is poetry. I mean great poetry, as contradistinguished from mere metrical matter – whether a legion of alliterative lines, a crowd of competent cadences, or a stack of staves.'[22] □

DOROTHY WHITELOCK

Thirty years after Tolkien's groundbreaking reading of *Beowulf* as a *poem*, it is curious to note that some critics were still intent on ignoring the literary merits of the text. Questions concerning the poem's authorship were matched by those regarding the possible audience of *Beowulf*. Perhaps one of the most important explorations of the latter topic is that of Dorothy Whitelock. Over the course of the winter of 1950, Whitelock gave three lectures in the Senate House, University of London; these texts were subsequently gathered together and published under the title *The Audience of Beowulf* (1951). It is also interesting to consider here why Whitelock may have wished to devote her attention to this particular topic:

■ And why my title? It will seem very trite and obvious to say that the effect of any work of art depends not only on the author's power and skill, but also on what is already present in the minds of its hearers, or readers, or – in the case of the visual arts – its beholders. Nevertheless, this consideration is particularly pertinent to the poem of *Beowulf*, partly because it is far removed from us in time, so that we are not entitled to assume without investigation that an audience of the poet's day would be moved by the same things we are, or, if by the same things, in the same way; but still more, because much of the poem is composed with a subtle technique of allusion, reminder, and suggestion, so that we cannot guess at the effect the poet was hoping to obtain unless we know something of the meaning and associations his hints and allusions carried for those for whom he composed his poem.[23] □

Whitelock is ultimately attempting, then, to discover 'what effect the poet was consciously striving to produce on the men of his own time'.[24] But who is this poet, and who is his audience? Whitelock sees it this way: 'By the "poet" I designate the Christian author who was responsible for giving the poem the general shape and tone in which it has survived, and by the "audience" the people whom he had in mind.'[25] The poet's relationship to his audience is exhaustively explored in Chapter Two of Whitelock's study, especially in relation to possible sources and analogues of *Beowulf*. Whitelock uses this approach in an effort to find out just how familiar the original audience of *Beowulf* may have been with the central storylines of the poem. After much deliberation she concludes that:

■ one cannot state with confidence that the audience knew the main plot of the poem beforehand; but neither can one state that it did not, for a poet might well be expected to tell his main tale fully and clearly, however vague he might be allowed to be about an illustrative parallel.[26] □

Chapter Three, the final section of *The Audience of Beowulf*, sees Whitelock assembling 'evidence which may help us to assess the audience's attitude to what the poet has to tell it'.[27] After a lengthy assessment of the historical, intellectual and cultural climates that inform the poem, Whitelock ultimately concludes that 'In short, it would be unsafe to argue that any part of England was in the eighth century insufficiently advanced in intellectual attainments for a sophisticated poem like *Beowulf* to have been composed there and appreciated.'[28] We find ourselves returning once more to questions of the dating and provenance of *Beowulf*. As can be seen, Whitelock opts for placing the composition of the poem as some time in the eighth century, but she rejects the theory that *Beowulf* was composed in Northumbria. Why the eighth century? This is to do with the Christian elements Whitelock identifies in the poem:

■ A little before the year 700 all England had been won, nominally, to Christianity, but it is to the eighth century that one must assign much of the steady, unspectacular advance which brought a deeper knowledge of faith to the ordinary layfolk all over the land, by the gradual establishment of parish churches and the provision of a permanent income for the church.[29] □

KENNETH SISAM

Another major work which needs to be mentioned in this chapter is Kenneth Sisam's *The Structure of Beowulf*. Sisam begins by acknowledging that though 'there is no one key to the appreciation of *Beowulf*', there are 'some structural problems, on which there are wide differences of opinion between scholars, especially between scholars of different periods'.[30] In terms of genre, Sisam defines *Beowulf* as 'an heroic narrative poem, composed to entertain an audience of Anglo-Saxons'. One of the most intriguing questions that Sisam asks in his book is: why is *Beowulf* so long? He adds that 'Before the twelfth century no secular poem approaching its scale is recorded from the vernaculars of western Europe.'[31] *Beowulf* is, as we know, by far the longest extant Old English poem. What might account for this? Here is what Sisam has to say on the matter:

■ At one time leading critics like [K.] Müllenhoff [in *Beowulf*, Berlin, 1889] explained the form and length of the poem by postulating a number of interpolators who worked over a more shapely, compact, and consistent synthesis of short lays. Recently Heusler [in *Die altgermanische Dichtung*, 2nd edn., Potsdam, 1943, p. 192] has given his authority to the view that *Beowulf* is the work of an ecclesiastic who emulated the epic breadth of Virgil. I prefer to think with [H.M.] Chadwick [in *The Heroic Age*, 1912, pp. 73 ff] that long secular poems were a native development, to be expected when story-telling was the principal entertainment in the northern winter, and when professional minstrels (*scopas*) had the training necessary to compose or recite an heroic poem that could entertain an audience for hours, even for days. There would be times when a continuous, slow-moving story would please better than the less restful succession of short pieces; and the length of *Beowulf* was well within the capacity of a memory accustomed to work without books.[32] □

Sisam continues on a related note:

■ Whether or not delivery in instalments based on the three great fights was contemplated, the plot seems to have been built up to meet the demand for another story about the hero who killed Grendel. A child who asks for another story about Jack the giant-killer expects more giant-killing.[33] □

This is a rather novel way of arguing for a tripartite structure to *Beowulf*; the poem is in three parts as it was (possibly) read in three instalments over three nights. We may imagine that each evening the poet finished with a cliff-hanger to keep his audience wanting more. This is further support for Sisam's belief that *Beowulf* was primarily created for entertainment purposes.

Sisam also offers an opinion on another popular subject, the Christian and pagan elements in *Beowulf*:

■ in this work the poet was not much concerned with Christianity and paganism. Beowulf was a hero mainly because of his deeds. All his adventures come from pagan stories, and the pagan motives and actions persist. Hrothgar is made eminent by his speeches, which were not governed by pagan tradition. The Christian poet was free to mould them as he wished, and so to make belief in God a leading feature of the character. He was likely to make the most of it, since Hrothgar is not just the pathetic figure of a king incapable through old age of protecting his people; he is a famous hero, still great because of his wisdom and goodness.[34] □

Sisam expresses two interesting opinions here, ones that go against the grain of much previous criticism: firstly, that the *Beowulf* poet was not overly concerned with religion and, secondly, that Hrothgar is, in part, a character with heroic qualities.

E.B. IRVING, JR.

The final critic to be discussed in this chapter is E.B. Irving, Jr, a prolific *Beowulf* scholar. Because of the sheer volume of his output, it is difficult to single out works for mention; nevertheless, choices must be made. For its novelty and insight, '*Ealuscerwen*: Wild Party at Heorot' (1966) will be the first of Irving's works to be discussed. *Ealuscerwen*, defined ultimately by Irving as 'ale-sharing', is found in the scene (761–790) where Grendel is attempting to escape from Beowulf's grip causing the *comitatus* (warrior band) to strike out at him, unaware that Grendel has put a spell on all weapons. What seems even more significant than attempting to define *ealuscerwen*, however, is the way that Irving discusses the poet's use of heroic irony in relation to Grendel:

■ The whole presentation of Grendel as a mock-warrior is one of the striking instances of heroic irony in the poem generally. Full discussion of this point would take many pages; it will have to be enough for our purposes here to remind the reader of a few specific examples of this kind of irony. Grendel is referred to as a *healðegn* (142); he lives in

Heorot (at night), even though he is not permitted to take part in the rit-ual of receiving gifts (164–9); in the *ealuscerwen* passage itself, he and Beowulf are collectively called *rewards* (770). This evidence alone should suggest that it amuses the poet (and is clearly a poetic advantage to him) to treat this giant troll Grendel as if he were really a human being: a lonely exile, a caller of Heorot, a would-be retainer (but where did all the other fellows go?), and perhaps also a guest at a party. In fact there seems to be some slight irony of this sort in the passage immediately preced-ing the *ealuscerwen* scene, where we are told that Grendel prefers to seek the *deofla gedræg*, the noisy company of devils, rather than the *drohtoð*, the society or company, which he has found in Heorot – quite unlike anything he has ever run into in his life before. To Grendel as sam-pler of various social milieus, this call on Heorot has turned out to be a mistake.[35] □

What is striking in the passage above is how much Irving diverges from the sympathetic readings of Grendel discussed earlier in the chapter. On the contrary, Irving believes that 'it amuses the poet' to portray Grendel as a lonely exile. As has been seen, other critics would disagree with this view and argue that the original audience of the poem would have felt some measure of pity for Grendel's plight. Additionally, Irving also draws attention to the way in which Heorot is portrayed in this passage involving Grendel: 'The answer must be that it is an impression of noise and of extreme physical violence, with the hall itself being, so to speak, the victim of both [...] it is a miracle that the hall itself does not collapse from such violence.'[36]

The characterization of Heorot will be returned to in the fol-lowing chapter of this guide. As will be seen, Irving is not the only critic who has some fascinating things to say on this subject. This present chapter, however, will conclude with a discussion of another work by him – *A Reading of Beowulf* (1968). Irving starts off by defin-ing the Ideal Hero and setting him against what is understood to be monstrous. A discussion of Grendel naturally ensues, and Irving reasserts his view that Grendel is a 'mock-thane.'[37] This claim is supported by a brief linguistic analysis of lines 972[b]–979: 'Perhaps it is significant that the words *guma* and *maga*, common words for man, are applied to Grendel in this passage, for what is stressed here is Grendel's sinfulness [...] and his ultimate responsibility for his actions in the face of the Last Judgment.'[38] Much of *A Reading of Beowulf* is given over, however, to the character of Beowulf himself for, as Irving confidently asserts, 'To write of the hero in *Beowulf* is to write of everything in the poem, for there is nothing that does not serve in some sense to illuminate the character of the protagonist.'[39]

In addition, speaking of the first three lines of the poem, Irving asserts that 'Memorable strength and courage, then, is the announced subject of the poem.'[40]

As we move to the next decade of *Beowulf* criticism, scholars themselves continued to 'write of everything in the poem' from a variety of different angles.

CHAPTER FIVE

Stock-taking: the 1970s

In *The Audience of Beowulf*, Dorothy Whitelock advises that 'From time to time in *Beowulf* studies it is desirable to do a sort of stock-taking, to see if received opinions have stood the test of time and the impact of new evidence.'[1] Though these words were written in 1951 they hold equally true for the 1970s – a time when the landscape of *Beowulf* scholarship was fast changing. Feminist criticism of the poem began to emerge, and there were ongoing attempts to define what exactly *Beowulf* was about. Marijane Osborn, for example, in 'The Great Feud: Scriptural History and Strife in *Beowulf*' confidently declared in 1978 that '*Beowulf* is the story of a culture hero who fights in succession three monsters that threaten the fabric of his society.'[2]

STANLEY B. GREENFIELD

The type of 'stock-taking' referred to by Whitelock above was also done by Stanley B. Greenfield, another leading Anglo-Saxonist, during this decade. In 1976, in his article 'The Authenticating Voice in *Beowulf*', he observed the critical scene in this way:

■ Two major concerns of recent Beowulf criticism have been (1) to establish the extent to which the poet used his pagan heroic narrative to shadow forth Christian meaning and (2) to establish the exact attitude of the poet towards his hero and towards the social institutions and mores [the customs and conventions] of his hero's day – which, as we know, was several centuries before the poet's own [...] such concerns about Christian meaning and authorial stance are not unrelated; and even back in 1936, in his important essay on the monsters, J.R.R. Tolkien was not unaware of a distinction to be made between the authorial voice and the sentiments expressed by the poet's characters. The distinction has been considered and explored in various ways since then, and my analysis of what I venture to call 'the authenticating voice' is but a continuation of such efforts. It is my hope in some measure to clarify, even if not to resolve, these related issues.[3] □

And here is the core of Greenfield's argument:

■ this authenticating voice [in *Beowulf*] responds to the narrative events and characters it presents in four major ways: first, by historicizing or distancing them from its own and its immediate audience's time and way of life; second, contrariwise, by contemporizing them, suggesting a continuity between the past and the present; third, by commenting on the morality involved in the actions of the characters; and fourth, by putting the accidents and eventualities of human existence into a perspective which emphasizes the limitations of human knowledge. Taken together, these responses of the voice should give us some insight into the *Gestalt* [form or shape] of the poem itself.[4] □

Ultimately, Greenfield's multi-layered approach yields the following conclusion:

■ Now, these concerns or responses of the authenticating voice may well call to mind the several levels of traditional Christian allegory: the historical [of or relating to the character of history], the allegorical [the representation of abstract ideas or principles by characters, figures, or events in narrative, dramatic, or pictorial form], the anagogical [a mystical interpretation of a word, passage, or text, particularly scriptural exegesis that looks for allusions to heaven or the afterlife] and the tropological [a mode of biblical interpretation that stresses the morally edifying meaning of figures of speech in the Scriptures]. Are they really the same?

Does this analysis lend support to those allegorical and patristic critics who would find, on other grounds, various specific Christian meanings in the poem? I do not think so. Though there is a resemblance, perhaps even an interrelationship, the voice of the poem authenticates a *literalness* of meaning; it insists on the value of *what is there*, concretely. It does not invite symbolic or typological [relating to the study of types or prefigurative symbols, especially in scriptural literature] or allegorical value-adding.[5] □

Greenfield's wariness over finding potential Christian allegory in *Beowulf* did not, however, prevent other critics during the 1970s from continuing to engage with this topic.

MARGARET GOLDSMITH

Margaret Goldsmith for example, in *The Mode and Meaning of Beowulf* (1970), provides a Christian reading of the Anglo-Saxon epic.

She begins her study (a more extensive discussion derived from her earlier work of the 1960s on a similar topic), however, by enumerating the challenges *Beowulf* presents to its audience. Many of these should by now be familiar to readers of this guide:

> ■ The central critical questions about *Beowulf* arise from its peculiar structure, the discontinuity of its narrative, and its abrupt changes of tone [...] a different cause of bafflement is that the author of *Beowulf* composed in chords reverberant to that audience, but now dead sound. All general studies of the poem have in some measure to fill in the silent intervals in the composition, but there is no unanimity on how this should be done.[6] □

One of the few things that the critics *do* agree over, it seems, is that there is a lack of unanimity amongst *Beowulf* scholars on almost all topics relating to this most enigmatic of poems. This aside, however, Goldsmith raises here an important point about the original audience of the poem – that it is, in many ways, a largely unknown quantity. All the critic can do is conjecture (though sometimes with the help of valuable historical information) and speculate in an attempt 'to fill in the silent intervals'. One such attempt by Goldsmith to do just this comes when she herself attempts to reconstruct the original audience of the poem, especially in relation to its class:

> ■ The best playwrights [Goldsmith is speaking here of Elizabethan drama- tists in particular] were not afraid to include subtle effects because the groundlings would fail to appreciate them: they addressed themselves to the nobility, as I think the *Beowulf* poet clearly does, and put in plenty of vigorous action to please the crowd. *Beowulf* in its present form has none of the marks of popular entertainment; the characters and their pastimes are aristocratic and no interest whatever is shown in any menial activity. The one category of person whose special interests are evident throughout the poem is the ruler.[7] □

Goldsmith shares the general opinion (one that is never really contested) that *Beowulf* is essentially an aristocratic poem, one aimed at the upper stratum of Anglo-Saxon society; epics, after all, were largely aimed at this group. What is also touched upon in the quotation above, how- ever, is the idea that one of the main subjects of *Beowulf* is kingship. If this is indeed the case, the poem may be viewed as a very early example of a Mirror for Princes/Mirror of Kingship text (along the lines of, say, *Il Principe* (The Prince) (1532), by the Florentine political theorist and historian Niccolò Machiavelli (1469–1527)). Writings of this kind were meant to hold a mirror up to a leader and teach him (these figures were almost exclusively male) the proper way to govern.

As with the original audience of *Beowulf,* the actual author of the text is also difficult to pin down. Goldsmith writes:

■ Even if we knew the poet in person, we should still have to 'conjecture' what his poem meant. Our remoteness from the Anglo-Saxons only makes more apparent the problem of any reader facing any poem, the difficulty of 'understanding the language'. The more we know of an author's life and upbringing, the more we can hope to share the mental experience recorded in the language of the poem, and the more we can know of what he has left unsaid. It hardly needs to be stated that 'associations' vary from person to person in every period. No one of us can, even theoretically, expect to recreate the author's *Beowulf,* or even Klaeber's or Tolkien's *Beowulf.* The 'plain meaning' is a figment.[8] □

Of course because *Beowulf,* like the majority of Anglo-Saxon poetry, is anonymous, we will never have any biographical information about its author. This in turn precludes the type of autobiographical reading often done of more modern literary texts. Goldsmith also argues here that the reading of literature is largely a subjective exercise, one reliant upon such things as individual personality, life experience and historical positioning.

In terms of the Christian underpinnings of the poem, Goldsmith initially refers to the overt didacticism of most Old English poetry and acknowledges that this can be something of a stumbling block for the modern reader: 'The poem's plain moral and religious statements can [...] be a source of difficulty.'[9] Earlier in her discussion she couches things in this way: 'All serious literary art contains an element of moral suasion, more or less concealed according to the conventions of the *genre* and the skill of the artist. In *Beowulf* as in other Old English poetry the moral intent is unmistakable.'[10]

What might this 'moral intent' consist of? As has already been noted, there is the possibility that *Beowulf* was meant to be read as a Mirror for Kingship (though Goldsmith herself curiously refutes this theory). A particularly good discussion of this theory is to be found in J. Leyerle's 'Beowulf the Hero and the King' (1965). *Beowulf* is also a poem that has much to tell us about the nature of the hero, though what is actually being said on this topic is problematic. The closing lines of the text use a series of superlatives to describe Beowulf; the most interesting of these is *lofgeornost,* which is regularly glossed as 'most eager for fame'. This desire for fame is seen as laudable in the heroic pagan context, but from the standpoint of Christianity it is something of a negative impulse because of its associations with pride (one of the Seven Deadly Sins). Also, the final moments of the poem flag up some tensions relating to the behaviour of the hero. We are shown, especially in Wiglaf's highly poignant speech, that when the hero (i.e. Beowulf) pursues the path of individual glory, many suffer. E.T. Donaldson translates these famous lines as follows:

■ Wiglaf spoke, the son of Weohstan: 'Often many a man must suffer distress for the will of one man, as has happened to us. We might by no counsel persuade our dear prince, keeper of the kingdom, not to approach the gold-guardian, let him lie where he was, live in his dwelling to the world's end. He held to his high destiny. The hoard has been made visible, grimly got. What drove the folk-king thither was too powerfully fated.'[11] □

Beowulf's death, therefore, provides him personally with a lasting reputation, but his people are left leaderless and vulnerable. In pursuing the extent to which Christianity is present in the poem, Goldsmith also examines a 'controversial question':[12] is Beowulf meant to be interpreted allegorically as a *figura Christi* (figure of Christ)? An early advocate of this reading was John Earle, who advanced it in his book *Anglo-Saxon Literature* (1884).

On a related note, Chapter Seven (entitled 'The Nature of the Hero') of Goldsmith's book is of particular interest here for it examines 'the degree to which Beowulf is given personality, and in what areas of human activity he has his being'.[13] Alvin A. Lee, in *The Guest-Hall of Eden: Four Essays on the Design of Old English Poetry* (1972, which is discussed further below), has also given this question some thought and provides this answer: 'There is almost nothing in Old English narrative poetry of what might be called interior mental event which would individualize the human figures presented.'[14]

Goldsmith goes on to note that 'the poet gives scant attention to Beowulf's private personal relationships [...] his marriage is not mentioned, though it is inferred from the presence of a mourning woman at his funeral.'[15] As has been seen in Chapter Two of this guide, however, there are many interpretations of this 'mourning woman' and there is no concrete reason to believe that she is Beowulf's widow (though the theory is a tantalizing one). Another compelling question which Goldsmith explores in Chapter Seven has to do with Beowulf's challenging of the dragon. Did he have free will/'moral choice' in this, or was his course 'chartered' as some critics argue?[16] This tension between fate (or *wyrd* in Old English) and free will is of major importance to the poem as a whole.

ANDREAS HAARDER

As has been seen, the 1970s were a time of 'stock-taking' for *Beowulf* criticism and one work which does this particularly well is Andreas

Haarder's *Beowulf: The Appeal of a Poem* (1975). Haarder offers an excellent and comprehensive overview of previous scholarship on the poem,
especially that produced in the nineteenth and early twentieth centuries. He responds in some detail, for example, to Sharon Turner's work
on *Beowulf* (which was considered in Chapter One of this guide), and to
the relevant writings by J.M. Kemble and Benjamin Thorpe. Haarder
also asks the ultimate question about the Anglo-Saxon epic:

■ Why is *Beowulf* important? The answer that has been most generally
given, and possibly the only answer agreed upon, is the following: It is
very old and it gives many glimpses of the life of our distant ancestors.
One cannot help but wondering what those ancestors – the first audience
of *Beowulf* – would do with an answer like that. Moving it back towards
Anglo-Saxon times it loses all meaning – or at least all the meaning now
attached to it. To anyone but the scholar who has his own investigations to
make, to anyone who wants to appreciate it in its own right, it is the wrong
answer. And in making *Beowulf* a scholarly problem – how old? What
glimpses? What ancestors? Etc. [sic] *ad infinitum* – it proved a bad answer.
The history of more than a century of *Beowulf* criticism shows how, with
some exceptions, belief in the problem was stronger than the belief that the
poem may have been worth creating.[17] □

In the above extract, Haarder returns to the issue that was so dear to
Tolkien's heart – the assessing of *Beowulf* as a work of art rather than as
a historical artefact. The dangers of the latter approach are also voiced
by Haarder: 'According to George Anderson, speaking in 1949, we
have tramped the fields of Old English poetry almost flat. Although
it is unlikely that any poetry, properly so called, would ever become
almost, not to say quite, flat.'[18] Haarder continues by opening up the
topic further: 'There has indeed both before and especially since 1949
been much tampering with that particular feature in Old English
poetry: the Anglo-Saxon *scop* [poet].'[19] Intent, then, on doing his own
'tampering' with this subject, Haarder offers this view of the Anglo-
Saxon poet:

■ The picture of the Anglo-Saxon *scop* as we are told of him in *Beowulf*
and many other places, inside and outside the field of Old English poetry,
is fascinating and has fascinated many students of Anglo-Saxon civilization. There is something awe-inspiring about it. In the Anglo-Saxon world
schools were reserved for the happy few, and especially for those who had
dedicated their lives to the church. To meet this performer who could hold,
through his art, the attention of a circle which included everybody, gives one
a feeling of being confronted with something that was really important to the
people involved, a feeling of being in touch with something the participants
could not do without. One has a feeling of being in touch with life.[20] □

It would be difficult to find a more impassioned advocacy of the importance of art than this. Haarder also implicitly contests here the idea that *Beowulf* was meant for an essentially aristocratic audience in his statement that the poem's audience 'included everybody'. In addition, he clearly sees *Beowulf* as being about much more than entertainment; it put its original audience 'in touch' with something that they 'could not do without'.

The hall is another topic explored in some detail in *Beowulf: The Appeal of a Poem* and Haarder shares much with E.B. Irving, Jr. in the way that he discusses Heorot:

■ The *dream* [Old English word for 'joy'] of the hall seems to bring up, through the very fact that it manifests itself, its own antithesis, the *ellengæst* [a word used to describe Grendel and meaning 'powerful demon'] from a different world, a world outside, a world of otherness and a world of darkness [...] It serves as a clear demarcation of the otherness of the world of monsters when man to lend meaning to it is forced to make it a copy of his own world. As the monster world is the quintessence of everything that is not human, i.e. not of the hall, any suggestion of a hall outside the hall of man instead of bridging the gulf widens it through its ironical implication.[21] □

Furthermore, 'The haunts of monsters in *Beowulf* may, in short, be anywhere outside the hall and life of man, in the water, in the air, in the earth. But the haunts are always *outside*.'[22]

Haarder brings this part of his argument to a close by introducing the topic of time, another important theme in *Beowulf*:

■ One could not help noting how clearly the poem offers a unity of place: the hall, and a unity of time: the time when the hall is nationally great, for the threat to intrude upon and for the action to take place in.

The hall is on the one side, the threat is on the other. To keep the balance between having and not having is man's concern.[23] □

Haarder provides us here with another way of looking at the structure of the poem. He also, in the final line of the above extract, identifies what *Beowulf is* potentially about.

ALVIN A. LEE

Another study from the 1970s which, partially at least, comments on the nature of the hall in *Beowulf* is Alvin A. Lee's *The Guest-Hall of Eden: Four Essays on the Design of Old English Poetry*. In the following extract from this work, echoes of Andreas Haarder can be found:

■ *Beowulf* is not about an individual as such but about a man of archetypal proportions, whose significance, in the broadest and deepest sense, is social. The poem is an imaginative vision of two kinds of human society, one symbolized by the gold-hall and banqueting and characterized by generosity, loyalty, and love, the other by monsters of darkness and bloodshed who prey on the ordered, light-filled world man desires and clings to.[24] □

The sentiments expressed above are very much in keeping with Haarder's view of *Beowulf* as a text with a tragic vision:

■ Beowulf is a poem about hell's possession of middle-earth. Within its overall tragic structure, the joys of the golden *dryht* [warrior band] and the actions of good kings and heroes are presented as capable of a splendid but precarious realization; the dominant vision, however, is the defeat of man in the kingdoms of this world by the powers of darkness.[25] □

Lee also argues, however, that man is oftentimes destroyed by the enemy within:

■ All fraternity, *Beowulf* seems to say, is potentially fratricidal, and brothers in the fallen world are brothers to dragons. The warring, schismatic, confused tribal world, then, in which Beowulf dies is symbolized by a dragon.

It is, finally, only death that can mark Beowulf off completely from the relentless vendettas of life in the northern lands, a life that has become an intricate, bloodstained pattern of accidental, vicious, or legally required murders. Beowulf's life has risen like a parabola [a type of curve] from an inauspicious youth to the role of mighty hero and king, but now that life sinks again, penetrated by the fire and venom of the serpent. What remains, once the rituals of lamenting have ended, is a large memorial barrow that is to serve other seafarers in the perilous floods of existence in middle-earth as a reminder of one truly exemplary life.[26] □

Lee's belief that, in Beowulf, the poet has created an exemplary hero goes against the view that the ending of the poem is problematic. Ironically though, whilst Lee mentions the 'rituals of lamenting' that accompany the hero's death, he fails to mention that these lamentations are partly based upon the fact that Beowulf's people are left vulnerable and leaderless in the wake of his (potentially selfish) final action.

KATHRYN HUME

At this juncture, it might seem that most critics problematize the image of the hall in *Beowulf*. This is not the full story, however. Critics like Kathryn Hume, for example, interpret Heorot in an altogether more optimistic light. In her article 'The Concept of the Hall in Old English Poetry' (1974), Hume writes that:

> ■ *Beowulf,* to my mind, seems relatively untroubled by tensions over worldly matters – 'fighting words' in the current state of scholarly dispute. Heorot seems to me to retain most of the positive power of the [...] hall-ideal. Granted that it is ultimately doomed, and granted the presence of ambition, envy and like dangers within its circle, Heorot nonetheless emerges as very attractive. If the *Beowulf* poet had meant to persuade his audience of the hall's shortcomings (let alone of its vanity, its identity as a Castle of Pride and new Babel), he could have destroyed its claim to heroism and joy just as [does] the *Judith* poet [*Judith* is found in the same manuscript as *Beowulf*].[27] □

'Fighting words' indeed. Hume also makes us aware of how important the image of the hall is in Old English poetry more generally: 'Moreover, because the hall is the focus for conflicting attitudes, the array of associations proves useful to a more general understanding of the nature of Old English poetry.'[28] And she concludes by saying that 'What the poems celebrate is, of course, not simply the hall as a building but the social system associated with it.'[29] It is interesting to note that much of Hume's research is based upon what has been learnt about the great halls of Anglo-Saxon England through archaeological discoveries. As might be expected, Sutton Hoo (the lavish Anglo-Saxon royal cemetery discovered in Suffolk in 1939) is of particular importance to Hume's argument. Indeed, since the discovery of this great treasure trove 'a quite considerable literature of descriptive material and various discussion has been published,'[30] and some of this material relates to *Beowulf*.

C.L. WRENN

C.L. Wrenn (another eminent Anglo-Saxonist), for example, produced a fascinating study in 1959, 'Sutton Hoo and *Beowulf*'. Wrenn primarily sets the Christian and pagan elements of the poem against the material reality of the Anglo-Saxon world as it emerged in this great archaeological discovery:

> ■ The rich variety and assimilative creativeness of Anglo-Saxon culture with its progressive adaptation of pagan elements into Christian contexts,

have often been remarked: and these features are well illustrated in both the Sutton Hoo cenotaph and by *Beowulf* [...] At Sutton Hoo were found expressions of pagan symbolism along with some clearly Christian arte-facts, just as in *Beowulf* the pagan sentiment and Christian thinking go together [...] Again, there is variety in the ages of the artefacts. The large sil-ver dish has the hall-mark of the Byzantine Emperor Anastasius I who died in the year 518; and the shield and helmet were some hundred years old when buried. Some of the jewellery, on the other hand, may well have been quite recent when placed in the cenotaph [an empty tomb which functions as a monument to a person buried elsewhere]. The stag which surmounts the iron standard-frame, which reminds us of the wondrous hall *Heorot* in *Beowulf*, suggests magic perhaps, as well as being another possible link with the cult of Woden.

[...]

That loving connoisseurship of treasures of aesthetic appeal which is so characteristic in the artefacts of Sutton Hoo, is equally strongly felt in *Beowulf*, where there is the same suggestion of sheer joy in the contem-plation and possession of treasures of the art of the goldsmith and the gem-cutter. That love of ordered ceremony and ornament which is so marked a characteristic of Anglo-Saxon culture, is apparent alike in the Sutton Hoo cenotaph and in *Beowulf*. Though there is much blending of authentic tradition from pre-Christian times with ideas drawn from contem-porary practice in the poet's accounts of the passing of Scyld Scefing, of the funeral rites of the slain in the fight between Hnæf's men and those of Finn, and in Beowulf's own funeral ceremonies at the end of the poem, all three suggest reminiscences of Sutton Hoo.[31] □

Wrenn raises many important points about Anglo-Saxon culture and the way it is reflected in *Beowulf*. What the above extract elucidates especially well, however, is the materialism of the Anglo-Saxons. The 'sheer joy' felt by Beowulf and Hrothgar in the gift-giving scenes in the poem is a perfect illustration of this, as is the focusing on the drag-on's hoard at the end of the poem and the lavish nature of Beowulf's funeral. Wiglaf even commands Beowulf's men to view the treasure one last time after the hero has died:

■ Let us now go quickly to view and visit for the second time the mound of precious jewels, the wonder under the walls. I shall lead you so that you may look at a satisfying selection of them at close quarters – rings and wide gold. Let the bier be prepared, speedily constructed, when we emerge, and then let us carry our prince, beloved man, where he shall long live in the protection of the Ruler. [Guide author's translation] □

Of course, the treasure itself is problematic and carries a heavy sym-bolic weight at the poem's close. Though Beowulf's death is a direct result of the stealing of a cup from the dragon's hoard, at the end of the day these earthly goods benefit no one:

■ In the barrow they [Beowulf's people] put rings and jewels, the very adornments that anxious earls had lifted previously from the hoard. They allowed the earth to embrace the wealth of warriors, gold in the ground, where now it remains still, as useless to men as it was once upon a time. [Guide author's translation] □

Aside from stressing the materiality of Anglo–Saxon culture, Wrenn's article on *Beowulf* also has much to say on Sutton Hoo and the genesis of the poem:

■ It may now seem appropriate to ask what new light the discoveries at Sutton Hoo may throw on the still quite unsolved problems of the date and place of the composition of *Beowulf*. Sune Lindqvist, in his now famous article *Sutton Hoo and Beowulf* [1948] which originally suggested the title of this paper, looks for the explanation of the apparent confusions and anachronisms in the poet's account of the passing of Scyld Scefing and of the funeral rites of Beowulf himself in the idea that phenomena like the Sutton Hoo ship-burial were still remembered at the time when the poem was composed: – 'The Christian skald [poet],' he says, 'imagined that lavish burials after the fashion of the one still remembered in his own day, at Sutton Hoo, and notions then current such as leaving the grave goods unburned in the ground, were the rule in more ancient times too.' He then goes on to suggest that the connexion between the Swedish elements in the subject-matter of *Beowulf* and the royal house of the Wuffingas of East-Anglia which the Sutton Hoo finds bring to mind, may be a reality. This is seen in linking the Wehha of the Wuffing genealogy with the Wiglaf son of Wihstan or Weohstan of *Beowulf* – that last of the Wægmundingas who alone stood fast by the hero in his last fight with the dragon, who was also a prince of the Scyldingas, the royal Swedish house (cf. *Beowulf* 2603, 2907 and 2813ff.) This Wiglaf was, in a sense, a hero of the poem second in nobility only to Beowulf himself: and he, through the equating of his father Wihstan with Wehha as mentioned above, was, it would seem, of the royal house of Uppsala of which the founder of the East-Anglian kingdom had first come from the family seat in Sweden. Such speculations as these may well lead to some complementary clarification of one another by the Sutton Hoo finds and *Beowulf*.

Such a view would tend (a) to place the date of the composition of *Beowulf* as early as possible; and (b) to suggest a search for the exact connexion between the making of the poem and the royal house of East-Anglia.[32] □

Amongst other things, Wrenn makes a convincing argument here for the vital importance of Wiglaf in the poem. That this character was 'a hero of the poem second in nobility only to Beowulf himself' is certainly something to note.

BERNICE KLIMAN

It was stated at the start of this chapter that the 1970s saw the advent of feminist approaches to *Beowulf*. One such study was Bernice Kliman's 'Women in Early English Literature, *Beowulf* to the "Ancrene Wisse"' (1977). Whilst Kliman does not explicitly mention Grendel's mother in her discussion of the women in the poem, she does observe something extremely apposite to the portrayal of this character:

■ A glance at the genealogical charts which accompany most texts of *Beowulf* will show that most females are unnamed. They are important in marriage as the invisible solder which welds man to man. As such, they need no name; only the son-in-law or the male issue of the marriage is named. For example, a daughter of Hygelac married Eofor and a daughter of Hrethal married Beowulf's father.'[33] □

Grendel's mother is, of course, also unnamed. All we know of her identity is in relation to her son. It would seem, then, that the world of the monsters in *Beowulf* is as patriarchal as the human one. Where Grendel's mother does deviate, however, from most of the other women mentioned in the poem is in her behaviour. She is physically strong (recall her fight with Beowulf) and she is an avenger – a role normally reserved for the men within heroic society. In contrast, women were meant to be peace-weavers. This is the role that Hrothgar's wife, for example, fulfils in the poem. As a result, Wealtheow is something of a dramatic foil to Grendel's mother. This relates to Kliman's remark that:

■ Through marriage, however, women can assume some of the prerogatives naturally inhering in the male. First, they can participate in strength not by being as strong as men but through their sons, as Hrothgar implies when he says that God was gracious to whoever brought forth Beowulf. God's grace to a woman is expressed by giving her a son who is valorous.

Secondly, they set the moral tone, as Beowulf reveals when he describes Wealtheow as a gracious hostess whose presence commands respect and attention. He calls her a 'mæru cwen' (great queen), the 'frithu-sibb folcu' (the peaceful tie of nations). Her description, in fact, follows and this is Beowulf's support for his statement that the Geats are a joyous people (2014–19).[34] □

Guide readers may like to be reminded of Beowulf's speech here:

■ There was joy amongst the comitatus. Never in my life under heaven's dome have I seen more mead-mirth of hall-sitters. At times the famous queen, peace-weaver and people's pledge, went through the entire hall, celebrated the young warriors; frequently she would give a man a ring-band before she retired to her place. At times Hrothgar's daughter carried the ale-cup to the thanes, to the men throughout the hall. I heard hall-sitters call her Freawaru when she gave the embossed cup to warriors. Young and gold-adorned, she is promised to Froda's handsome son. [Guide author's translation] □

It is interesting to note here how the poet elides his description of Hrothgar's wife with that of his daughter. Both generations of women essentially function in the same way, as 'peace-pledge[s] of the people'. The allusion in the final line of the above passage confirms this as Freawaru was given in marriage to Froda, future king of the Heatho-Bards, in settlement for the long-standing feud between the Heatho-Bards and the Danes. The history of the period is full of such matches, as Bede's *Ecclesiastical History* attests, for example. Those interested in the character of Wealtheow may also wish to consult Fred C. Robinson's article 'Is Wealhþeow a Prince's Daughter?' (1964).

PAUL ACKER

Kliman's study provides an interesting contrast to more recent scholarship on women in *Beowulf*, especially in relation to their all-important role as mothers. There is, for example, Paul Acker's 'Horror and the Maternal in *Beowulf*' (2006). The article (also noteworthy for its excellent and comprehensive bibliography) begins with an acknowledgement of J.R.R. Tolkien's influence on any subsequent study of the monsters in *Beowulf*; one of Tolkien's prime achievements being in 'placing the monsters at the center of the poem rather than at the periphery'.[35] Acker does find fault with Tolkien, however, in what he regards as Tolkien's failure to see the interrelationship between myth and society: 'The poet of *Beowulf* presents us with real monsters incarnate in a fictive world, Tolkien implies [...] Eventually Tolkien agrees with W.P. Ker that the monsters mythologically embody (not symbolize, exactly) the forces of "Chaos" and "Unreason" eternally pitted against gods and men.'[36] Acker also, however, draws upon previous work involving literary hermeneutics and psychoanalytic theory (especially that of Sigmund Freud (1856–1939) and Jacques Lacan (1901–1981)), and his article is also somewhat dependent on *Powers of Horror: An Essay on Abjection* (1980) by Julia Kristeva (born 1941):

> ■ We may nonetheless seek traces of long-term (but not timeless) cultural preoccupations as expressed in literary and historical sources; one approach to the monsters would then be to examine them as projections of Anglo-Saxon cultural anxieties. I focus here on the one monster Tolkien, oddly enough, ignores almost completely: Grendel's dam, or mother. I argue that through her is projected an anxiety over the failure of vengeance as a system of justice and that her 'powers of horror' (borrowing Julia Kristeva's phrase) partly reside in (or are attributed to) her maternal nature. In so doing, I make use of contemporary psychoanalytic theory even when questioning to what extent such theory, based on a modern construction of the personal subject, applies to the processes of socialization and acculturation operative roughly a thousand years ago. Other questions can be raised about such approaches: should they address authorial psychology [...] the political unconscious [...] or a textual unconscious [...]? Given the lack of any life records for the *Beowulf* poet [a situation noted previously in this guide] and of a specific political milieu, I have settled on 'cultural preoccupations' as the element most likely to be discernible in a traditional work, one that begins by calling attention to (Hwæt!) the heroic legends that 'we' (the poet and the poet's Anglo-Saxon audience) have heard of (1–3).[37] □

Acker raises a number of legitimate questions here about the application of contemporary literary theory to ancient texts. It is clear, for example, that the notion of the self was thought of quite differently in the Anglo-Saxon period from the way it is now. In support of this, Acker admits that 'we must consider that the way in which a subject will be constituted, as well as our interpretation of that process through a particular model of psychoanalysis, will be rooted in a particular historical and social moment.'[38] So how is Grendel's mother as a subject constituted in *Beowulf*? Initially, as Acker notes:

> ■ The reader of *Beowulf* may be struck by how Grendel and his mother are not introduced into the narrative [as, say, Beowulf is] so much as they suddenly materialize within it [...] The sudden appearance of Grendel's mother is preceded by the narrative presentation of two other maternal figures, Hildeburh and Weahltheow [...] Grendel's mother thus appears on the scene as a type of feminine antitype.[39] □

The idea of Grendel's mother as a 'feminine antitype' is at the core of Acker's argument, and he develops it in the following manner:

> ■ That a female creature and more particularly a maternal one takes this revenge [for the death of Grendel] may have highlighted its monstrousness.

Unlike Hildeburh and Wealhtheow, Grendel's mother acts aggressively, arguably in a fashion reserved for men. The similarity of her actions to that of her son, the fact that she is following in her son's (bloody) footsteps, is emphasized [...] Given that Grendel's mother will carry off a warrior just as effectively as her son did, does it really matter that her strength may be a bit less or that (as the poet also feels compelled to remark in line 1292) she is in rather more of a hurry to leave Heorot? Furthermore, it can be argued that Beowulf's confrontation with Grendel's mother is every bit as horrifying, as life-threatening, as his comparatively easy dispatching of Grendel, if not more so.[40] □

Acker continues in a similar vein:

■ Grendel's dam may have seemed monstrous not only because she was a female exacting revenge but more specifically because she was a mother [...] Seen from the socialized world of the hall, such a figure could only be a monster from the frontiers of the human world, on the borders of the animal world, in which for instance a mother bear might come roaring from her den to protect her cub [...] The audience of *Beowulf* [...] would have had a more vivid, experiential sense of mother animals protecting their young than most of us do today, and that sense would have resonated in the setting of Beowulf's second fight deep in the lair of a half-humanoid, half-bearish creature.[41] □

It would seem then, that there are degrees of 'monstrousness' in *Beowulf.* Whilst Grendel may be a monster, his mother is even more of one given her gender and her atypical behaviour. This illustrates another cultural anxiety at work, the all-pervasive fear of the female found in many (especially later) mediaeval texts. Misogyny is also at work here – an attitude often associated with patriarchal cultures. Aside from the issue of gender, however, Acker speaks here of some essential differences between the Anglo-Saxon worldview and our own. Because of the fact that 'The audience of *Beowulf* [...] would have had a more vivid, experiential sense of mother animals protecting their young than most of us do today,' it can be argued that a figure such as Grendel's mother was more 'real' to her original audience than to subsequent ones. Despite this stressing of cultural dissimilarities throughout, Acker ends his article by contemplating a possible point of commonality:

■ One indication that Anglo-Saxon psychodramas might have been at least comparable to ours (as described by Kristeva), however, is the preoccupation in *Beowulf* with primal loss – loss of a golden age with Scyld, loss of Heorot to Grendel and his mother and eventually to fire, loss ultimately of the heroic age of which the poem is a nostalgic mirror.[42] □

The passage above provides us with another way of thinking about *Beowulf* as a poem with a tragic vision, one based upon anxiety and fear of the unknown: what Acker's study illustrates particularly well, however, is just how much Grendel's mother contributes to this sense of 'primal loss'.

The 1970s also produced such works as Thomas Cable's *The Meter and Melody of Beowulf* (1974), a rather technical study 'of traditional metrical analysis' of the poem. In addition, Cable asks an intriguing question about the metrical patterns of *Beowulf*: 'What kind of psychological and aesthetic reality could this quasi-mathematical system have had?'[43] He continues:

> ■ In originally turning to acoustic and musical patterns, I was looking for an external kind of confirmation: the assurance that the sort of abstract pattern that I posit for Old English verse exists elsewhere, in theory or in history. The preliminary investigations beyond the narrow area of my competence have revealed certain relationships too striking to be dismissed as an amateur's fancy.[44] □

And at the close of his study, Cable reaches a striking conclusion:

> ■ If the Old English verse-form has its own logic, it also has an aesthetic reality that the poet and his audience perceived. In translating the abstract pattern of meter into the related patterns of linguistic and musical pitch, I have tried to ask appropriate questions about that perceived reality so that adequate answers may eventually be given. Then we may be able to recapture something of a lost mode of perception and understand better an unfamiliar form of poetry.[45] □

JEFF OPLAND

The subject of the poet was also returned to again. There is, for example, Jeff Opland's '*Beowulf* on the Poet' (1976). Opland opens with a refrain familiar since the days of Tolkien's famous essay on the poem: 'In recent years many literary studies of Old English poetry have appeared in print; scholars tend no longer to treat the extant poems exclusively as artifacts of value to the philologist or social historian.'[46] Opland's ensuing argument is that the more Old English poetry is valued as art, the more central the figure of the poet becomes to any study of it. This is especially true in relation to *Beowulf*:

> ■ Of these extant writings, the heroic poem *Beowulf* has proved to be the principal source for all studies of the Anglo-Saxon poet. Unfortunately, scholars have tended to take at face value all the information the poem

seems to yield, frequently allowing the testimony of this single source to weigh against the testimony from all other primary sources of information. In this article I propose to assess those passages in *Beowulf* that deal with poets and poetry in an attempt to determine what can reasonably be deduced from them.[47] □

Opland then proceeds to explain why 'poetry might be less reliable than prose as evidence of social activity':[48]

■ (1) Our interpretation of Old English poetry is often influenced by the editor's treatment of the text or by the lexicographer's glossing of words in the text both of which in turn occasionally depend on their interpretation of what the text means. (2) As a result of the metrical or alliterative demands of his tradition, the poet may have had occasion to choose a less precise word than the writer of prose could choose. (3) In assessing the evidence of poetry about poetic activity one might have to make allowances for the conventional diction of the tradition, which may, for example, retain descriptions of objects or practices long after they have ceased to be current.[49] □

In his specific analysis of *Beowulf*, Opland begins by examining 'those passages that describe the poet performing in Heorot in order to relate them to the traditional poetic theme of joy in the hall'.[50] It would seem, then, that the image of the Anglo-Saxon poet can never quite be separated from that of the hall. In *Beowulf*, the poet performs in Heorot on three notable occasions, as readers of the text may recall. Opland also alerts us to the fact that:

■ Donald K. Fry has defined a theme in Old English poetry as 'a recurring concatenation of details and ideas, not restricted to a specific event, verbatim repetition, or certain formulas, which forms an underlying structure for an action or description.' What we are dealing with here is the theme of joy in the hall, which the *Beowulf* poet establishes for his audience in these passages [the ones where the poet performs in Heorot]. The theme consists of a concatenation of details depicting joy (*dream, gamen, gleo*), music (*gid* (?), *sang, sweg*), the harp (*hearpe*), and a poet (*scop*).[51] □

And, additionally: 'The *Beowulf* poet's depiction of joy in the hall is unique in Anglo-Saxon literature: no other poem associates the *scop* with any of the other traditional elements. In no other poem is the *scop* associated with music: in all the extant writings from Anglo-Saxon England, it is only in this poem that the *scop* is associated with music, joy, or a harp.'[52] This suggests that the *Beowulf* poet was doing something unique with his characterization of the *scop* of Heorot. One must not, however, take this portrait as 'evidence of social practices current in Anglo-Saxon times'.[53] In relation to this, Opland concludes that:

■ Scenes in *Beowulf* have often been taken as an accurate representation of the life of the time. As far as its references to poetry are concerned, we should note that *Beowulf* provides unusual evidence of the activity of the *scop*, and that in a number of crucial passages its evidence is not always unambiguous.[54] □

As we shall see in the following chapter of this guide, critics were still pondering the ambiguities of the poem into the 1980s. These ambiguities include the role and exact nature of Grendel's mother (and that of women in general in *Beowulf*), the character of Beowulf himself, and the relationship between Christianity and paganism.

CHAPTER SIX

Critics on the Crest of a Wave: the 1980s

In 1993, J.D.A. Ogilvy and Donald Baker noted in *Reading Beowulf* that 'The past 30 years have seen an enormous surge of critical interest in *Beowulf*'[1], and the 1980s were on the crest of this scholarly wave. This is supported by Seth Lerer's observation that 'Since the early 1980s, approaches drawn from deconstruction, semiotics, cultural studies, and psychoanalysis have sought to relocate *Beowulf* in the shifting canons of contemporary academic debate.'[2] In the field of psychoanalysis, for example, there is James W. Earl's 'The Role of the Men's Hall in the Development of the Anglo-Saxon Superego' (1983), which takes a Jungian approach to a subject that readers of this guide are by now very familiar with. Earl also talks about masculinity here, which makes this article a very early example of a critical application of masculinity studies to Old English literature. This is not to say, however, that earlier attempts were not made to apply psychoanalytic theory to *Beowulf*; Jeffrey Helterman's '*Beowulf*: The Archetype Enters History' (1968) particularly comes to mind here.

JEFFREY HELTERMAN

Helterman returns to the idea (one which has previously been discussed in this guide) of *Beowulf* as myth and states that:

■ Myth, in its most general sense, provides a link between the eternal and the human, as manifested *in the human*. That is to say about Beowulf what is readily apparent: he is more than a man and yet no more than a man. Under this double aspect, Beowulf can surpass man's tragic limitations and yet is involved in them. Myth fuses the world of actuality with the world of desire or in psychological terms, the dream world with the waking one.[3] □

The extract above provides a working definition of 'myth', but what of 'archetype'? Helterman goes some way to explaining this term in the following:

■ Margaret Goldsmith [1962], extending the Christian viewpoint [found in the poem], uses the example of [William] Blake [the Romantic poet and painter (1757–1827)] to remind us that *Beowulf* 'stems directly from the poet's inbred beliefs about man and the universe, so that the work itself embodies his conception of reality,' yet her analysis deals chiefly with the poem as a didactic work. [Helterman believes that 'the poem remains theologically unspecified.']⁴ □

The comparison with Blake might also suggest that we look at the poet as *creator* of myth and that we take 'inbred' in a psychological rather than a social sense:

■ This is to deal with Beowulf as an archetypal figure, and although we need not accept [the] theory of the collective unconscious [developed by Carl Jung (1875–1961)], his descriptions of the manifestations of the archetype may prove fruitful. Suffice it to agree with Northrop Frye [(1912–1991)] in his famous *Anatomy of Criticism* (1957) that the continuity of the human mind and its response to the universe provide a basis for the appearance of archetypal patterns in dream and folk-lore. If Beowulf is an archetypal figure, his actions will correspond to, although not necessarily be derivative from, ritual patterns discovered in anthropological research and dream patterns uncovered by psychiatry. In these patterns, we may hope to find a design for the over-all structure of *Beowulf*.⁵ □

At the core of Helterman's argument, however, is Jung's theory that the 'archetype is bipolar, embodying the dark side as well as the light.'⁶ He relates this to *Beowulf* by asking 'to what extent is Beowulf Grendel?'⁷ This suggests that Grendel is Beowulf's shadow aspect (or shadow), one of the most recognizable Jungian archetypes. Jung argued that the shadow was instinctive and irrational and could be extremely ruthless if faced with conflict. Connections between this archetype and Grendel are not difficult, therefore, to discern. Helterman expands his Jungian reading of *Beowulf* by saying that 'Beowulf's battle with Grendel has psychological as well as cosmic import.'⁸ Furthermore, it:

■ externalizes the struggle of opposing forces within one man. This externalization of psychological conflict is a common literary device often imbued with ritual significance [...] If we use the textbook description of the epic hero as the ideal representative of his society, the psychological struggle also symbolizes the conflicting forces within that society [...] Beowulf's refusal to use armor against Grendel allows for the complete fusion of the two figures [...] Beowulf's battle with Grendel reveals the potential for destruction in his society [...] Verbally, it becomes almost impossible to distinguish the two antagonists in Heorot. Beowulf is described as *gram* [enraged], a word typically reserved for the forces of evil, while Grendel is called *se mæra*. The opponents are equated in one phrase: 'Yrre wæron begen,/reþe renweardas' [furious/hostile hall guardians] (769–70).[9] □

Helterman's work on the shadow aspect also leads him to believe that Grendel's mother is the shadow of Wealtheow. Taken together, these two figures are seen to 'form what Jung calls the dual mother.'[10] Under Wealtheow (the Good Mother), 'Heorot becomes the paradise of the warrior,'[11] whereas 'Grendel's mother is the Lilith, who is the demon wife of Adam, corresponding to Eve. She is the whore of Babylon, the other face of the Virgin Mary.'[12] Additionally, she 'symbolizes the feud aspect of the web of peace'.[13] We see Grendel's mother again displaying masculine characteristics.

As Helterman's primary concern is to read Beowulf and his three adversaries in a psychologically symbolic way, he also of course discusses the dragon. After arguing that Beowulf will be 'marked by *hamartia*' [a fatal error as opposed to a tragic flaw] in his final battle, Helterman goes on to say that:

■ When the dragon decimates Beowulf's *gifstol* [gift-seat], he symbolically destroys the hero's effectiveness as an archetypal figure. Beowulf no longer has a center of power to defend – a place in which he can repeat the archetypal act of creation. Yielding ground to the dragon means giving up one's place of refuge from the process of time and involves man in mortality [...] The fiery dragon is doubly appropriate as a symbol of the destruction of Beowulf's society. Not only will Heorot end in fire as a result of *ecghete* [sword-hate], but each warrior ends his days on the pyre.[14] □

Helterman's conclusion also revisits a familiar topic – the problematic and ambiguous way in which the *Beowulf* poet portrays treasure and worldly goods:

■ there is pathos in his [Beowulf's] belief that the gold obtained by his death will be the salvation of his people. Instead, it lies buried in the ground, a reminder of man's futility in attempting to order the world of time. The closing juxtaposition of the towering barrow and the useless treasure symbolizes undaunted courage in the face of physical defeat.[15] □

Ultimately, then, Helterman is arguing against the view of *Beowulf* as a poem with a tragic vision. At the end of the poem, he seems to suggest, the glass is half full rather than half empty and the reason for this is that the final image the audience is left with is one of the hero's 'undaunted courage in the face of physical defeat'. In other words, Beowulf's spirit has triumphed at the moment of his bodily death.

As can be seen, Helterman's reading of *Beowulf* incorporates a significant amount of material on the way in which gender roles operate (especially symbolically) in the poem. In this respect it anticipates the *Beowulf* scholarship of the 1980s, as this was a time when feminist readings of the poem began to be much more commonplace.

ALEXANDRA HENNESSY OLSEN

An excellent summary of the situation is found in Alexandra Hennessy Olsen's overview in *A Beowulf Handbook*, where she identifies the major contributions to feminist interpretation of *Beowulf* during this particular decade. Here is a selection of significant dates and critics:

- *1983*: Jane-Marie Luecke uses modern anthropology to suggest that *Beowulf* reflects an early Germanic matrilocal or matrician culture rather than the patriarchal society in which it was composed.

  1983: John D. Niles argues that *Beowulf* displays evidence of ring composition [a structural principle or rhetorical device in which an element or series of elements are repeated at the beginning and at the end of a poem or narrative unit, thus comprising a 'ring' framing a core which is not a ring] and that the battle with Grendel's mother is the centre of the poem.

  1983: Richard J. Schrader in *God's Handiwork: Images of Women in Early Germanic Literature* (1983) examines the principal women of *Beowulf* and argues that their roles are derived from Mary and Eve.

  1984: Kevin S. Kiernan discusses the actions of Grendel's mother in terms of Germanic feud structure.

  1984: Alexandra Hennessy Olsen discusses the women of *Beowulf*, arguing against interpretations of them as passive.

  1985: Michael Murphy points out that women in Germanic literature played the role of goaders who spurred men into action and suggests that this role underlies the scene between Wealtheow and Beowulf.

  1986: Jane Chance discusses the social role of women as peace weavers in Anglo-Saxon society and identifies two literary types, Mary (who underlies the conventional queens) and Eve (who underlies Grendel's mother and Thryth).

  1986: Setsuko Haruto reviews the women in *Beowulf* as passive sufferers and peace-weavers, concluding that they help enhance the poem's worldview by depicting the side of society that complements the warriors.

  1988: Michael J. Enright examines the relationship of Wealtheow and Hygd to king and *comitatus* to conclude that the queen helps establish rank and succession.[16] □

Alexandra Hennessey Olsen herself is a major feminist critic of Old English literature. As a consequence, she has a comprehensive knowledge of this field of scholarship. Here is how she summarizes the state of play in relation to *Beowulf*:

■ Traditionally, the study of gender roles in *Beowulf* has been based on the assumption that, since men were responsible for public functions like king, warrior, and avenger, they also held the power in the world of the poem. Women, it was assumed, held more passive and private roles as hostesses, peace weavers, and ritual mourners and were therefore marginalized by the poet. Critics of *Beowulf* have tended to minimize the importance of women in the poem because of the obvious importance of male heroism. This view is widespread.

[...] In recent years, the accuracy of such views has been challenged by both men and women, in a way that parallels similar revaluations in social history, anthropology, and the study of other Germanic literatures. Carol J. Clover [1993] argues that we misinterpret gender roles in Germanic society by viewing them in the light of beliefs developed in the late eighteenth century [...] She suggests that these roles should be viewed in terms of power and the lack thereof rather than in terms of biological sex [...] A more inclusive view of power in general and *Beowulf* in particular helps us appreciate the actual social order presented by the poem.[17] □

Olsen then goes on to examine the three main roles that women have been seen to fulfil in the poem: the peace-weaver, the hostess and the ritual mourner. A fair amount has already been said in this guide about the first two figures, but the third, because of its highly enigmatic nature, merits further discussion. Various interpretations have been advanced about the identity of the ritual mourner. As has been seen, at least one critic believes her to be Beowulf's wife though there is no actual evidence in the poem to support this theory. Other scholars, as Olsen notes, have had this to say about the character:

■ Tauno F. Mustanoja studies the occasion of Beowulf's death, when a 'meowle' (maiden, 3150b) sings 'sorgcearig' (sorrowful, 3152a). He links this mourning woman to an international tradition of ritual mourning, 'an essential traditional feature in the funeral ceremony' (1967, 27). [Helen] Bennett, however, objects that 'the passage in *Beowulf* dealing with the female mourner [...] does not actually exist' (1992, 35); the existence of the mourner is problematic because 'almost all that is legible on this page [has been] freshened up in a late hand' [...] The scholarly acceptance of the traditional text reinforces the idea that women are passive because, as Bennett notes, traditional interpretations have viewed the mourner as 'another example of the passive female victim in Old English poetry [...] Analogues, however, can produce a quite opposite picture of the female mourner as strong and enduring'.[18] □

Bennett's point is a sound one, and one that has much bearing on the study of Old English literature as a whole. When a text is corrupt, as the *Beowulf* manuscript is in the passage 'dealing with the female mourner', we become reliant upon the opinion of editors. A particular reading begins to circulate and is eventually taken as given. In the case of the 'female mourner' passage, the received interpretation reinforces traditional beliefs about women's roles in Anglo-Saxon society.

J.D.A. OGILVY AND DONALD BAKER

Aside from the rise of certain types of critical approaches to *Beowulf* in the 1980s, seminal single studies of the poem were also produced. One of these was J.D.A. Ogilvy and Donald Baker's *Reading Beowulf.* Much of this study is given over to a discussion of the importance of 'The Monsters and the Critics'. Almost 50 years after the delivery of this famous Sir Israel Gollancz Memorial Lecture, Ogilvy and Baker were well placed to assess the lasting impact of Tolkien's work:

■ At any rate, Tolkien's essay, emphasizing the reasonableness of the poet's materials in relation to the themes of the poem, the balance of the parts and the unity in effect, and assuming a single poem by a single author, caught a critical tide at the full. The 1930s were, of course, a very active period of literary criticism – the golden period of those critics who to a great extent, formed our ways of looking at literature – T.S. Eliot [1888–1965], Ezra Pound [1885–1972], John Crowe Ransom [1888–1974], Cleanth Brooks [1906–1994] – in short, the founders of the New Criticism – who were then approaching the zenith of their influence. *Beowulf*, hitherto protected by the barriers of language from much 'belletristic' [written and regarded for aesthetic value rather than content, but can also refer more generally to literature] criticism, became more accessible through Tolkien's brilliant demonstration that it was, above all other things, a poem. Because it was still in Old English, there was no great rush by the major new critics to consider it, but the way was prepared for those whose interest lay mainly in the critical analysis of poetry [...] But there is a sense in which all criticism since Tolkien has either affirmed or attacked his views.[19] □

Ogilvy and Baker see a certain integrity to Tolkien's reading of *Beowulf.* They do not, however, find this virtue in much of the subsequent criticism of the poem: 'On many occasions the twentieth century appreciation of complexity and subtlety in literature has led to a reading of *Beowulf* that has amounted to the creation of a new poem with little resemblance to the eighth century masterpiece left us.'[20] So what are their actual views about the poem, especially in relation to subjects already familiar to readers of this guide? What about the character of Beowulf, for example? Ogilvy and Baker see him as 'a selfless hero'[21] who 'emerges not only as a paragon of courtly behaviour but also as an individual.'[22] In relation to this point, the authors have some very interesting things to say about the *Beowulf* poet: 'The author of *Beowulf* was to the manner born'[23] and 'Among later English authors only Jane Austen [1775–1817] equals him in her concern for the proprieties. In fact, *Beowulf* has sometimes been called the first English book of manners.'[24] This seems a valid point. Most readers of the poem will have noticed the care and attention paid to social etiquette and acceptable codes of behaviour (by both the poet and the characters themselves) in the scenes of gift-exchange within Heorot. Beowulf, Hrothgar and their aristocratic circle are also at pains to speak well and with the appropriate courtesy to one another on every occasion.

The figure of the poet and that of his creation, Beowulf, are brought together in Ogilvy and Baker's comment that 'it is possible that the character of Beowulf is largely a creation of the author.'[25] This conjecture is of course at odds with critical readings which argue that Beowulf has some basis in historical reality. The potential originality of Beowulf is matched by what these two critics point out about the unusual length of the poem. As is well known, *Beowulf* is the longest of all the extant poems in Old English. Ogilvy and Baker address the issue in this way: 'we have no evidence of [other] poems of the scope of *Beowulf* [...] it is not impossible that *Beowulf* was unique [...] *Beowulf* is unique not only in scope and method but also in subject matter.'[26]

But how are we to judge the exact nature of the poem's 'method' when Ogilvy and Baker also acknowledge that: 'Although essential human nature probably has changed very little since the eighth century, many conventional beliefs have been altered [...] Fashions in narrative change'?[27]

In addition, Ogilvy and Baker implicitly challenge those scholars who see the ending of the poem as being problematic, especially in its delineation of the hero: 'Beowulf's death has been the cause of a good deal of unenlightened comment [...] For a hero-king the best death imaginable is death in a battle fought to save his people, and that is the death the poet gives Beowulf.'[28]

Thus, we see another instance of critics arguing against the notion of *Beowulf* as a poem with a tragic vision.

As has been seen, most discussions of the poet of *Beowulf* take in a number of issues: is there any way that the poet might be identified? Is there more than one author behind the text? What was the poet's religious orientation? Whilst Ogilvy and Baker do not offer a possible solution to the first question, they do cite A.S. Cook, an eminent scholar of Old English literature, on the subject: 'A.S. Cook argues that King Alfred (685–705) might be the author of *Beowulf*.'[29] A theory such as this is based upon the idea that a poem as sophisticated as *Beowulf* must be the creation of an exceptional individual. King Alfred was one such figure, and he was responsible for a type of Renaissance in learning and the arts. Critics such as Cook see *Beowulf* as being a product of this period of cultural flowering. Ogilvy and Baker, whilst not explicitly advancing the King Alfred theory, do see *Beowulf* as the work of a single author.[30] And in terms of this author's religious background and how it manifests itself in *Beowulf*, they suggest that 'the Christian veneer has been applied not to the poem but to the inherited pagan beliefs of the author.'[31]

Reading Beowulf closes on a high note, with an important overview of (relatively) recent scholarly approaches to the poem:

■ In summarising the critical trends of the past 30 years, we believe that, in spite of some of the controversies we have chronicled, scholars have moved to a position of fairly general agreement. The impetus given by Tolkien's lecture has pushed criticism to the point that it is now widely accepted (1) that *Beowulf*, as it stands, is the work of a single man of genius of a literate era, writing or composing within the modes of a previous and still-influential tradition of oral literary creation; (2) that this single man of genius was a Christian who consciously created his poem out of pagan materials; (3) that the resulting poem, while not an allegory, owes much of its intricate structure to a Christian view, as well as to the poet's knowledge of how to put together a long poem; and (4) that the resulting *Beowulf*, with its balances, its intricate weaving of themes, its diction strikingly original within a traditional frame, is one of the supreme creations of Anglo-Germanic literature. Most students of *Beowulf* would, we believe, subscribe more or less wholeheartedly to these conclusions. Although many corners of *Beowulf* have been illuminated since Tolkien's lecture, and our understanding of Anglo-Saxon poetry has advanced since that time, one may note with some awe that the conclusions above are still, in outline, those of Tolkien.[32] □

Another point should perhaps be added to the above summary of Tolkien's legacy, and this is that the author of *The Lord of the Rings* (1954–5) promoted the idea that *Beowulf* should be read as far as possible from its own historical vantage point. This makes one mindful of Fred C. Robinson's warning, in 'Teaching the Background: History, Religion, Culture' (1984) of the problems faced by modern readers of the poem. We must be aware, he argues, of:

■ instances where a theme or subject of *Beowulf* had markedly different cultural significance for the poet and his audience than it has for the modern student of the poem. Consideration of six such topics will help readers free themselves from their own cultural preconceptions and project themselves into the imaginative world of *Beowulf*: love and friendship, shame culture and guilt culture, vengeance, descriptions of artifacts and nature, gift giving and fate.[33] □

The ultimate underpinning of Robinson's argument is the belief that 'Understanding literature for another time and land is an exercise in projecting ourselves imaginatively into other people's minds, and lives and languages.'[34]

BERNARD HUPPÉ

Another critical study of the 1980s which betrays an implicit indebtedness to Tolkien is Bernard Huppé's *The Hero in the Earthly City* (1984), as Huppé (like Tolkien) expresses here the desire to challenge those critics who see *Beowulf* 'as a primitive work of art'.[35] Tolkien, as we know, also wished to exonerate the poem from charges of primitivism. More broadly, however, Huppé's work aims 'to present a coherent view of the theme and structure of the poem in the context of the poet's inescapable Augustinian [of or relating to the Latin Church Father Saint Augustine of Hippo, 354–430, or his doctrines] frame of reference'.[36] In terms of the structure of *Beowulf*, Huppé believes it to be 'mathematical [...] based on the counter pointing of two and three'.[37] He then develops this argument a little further: 'Number symbolism, a significant element in the Augustinian conception of typological correspondences, was part of the Old English poet's scheme, the counter-pointing of the dualism of the two cities [the earthly and the heavenly] and the unity of the Trinity being of primary importance.'[38] Ultimately, Huppé wishes to 'rediscover the territory of the poet's mind'.[39] Those who approach *Beowulf* in this way are compared to 'the makers of historical maps who plot the routes of communication of a forgotten past'.[40] Readers of this guide may also wish to know that Huppé's volume contains an interesting feature: in Chapter Five he provides a translation of *Beowulf* that 'aims to present the shape and form of [his] reading of the poem'.[41]

FRED C. ROBINSON

In 1985, the year after *The Hero in the Earthly City* was published, Fred C. Robinson came out with *Beowulf and the Appositive Style*. The chapters comprising this work were originally 'presented as the John C. Hodges Lectures in Knoxville in 1982, [and] they bore the title "Dark Age Heroism and Christian Regret: The Appositive Art of

Beowulf" '. For those unfamiliar with Robinson's key term, a definition is offered:

> ■ A recent edition of John C. Hodges' *Harbrace College Handbook* defines 'appositive' as 'a noun or noun substitute set beside another noun or noun substitute and identifying or explaining it.' Thus in the sentence 'the hero of the poem is Beowulf, king of the Geatas,' 'Beowulf' and 'king of the Geatas' are in apposition, since they stand next to one another, have no word connecting them, and have the same referent, one element explaining or identifying the other.
>
> [...] The distinguishing feature of apposition (or variation) is its parataxis – its lack of an expressed logical connection between the apposed elements.[42] □

But how is this technique central to *Beowulf* ? Robinson's answer is that:

> ■ The appositive method is used repeatedly to characterize Beowulf. After the hero's victory over Grendel, a *scop* celebrates his prowess by singing not about Beowulf but about two earlier figures from Germanic legend: Sigemund, the prototype of Germanic heroes, and then Heremod, the violent ruler who turned on his own subjects, by whom he was ultimately banished. The point of this curiously indirect way of characterizing Beowulf is never spelled out, but the implication is clear: Beowulf is like Sigemund, unlike Heremod. And here again the names of the two opposed figures signal a contrast. *Sigemund* means 'victorious protector' (a precise description of the man who has just saved the Danes from Grendel's depredations), while *Heremod* means 'hostile temper' (the defect of character which Beowulf, near the end of his life, prides himself on having avoided [2741–3]). Scholars have seen a similar contrastive intent in the Hama-Hygelac passage in *Beowulf* 1197–1214, and the character Unferth has been seen as existing primarily to serve as a foil to Beowulf.[43] □

According to Robinson, however, the appositive method is used much more widely than simply to characterize Beowulf:

> ■ The most forceful expression of the youth-and-age theme in the poem is yet another apposition of narrative segments, the apposition that controls the structure of the entire narrative. *Beowulf* consists of two starkly juxtaposed episodes in the hero's life divided chronologically by a chasm of 50 years and hinged together across that chasm by a single transitional sentence (2200–9).[44] □

It would seem, then, that Robinson is in the critical camp which sees *Beowulf* as a poem of two, as opposed to three, parts.

In addition, Robinson identifies the themes of artifice and nature as being central to the poem, and he shows how they too are presented in an appositional manner:

■ In the story of Beowulf we see a similar opposition of artifice and nature. The hall Heorot, whose construction receives such mythopoeic [myth-making] emphasis, is a bastion of order and safety which throws light into the surrounding darkness (309–11). Beyond Heorot, its adjacent *buras* [dwellings], and their protective *weall* [wall] lie the forest, the fens, and the mere, swarming with reptilian and monstrous life. The story of the Grendelkin is the story of the invasion of the citadel – the place of light and order – by the creature from the vernal shade who strives against human order [...] Beowulf frees the artifact of Heorot from Grendel's hold and returns the wise creator of the hall to power. Similarly, at the end of the poem Beowulf wrests from the dragon's hold the artifacts in the treasure hoard and returns them to the possession of men.[45] □

Perhaps the greatest apposition in the poem, however, is that between the Christian and pagan religions. Huppé's argument is that the *scop* of *Beowulf* was a Christian looking back with regret at the paganism of Beowulf and his noble contemporaries. As a consequence, 'a combined admiration and regret is the dominant tone in *Beowulf*'[46] – though the poet may have admired Beowulf, he also knew that because he was a pagan he could not enter into the kingdom of heaven. This sympathy, however:

■ profits the souls of Hrothgar and Beowulf but little, although it does give the poet's audience a brief moment of fellowship with those Germanic ancestors, since both stand in the presence of inscrutable powers. But that fellowship can be of no lasting union, for the people of Christian England can never reenter the severe, benighted world of the men of old, nor would they. All the poetry of *Beowulf* can do is bring the two together in a brief, loving, and faintly disquieting apposition.[47] □

LINDA GEORGIANNA

Linda Georgianna, in 'King Hrethel's Sorrow and the Limits of Heroic Action in *Beowulf*' (1987), expresses a similar view. She argues that 'the poet seems intent on disengaging his audience from the forward movement of the heroic story in order to suggest the limits of heroic action and perhaps of heroic narratives as well.'[48] In part, a pagan hero is limited because he 'cannot hope to transcend [in the way that a Christian can] the need for earthly joy'.[49] Georgianna further develops this extremely interesting argument in the following passage from her article:

■ [there is] a more general confusion and paralysis at the heart of heroic society, the cause of which is ultimately a lack of belief and hope for meaningful or permanent change. Beowulf knows as well as any Christian that 'life is læne,' [on loan] but Beowulf's choices in the face of life's transitoriness come to seem extremely limited [...] A man either fights as a hero or flees as a coward, and each fight requires this heroic choice, without regard for what may lie beyond the next fight or even the last fight. The rewards the hero seeks in return for fighting – fame, vengeance, and treasure – come to seem equally limited and shortsighted. Beowulf deserves and gains all of these rewards before he dies, but the Christian poet cannot help asking his audience to consider, even if only from time to time, what such gains are ultimately worth. Ultimate values, causes, and effects are not invoked often in the poem, which commemorates more often than it moralizes the past, but when they are invoked, the result is to unsettle the narrative profoundly, to disorient the audience enough to disengage it from the lure of heroic narrative. In short, lack of steady advance, rather than being a defect of the poem, is the point. By the end the poem is not so much a heroic narrative as it is *about* heroic narratives, in which, the poet suggests, advances and retreats are equally illusory.[50] □

STANLEY B. GREENFIELD

Stanley B. Greenfield, in *Hero and Exile: The Art of Old English Poetry* (1989), also sees the *scop* displaying a certain sympathy for Beowulf. This is clear in Greenfield's discussion of the poet's treatment of the hero's fight with the dragon: 'by revealing a weakness in the aged Beowulf he [the poet] has somewhat humanized his hero's nature, making him easier of empathetic access to an audience's sensibilities.'[51]

The issue of genre is explored by Greenfield as well. He debates, in the first instance, whether *Beowulf* is an epic or a dramatic tragedy and he opens with a question: 'Is there only one kind of *tragic*? Or do epic and dramatic tragedy have real and differing qualities to which we respond in distinct and separable ways?'[52] Furthermore:

■ Both epic and dramatic tragedy derive from and thrive on a tension between skepticism and faith; yet the tensions differ. They reflect the ages in which these genres predominate. Epic flourishes in the last days or in the aftermath of a nation or Weltanschauung [world view], not in the heyday [...] Dramatic tragedy flourishes at the peak of an era in which man has been apotheosized [elevated to quasi-divine status], but in which the events of the time give rise to doubts and uncertainties about his ultimate control of matters.[53] □

Is it better, then, to be an epic or a dramatic tragedy? From what Greenfield says above, it seems like six of one and half a dozen of the other. And, when all is said and done, he himself admits that 'perhaps the question of whether *Beowulf* is epic, or heroic elegy, or heroic tragedy becomes academic.'[54] Greenfield may have ultimately viewed this question as 'academic' but, as the next chapter of this guide will show, scholars continued to generate debates concerning the poem's genre.

CHAPTER SEVEN

An Embarrassment of Critical Riches: the 1990s to the present

The period from the 1990s to the present offers an embarrassment of riches where *Beowulf* criticism is concerned. Scholars during this period were especially prolific, though this in part has something to do with the nature of the poem itself. As Natalia Breizmann has noted in '*Beowulf* as Romance: Literary Interpretation as Quest' (1998), 'The curiously "unfocussed" compositional organization of *Beowulf* renders the process of the poem's interpretation potentially infinite, and is thus responsible for the endless deferral of the meaning of the poem.'[1] As a consequence, it is difficult to know where to begin the present survey of scholarship.

NICHOLAS HOWE

Perhaps, though, the obvious choice is Nicholas Howe's *Migration and Mythmaking in Anglo-Saxon England*, for it spans the period from 1989 to 2001. Initially published in 1989, the volume was then revised by Howe and reissued in 2001. Howe informs his readers that during this time he moved from a deconstructive approach to a historicist one, though his work is also indebted to post-colonial theory as the following quotation demonstrates:

■ Anglo-Saxon England had its origins, at least in the realpolitik of the migration myth, in the post-colonial void created in the early fifth century when Roman legions withdrew from that outpost of empire known as Britannia. Anglo-Saxon England was always already post-colonial, even as it continually redefined its ties with the imperial center of a Rome turned Christian through the conversion of a British mercenary, Constantine [272–337; Emperor of Rome 306–37].[2] □

Despite this, at a later stage in his argument Howe observes that the Anglo-Saxons left behind no migration myth of their own: 'We should remember that there is no surviving Old English poem that relates the ancestral migration as explicitly as the *Aeneid* narrates the founding of Rome.'[3] Nevertheless, because of the poet's 'dexterous handling of geography'[4] and the 'geographically ordered narrative of *Beowulf*',[5] *Beowulf* itself makes use of the 'migration myth'[6]: 'The myth of migration gave the English as a *folc* a common identity by teaching them that they were descended from those who had made the exodus in the mid-fifth century.'[7] And, according to Howe this myth grew 'organically' and fostered the idea of the Anglo-Saxons as a 'chosen people to whom a promised land had been entrusted by virtue of their migration'.[8] In addition, 'the rhythm of home and abroad provides the poem with its source of causality.'[9] Howe also links the geography of the poem with its positioning in time: 'The setting of *Beowulf* may be understood as the homeland before conversion. While thoroughly pagan, it is viewed through the sympathetic eyes of a Christian poet.'[10]

Howe's reading of Grendel, Grendel's mother and the dragon in *Beowulf* is also worth mentioning here. They are ultimately figures of the Other, awful in their difference and bent on obliterating the all important joy of the hall: 'Throughout the poem, monsters are depicted as terrifying because they destroy the hall and with it all possibility of communal life.'[11] It could be argued as well that the monsters are as much products of pagan as Christian culture (symbolic interpretations of Grendel have, for example, already been discussed in this guide). On a more general note, here is what Howe has to say about the religious bias of the poem:

■ To interpret *Beowulf* as a critique of the pagan culture that survived in the homeland is to read the poem through the perspective of Anglo-Saxon England. [...] While it would seem crucial to know something about where the poem was composed, history tells us little about the English milieu of *Beowulf* that cannot be deduced from its language [...it] was composed in the vernacular of Anglo-Saxon England.[12] □

Howe also does not believe that we are meant to see Beowulf as being a Christian: 'The poet does not smuggle Beowulf into the poem as a latent Christian – a concept so anachronistic that it would have been beyond his comprehension.'[13]

There are some interesting points of commonality between Howe's work and Gillian R. Overing and Marijane Osborn's *Landscape of Desire: Partial Stories of the Medieval Scandinavian World* (1994). The basis of this book is the authors' re-creation (as well as re-imagining) of Beowulf's voyage to Denmark – specifically, to Heorot – and their approach is an unusual one: referring to the idea of the 'thick description', devised by the anthropologist Clifford Geertz (1926–2006) they inform us that the book's intention:

■ is to 'thicken' (borrowing Clifford Geertz's term) the reality of the northern world of medieval literature for the reader, to make it accessible to the imaginations of those who actively enter into a world when they read fiction. Not everyone does this or wishes to, but this book will not appeal to those who read solely academically.[14] □

Like Howe, therefore, Overing and Osborn are primarily concerned with geography:

■ Our goal was to examine the suggestion of Klaeber and others that the poet was using geography indiscriminately. Instead, we thought, we might be able to show that he had some sense of the geographical relationships of the northern tribes he mentions. Another good reason to undertake such a project was the fact that no one else had done so.[15] □

A related fact is that 'studies have demonstrated that the *Beowulf* poet had a sound sense of the history and material culture of the period of his poem.'[16] Overing and Osborn also share with Howe the belief that *Beowulf* was in some ways the closest that the Anglo-Saxons came to producing a migration myth: 'The poem itself may be the greatest monument ever raised to a Germanic hero, and this has implications for the imagined ancestral origins of the Anglo-Saxon audience for whom the poet composed.'[17]

Like Overing and Osborn, Raymond P. Tripp, Jr., in his essay 'Humour, Wordplay, and Semantic Resonance in *Beowulf*' (2000), approaches the poem from an unusual angle. In his 'iconoclastic reading',[18] Tripp rather provocatively asserts that: 'there is much in *Beowulf* to suggest that the poet took Christianity as the last laugh of history.'[19] Somewhat paradoxically, perhaps, he sees the topic as a very serious one: 'From the very beginning of the poem everything depends upon the linguistic effects of reading from the point of view of an old heroic or a new Christian seriousness.'[20] More specifically, Tripp sees (absurd) humour in Beowulf's second great fight when Grendel's mother sits on the hero (l. 1545). In relation to this, it has been observed by others that the female monster lacks appropriate hall etiquette here; it is clearly bad manners to a 'lord' to sit on a guest! When all is said and done, however, Tripp does acknowledge that *Beowulf* is not traditionally noted for its humour:

■ One reason *Beowulf* seems so unfunny is that such a critical stranglehold has evolved as to what the poem means and how it looks. The fossilization of that view is evident in the hold that Klaeber's edition still retains some 75 years after it was first published.

It might also be suggested that failure to identify the 'funny bits' in the poem comes partly from the fact that we now largely access the text through reading, as opposed to hearing, it. There is no doubt that much irony, humour, and other subtleties of tone were conveyed by the *scop* in his performance.[21] □

Tripp foregrounds two very important points here. Firstly, he makes us consider how one critic can come to dominate the way a poem is read. His second point is equally crucial; that we cannot underestimate the relationship between *Beowulf*'s orality and the complexities of its tone.

ALLEN J. FRANTZEN

A study of humour in *Beowulf* is a rare thing. What was also uncommon before, at least, the publication of Allen J. Frantzen's *Before the Closet: Same-sex Love from Beowulf to Angels in America* (1998) were readings of the poem encompassing the issue of same-sex love. Frantzen explains the meaning of this term in the introduction of his book, whilst also acknowledging that 'Queer theory would [...] have been impossible without Michel Foucault, chief architect of the hide-and-seek economies on which queer theory depends':[22]

■ I call this a book about 'same-sex love' because the obvious choice, 'homosexuality', is, for periods before the modern era, inaccurate. 'Homosexuality' and 'homosexuals' were not recognized concepts in the Middle Ages or in the Renaissance, although we can safely assume that there were, then as always, men and women who preferred to be intimate only with those of their own sex. Rather than try to establish identities for medieval people, I describe 'same-sex love' and 'same-sex relations' that range from sexual intercourse to expressions of non-sexual affection, acts seen not in isolation but as part of the 'activity and interactions' that make up a social world. By 'same-sex' I mean no more, and no less, than that the partners involved in a given exchange are of the same biological sex, a determinant to which the gender roles assumed by either or both of the parties may or may not correspond.[23] □

Furthermore:

■ The thesis of this book is that the existence of the closet was not recognized by the men and women of Anglo-Saxon England. Hence I describe theirs as a culture 'before the closet'. Explaining the Anglo-Saxon evidence as specific and straightforward rather than closeted and queer is [one of my objectives].[24] □

In Chapter Two of his book, provocatively titled 'Kiss and Tell', Frantzen turns his attention to *Beowulf* – particularly, as might be expected, to the relationship between Beowulf and Hrothgar. The scenes that Frantzen concentrates on are (1) Hrothgar's lavish rewarding of Beowulf after the hero has killed Grendel (1046–1048) and (2) where the old king bids farewell to the young warrior (1870–82). Of the first episode, Frantzen writes that:

■ *Beowulf* describes two of the most manly men in Old English literature – Hrothgar, the aged Danish king whose kingdom is collapsing, and Beowulf, the young hero who rescues it. Having heard of Hrothgar's powerlessness before a monster who ransacks Hrothgar's hall, Beowulf appears to fight and kill Grendel. The deed done, Hrothgar fittingly rewards the hero, and the narrator approves.

[...] So manfully did the glorious prince, hoard-guard of heroes, repay the battle-rush with steeds and treasure that no man will ever find fault with them. [1046–48]

[...] The poet seems to be assuring the audience that Hrothgar, whom we have come to see as weak and ineffective, is as much a man as the young hero who has just killed Grendel. The audience is implicitly challenged to affirm its manliness – its humanity, but also its sense of what is appropriate – by approving of Hrothgar's gesture.[25] □

By stating that the audience of *Beowulf* 'is implicitly challenged to affirm its manliness' Frantzen assumes that this group is predominantly male and that their response to the poem is inevitably a gendered one. But what of the women in the audience? How would they have responded to the scenes between Hrothgar and Beowulf? By virtue of the parameters of his research, Frantzen does not tackle this issue. The following passage, however, contains Frantzen's interpretation of the moment of Beowulf's departure from Heorot where Hrothgar weeps:

■ Beowulf is socially subordinate, but he dominates the narrative [...] Hrothgar's tears mourn Beowulf's departure, not his rash actions. There is no conjugal language used to describe their relationship, no domestic details – one partner preparing food and serving it to the other, for example – and the language of kinship that connects them is carefully limited. Hrothgar's implicit attempt to 'adopt' Beowulf is thwarted by Hrothgar's wife, Wealhtheow, in a famous defense of her sons and their rights (1175–91). No women are associated with Beowulf, but his manliness is never in doubt. His comments on relations between men and women are incidental, such as his prediction that the warrior Ingeld's 'wiflufan' ('woman-love') will be cooled by hatred for his enemies (2063–66). Hrothgar's marriage, by contrast, is prominent. There is no point at which he and his hero constitute a closed, exclusive, and intense or heroic pair.[26] □

As has been observed previously in this guide, it is intriguing that 'no women are associated with Beowulf' as it is a literary commonplace for the hero-king to have a wife and carry on his dynasty (as well as his memory) through the producing of children. It is difficult to know exactly how to interpret Beowulf's single status, but Frantzen does a good job of implicitly suggesting that it provides a profound point of contrast between the hero and Hrothgar. And whilst these two male figures may not be an 'exclusive and intense or heroic pair', they are certainly dramatic foils for each other. This is confirmed by Frantzen when he says that:

> ■ I also think that Hrothgar's secret longing for Beowulf might have more to do with Hrothgar himself than with the young man. As he says farewell to the hero, Hrothgar is forced to realize that he long ago bade farewell to the young hero within. It is not just Beowulf's departure that grieves him (we must remember that he long ago said goodbye to Beowulf's father) but the passing of his younger and more valorous – may I say more manly? – self.[27] □

Similarly to *Before the Closet, Medieval Masculinities* (2006) also set out to explore men's culture in relation to early period literature. Thelma Fenster, in the preface (titled, fittingly enough, 'Why Men?') to this edition, asserts that 'as this volume goes to press, the discipline of men's studies, and gender studies along with it, has earned its place in scholarship.'[28] And she answers the question 'Why men?' as follows: 'The study of men's culture, through its challenge to an intellectual process that left men above examination, also corrects the peculiar "objectification" of women that feminist studies produced by studying women alone as gendered.'[29] Clare Lees, in the volume's introduction, adds that 'The question that runs throughout this collection in various formulations is, What does it mean to be a man in this historical period.'[30] Overlaps with Frantzen's approach are obvious here. For the purposes of this guide, it is also important to note here that Chapter Eight of *Medieval Masculinities*, written by Lees, is devoted to *Beowulf* and primarily explores two related questions: 'First, how does *Beowulf* criticism use masculinity as a beginning for interpretation? And second, in what ways can the poem's masculinity be understood?'[31]

JANE CHANCE

Gender-related *Beowulf* criticism of the 1990s was not, of course, exclusively devoted to the men in the poem: feminist readings

continued to proliferate during this time. One important contribution to this field was *New Readings on Women in Old English Literature*
(1990), a collection of essays edited by Helen Damico and Alexandra
Hennessey Olsen. For the purposes of this guide, the most relevant
piece to consider here is Jane Chance's 'The Structural Unity of
Beowulf: The Problem of Grendel's Mother'. Whilst Chance covers
some by now familiar ground in her assessment that Grendel's mother
'inverts the Germanic roles of mother and queen, or lady',[32] she does
bring some new insights to the critical table as well by identifying the
sexual nature of Grendel's mother's fight with Beowulf. The allusion
here is to the famous scene where the female monster sits on/astride
the male hero. Chance argues that Grendel's mother's desire to be on
top here signifies the evil nature of her being. Comparing *Beowulf*
with *Judith* (both poems are, of course, from the same manuscript),
Chance observes:

> ■ The poet's point in each case is that a perversion of the sexual roles
> signals an equally perverse spiritual state. Holofernes' [the evil king whom
> Judith, in the Old Testament of the Bible, beheads to save her people]
> impotence is as unnatural in the male as the *wif's* [Grendel's mother] is
> unnatural in the female; so the battle with the heroine or hero in each case
> is described with erotic overtones to suggest the triumph of a right and
> natural sexual (and social and spiritual) order over the perverse and unnat-
> ural one.[33] □

Despite, or perhaps because of, her perversity, however, Grendel's
mother is seen by Chance as having an extremely important role in
the poem:

> ■ Grendel's mother does occupy a transitional position in the poem: as
> a 'retainer' attacking Heorot she resembles Grendel, but as an 'attacked
> ruler' of her own 'hall' she resembles the dragon. As a monstrous mother
> and queen she perverts a role more important socially and symbolically
> than that of Grendel, just as the queen as peace-pledge or peace-weaver
> ultimately becomes more valuable than the retainer but less valuable than
> the gold-giver himself.[34] □

Chance makes a convincing argument here for Grendel's mother's
'transitional position' in *Beowulf*. Her interpretation also brings out
the striking similarities between the monsters and the men of the
comitatus. Grendel, Grendel's mother and the dragon are, as we have
seen, shadow figures of characters like Beowulf, Hrothgar and Wiglaf.
In relation to this point, readers of this guide might also take a look
at Christine Rauer's *Beowulf and the Dragon: Parallels and Analogues*
(2000).

GILLIAN R. OVERING

No discussion of gender in *Beowulf* would be complete without some engagement with Gillian R. Overing's *Language, Sign and Gender in Beowulf* (1990). The final chapter of this study, 'Gender and Interpretation in *Beowulf*' (reprinted in Peter Baker's *The Beowulf Reader*), is of especial interest here. In this chapter, Overing draws upon Freud's concept of desire in 'Beyond the Pleasure Principle' (1920), where it is stated that the 'ultimate object of all desire' is death.[35] As a consequence, Freud's influence reverberates throughout Overing's argument, and no more so than in the following passage:

■ At first, and even second glance, *Beowulf* seems to be a poem about death: how to die, how to seek out death, how to meet it head on, how to make it so commonplace that it becomes an old familiar, how to choose it, privilege it, embrace it. Everywhere in the poem this deathly embrace spawns a variety of forms of closure, a continual need for resolution, the notion that choice is heroic, inescapable and reducible to simple binary oppositions – one or the other. And the other always loses. *Beowulf* is also an overwhelmingly masculine poem; it could be seen as a chronicle of male desire, a tale of men dying. In the masculine economy of the poem desire expresses itself as desire for the other, as a continual process of subjugation and appropriation of the other.[36] □

If this is indeed the case, it is no wonder that the women in the poem have been described by Chance (with a heavy nod to Hélène Cixous, the French feminist theorist and writer born in 1937) as 'marginal', 'excluded' hysterics: 'Characterizing the women of *Beowulf* as hysterics not only allies them with ambiguity, but is also a means of avoiding a reductive critical approach.'[37] And, furthermore, 'There is no place for women in the masculine economy of *Beowulf*; they have no space to occupy, to claim to speak from.'[38] If one takes the view that women occupy a marginalized position in the poem, this may potentially provide another explanation as to why the hero is not married. For as Fred Robinson has stated, in 'Teaching the Background: History, Religion, Culture' (1984) in *Approaches to Teaching Beowulf*, '*Beowulf*'s marital status was of insufficient interest [to the poet] to warrant mention in the poem.'[39] The gist of Robinson's argument is that women are largely invisible in this most masculine of poems. 'Human women', perhaps, but this reading does not take into account the prominent position that Grendel's mother has in the text.

Before we leave our discussion of gender, a brief mention of another relevant study might be of interest to readers of this guide. This is Henrietta Leyser's *Medieval Women: A Social History of Women in England, 450–1500* (2002). Leyser addresses, though she does not explore in detail, the issue of gendered reader responses to *Beowulf*. Is reading the poem 'as a man' a different experience from reading it 'as a woman'?[40] From what has been said earlier in the present chapter of this guide, the answer is unquestionably yes. Leyser also spots an interesting linguistic connection between descriptions of Grendel's mother and the 'human women' of *Beowulf*:

■ Modthryth shares with Wealhtheow, Hildeburh and Grendel's mother – at first sight a strange assortment – the distinction of being described as an *ides* [glossed variously as woman, wife, lady, queen]. The meaning of this word has been a matter of some debate among philologists.[41] □

Whilst acknowledging the enigmatic nature of the Old English *ides*, Leyser herself believes that the word is 'morally neutral' and signifies 'power'.[42] Though it is problematic, especially given Chance's argument above, to describe any word used of Grendel's mother as 'morally neutral', it is obvious that the female monster is a figure of power (however malevolently wielded) in the poem.

JAMES W. EARL

During this time of rapid expansion in *Beowulf* criticism, James W. Earl's *Thinking about Beowulf* pushed the boat out in terms of the way that it approached the poem. Earl's method is twofold. In the first half of the book, his method 'is mostly phenomenological', an approach that focuses on consciousness and the objects of direct experience.[43] The second half of the volume, however:

■ is dominated by psychoanalysis. This interest began with psychoanalytic anthropology, under the influence of Victor Turner [1920–83] and René Girard [born 1923]; but Freud drew me on to issues of individual consciousness, creativity, and reader response. I end by probing the creative autonomy of the *Beowulf* poet, as well as the reader, and our mutual interest in the hero's freedom beyond his fate.[44] □

In his explanation of his methodology, Earl introduces a question already familiar to readers of this guide; does Beowulf have free will? The issue of the hero's ultimate fate is also linked to something that Earl brings up a little later in his work:

■ The distinctive psychology of mourning, with its blend of love, devotion, obsessive memory, guilt, self-mortification, anger, renunciation, and relief, might account for the poem's complex tone better than the more conventional theory of cultural nostalgia.[45] □

Nevertheless, nostalgia is present in the poem, as Earl suggests in his discussion of the significance of the hall in Anglo-Saxon culture:

■ The hall remained the locus of social-political (though not sacral) power and still embodied a heroic ethic, expressed in poetry in which idealized history shades imperceptibly into mythology. Poetry, as an essential component of hall life, remained a tradition of an Anglo-Saxon aristocracy that still considered itself, long after the conversion, as a warrior class.[46] □

The argument that the Anglo-Saxon aristocracy, even once it was Christianized, still considered itself to be a 'warrior class' is supported by *Beowulf* and other poems of the time. This may also, of course, account for some of the Christian–pagan tensions in the poem. Earl, however, identifies additional problems faced by scholars who wish to get to the heart of the matter:

■ An important difficulty is that while early Christianity is well documented, almost nothing is known about the native religious belief of the Anglo-Saxons, which we can detect only in the shadows that it cast on the Christian belief that supplanted it.[47] □

In Chapter Four of his work, '*Beowulf* and the Men's Hall', Earl indulges in some rather pyrotechnic rhetoric as he tests 'the usefulness of psychoanalytic anthropology as an approach to *Beowulf*':

■ I would not want students to catch me calling *Beowulf* a 'hallucinatory wishful psychosis' or a 'libidinal hypercathexis,' but heroic poetry generally does serve to prolong a culture's identification with a lost past while at the same time acknowledging that past as irretrievably lost.[48] □

It might seem best to let Earl have the last word, but Mary Clayton's 'Constructing Identities: Angles, Angels and English' (2002) seems relevant here. Clayton, however, opens up the topic of nostalgia and links it to the nationalistic undercurrents identified in the poem – a subject already familiar to readers of this guide. She states:

■ Hrothgar, whose court dominates the first two thirds of the poem, is descended from Scyld; this same Scyld is the one added in the genealogy on [King] Alfred's time [he reigned from 871–899], so the beginning of *Beowulf* celebrates an ancestral king of the Danes *and* English. Paradoxically, then, despite, the notable absences of England in the poem, *Beowulf* can be read as a kind of English national epic which, in invoking an Anglo-Danish past, works to assimilate English and Danes. This Anglo-Danish heathen past is viewed by the Christian poet as noble but doomed because of its paganism – one of the cultural tasks performed by the poem is, I think, to facilitate assimilation of Danes in a Christian England. It is a national project, not an ethnic one; it is ethnically inclusive in terms of national identity, but only if everyone is Christian.[49] □

NATALIA BREIZMANN

Though discussions of genre are sometimes considered old-fashioned, a fresh, partly Foucauldian, approach to the topic appeared in 1998 in the form of Natalia Breizmann's '*Beowulf* as Romance: Literary Interpretation as Quest'. Breizmann admits from the very outset that 'The problem of genre has long been subject to intense scholarly debate.'[50] She continues by saying that:

■ The remarkable diversity of the poem's generic makeup allows for a wide range of interpretations, which argue both for and against the traditional definitions of *Beowulf* as heroic epic. The generic aspects to which the critics assign primary importance in the poem include fairy tale, elegy, heroic lay, oral-formulaic poetry, historical and legendary narrative, and Christian allegory [...] This essay will discuss the possibility of reading *Beowulf* as a romance.[51] □

It is intriguing to think of *Beowulf* as a fairy tale, though not everyone will be convinced that this is an accurate way to describe the text. One of the best discussions of this subject, however, is to be found in G.T. Shepherd's '*Beowulf:* An Epic Fairy Tale' (1984) in Boris Ford's edition of *The New Pelican Guide to English Literature*. According to Shepherd, *Beowulf* is a fairy tale, if a rather equivocal one. It is:

■ a fairy story wrapped up quite confidently in an inexplicit Christian metaphysic. There may be bits of a more ancient mythology sprinkled though it, but the old myths cannot be reconstructed. It suspends even the normal workings of a fairy tale. At the very points where magic is brought into play – for example, when the gift sword Hrunting should be put to use – the poet substitutes and emphasizes instead the efficacy of human virtue and divine providence. There are marvels in the world of *Beowulf*, but no magic.[52] □

What allows Breizmann to categorize *Beowulf* as a romance is her belief that 'genre is a flexible category both in terms of historical period and formal features.'[53] The upshot of this is that, crucially, it enables 'critical approaches traditionally conceived of as modern to be used with some modifications, for reading medieval texts'.[54] Breizmann's definition of romance is illuminating:

■ If epic can be described as a narrative of society, then romance is a narrative of the individual. The plot of *Beowulf* presents a fictive history of a nation and is in this sense 'epic'. However, the plot also resembles an archetypal quest story, of the sort that reaches its apogee [highest point] in the courtly literature of the High Middle Ages – a story with elements of fantasy. The motif of adventure in which the protagonist fights monsters as well as human opponents and performs other deeds of valor is widespread in medieval romance.[55] □

James W. Earl, in '*Beowulf* and the Origins of Civilization' (1991) provides us with a much more expansive definition of epic (one heavily influenced by Freudian psychology):

■ As a genre, epic is involved with the task of superego construction, at the individual and cultural levels. Freud summarizes: 'Strengthening of the superego is a most precious cultural asset in the psychological field. Those in whom it has taken place are turned from being opponents of civilization into being its vehicles.' That strengthening is one of the tasks of epic, the poetic accompaniment of the birth of civilization.

   But the epic cannot discriminate among its audiences: it sets about constructing our superegos as well as its original audience's. So in the case of epic especially, interpretation is likely to express our own invaded psychologies as well as the author's. In this regard, *Beowulf* is an extreme, and therefore an extremely interesting, case.[56] □

If Breizmann feels that genre is a 'flexible category', Earl correspondingly sees the interpreting of *Beowulf* as being even more fluid and subjective. Readers interested in psychoanalytic readings of the poem might also like to consult Judy Anne White's *Hero-Ego in Search of Self: A Jungian Reading of Beowulf* (2004) and Janet Thormann's '*Beowulf* and the Enjoyment of Violence' (1997).

   Returning to the subject of romance, however, Breizmann offers further elaboration:

■ In romance the hero's character is central. To understand this character it is crucial to read and interpret the hero's words and actions. Furthermore, being aware of the fictional nature of his work, the author of romance attaches particular importance to the act of composition and writing – to such an extent that he allows his characters to share in the creative aspect of this process. Romance represents the individual as both the object and the subject of literary production: he is the hero and the creator of his own story, as well as a contributor to the larger narrative of his culture.

As a consequence, romance characters are often found listening to and telling stories – stories about themselves and others. (Examples of such stories can be found in Arthurian romances, such as Wolfram's *Parzival*: the narrative of Orgeluse or Trevrizent; Chrétien's *Yvain*: the narratives of Calogrenant, Lunete, etc.) It can be noted that *Beowulf* abounds with such stories, from the protagonist's monologue accounts of his exploits to extended legendary narratives.[57] □

Breizmann's comment that 'the author of romance attaches particular importance to the act of composition and writing' may partly explain why the figure and craft of the poet are so important in *Beowulf*. And if 'the hero's character is central' in romance, what does Breizmann make of the character of Beowulf? For one thing, she certainly sees the hero as possessing a potentially fatal flaw when she identifies 'The problem of pride as a possible major factor in Beowulf's destruction'.[58] This same pride is, of course, potentially responsible for the uncertainty that faces the hero's kingdom once he is dead for, as Breizmann notes:

■ Beowulf's conquest of the hoard is in vain – the gold that he receives as a trophy is to burn with him on the pyre. He freed his subjects from the dragon, but now they are left without rule and protection, threatened by hostile invasion. The Messenger, who brings the news of Beowulf's death to his people, glorifies the deeds of his slain king, yet also prophesies the ruin of the Geats – a ruin that is inevitable following the death of the leader and defender. The fundamental discrepancy between Beowulf's loyalty to his people and the demands of his ambition is finalized in the very last line of the poem, which describes him as both most kind and most eager of fame. This characterisation juxtaposes the mortal sin – vainglory – and the highest virtue – charity – and leaves the task of resolving this dilemma to the audience. With the end of Beowulf's adventure the quest of the reader begins – the quest for reading and understanding the poem's ideological message.[59] □

As readers of this guide may have guessed by now, the quest for reading and understanding the poem is seemingly endless.

SETH LERER

As is to be expected in any work of criticism, Breizmann makes reference to a number of other scholarly studies in her article. For our purposes, the most important of these is Seth Lerer's 'Grendel's Glove' (1994). Lerer thinks of Beowulf as 'a poem of the body', and:

■ Its actions celebrate that strength of sinew, mastery of breath, or power of the grip that define Beowulf as the victor of social challenge or monstrous invasion. Elaborate armaments and ornaments, while dressing and protecting the heroic form, more often fade into the background, or even fail, before the prowess of the victor or the wiles of the vanquished. The fight with the sea monster during the swimming match with Breca, the combat with Grendel in Heorot, and the vanquishing of Grendel's mother in her lair, all center on the hero's maintenance of the intact body. By contrast, the result of these victories, and indeed, the consequences of non-Beowulfian encounters with such creatures, leave dismembered bodies. The poem's landscape is littered with ripped trunks, severed heads, and fragmentary limbs. Grendel's arm, Æscere's head, and the decapitated forms of the monster and his mother become the landmarks along which the poem's characters and its readers mark their progress towards heroic victory. And at the poem's end, when Beowulf's blade fails and his mail cannot save him from the dragon's fiery breath, it is a war of body parts that he loses, as the dragon's head-bone breaks the sword Nægling and the hero's own hand fails.[60] □

Lerer's argument inspires Breizmann to suggest that 'This interpretation is consistent with the Foucaldian view of epic as a narrative of destruction, and romance as one of restoration, of the body.'[61] Lerer also, however, links his work on the body with the figure and craft of the Anglo-Saxon *scop*. It is an original argument, and is based on the episode in the poem where 'Returning from his exploits at the Danish court, Beowulf comes home to Hygelac to tell of his adventures.'[62] Lerer continues:

■ But in the middle of the narrative, Beowulf proffers information neither we nor they have heard before. There is the naming of the first Geat killed, Hondscio (2076), and the description of Grendel's monstrous glove in which he was wont to put his victims (2085b-88). Moreover, in its protestations of excessive length and its self-consciousness of telling, Beowulf's story of the fight seems strikingly unlike anything he has performed before.

[...] Beowulf's conjuring of Grendel's glove [which Lerer sees as signifying 'the gross processes of digestion'[63]], then, testifies to his command of the poetic resources of his culture. His performance is, in one sense, a social ritual: a fulfilling of a contract between the returning hero and the welcoming community for an account, both entertaining and instructive, of his adventures. It is, too, in another sense, a reflection on the problems of ritual itself: a recognition of the place that bodily dismemberment has in the deeper forms of cosmic, social, and poetic self-representation and explanation. To speak of a poetics of dismemberment, then, or to find in Beowulf's performance a commanding display of traditional materials and methods, is to speak of poetry itself and to see how the hero's literature takes the shards and fragments of dead bodies or inhuman artifacts and transforms them into reflections on the poet's craft and on the place of imaginative fiction in society.[64] □

Lerer's remark that the hero's performance is 'both entertaining and instructive' is an important one, for it gets to the very heart of how the Anglo-Saxons and people from the Middle Ages viewed art. Though art was primarily meant to be didactic, elements less lofty crept in from time to time and were clearly enjoyed by audiences. All we need do is think back to our earlier discussion of humour in *Beowulf* as proof of this point. Looking ahead to poems like *The General Prologue* to *The Canterbury Tales,* it is clear that Geoffrey Chaucer (*c.* 1343/4–1400) is also writing to this brief for he has the Host tell the pilgrims that they must tell 'Tales of best sentence and moost solaas'. [l. 800] In other words, tales which provide both meaning ('sentence') and solace/merriment ('solaas').

GALE R. OWEN-CROCKER

In 2000, a valuable study of the structure of the poem was published – Gale R. Owen-Crocker's *The Four Funerals in Beowulf.* Owen-Crocker begins by stating something that has been reinforced throughout the course of this guide: 'Since its first appearance in the nineteenth century, the Old English heroic poem known as *Beowulf* has attracted a great amount of critical attention and a dazzling variety of analyses and interpretations.'[65] She then speaks in a very specific way about the poem's structure: 'Until now [...] *Beowulf* scholars have accepted that the poem contains *three* funerals (as there are three monster-fights).'[66] Owen-Crocker extends this number by one, however, and identifies the four funerals in her Contents table as follows: 'The first funeral: Scyld Scefing's ship of death; The second funeral: the cremation of Hildeburg's kin; The third funeral: the Last Survivor's lament; The fourth funeral: Beowulf's complex obsequies.' In Chapter Eleven, 'Coexistent structures: three movements and a coda: *Beowulf*'s feminist middle; elements and seasons', the author elaborates more fully on the significance of her discovery:

■ Given the new identification of an additional funeral in the body of the text, it is possible to see that *Beowulf* has [...] a linear structure of three movements, each with an introductory funeral and each containing a monster-fight. The final funeral, Beowulf's, acts as a coda to the whole.[67] □

In what way, though, is the hero's funeral 'a coda of the whole' poem? Here is Owen-Crocker's elegantly argued response (line numbering is from Klaeber's edition):

■ Beowulf's complex funeral is a reprise of the diagnostic features of all the funerals that have gone before. The body is disposed of by cremation as the corpses were at Finnsburg, and the barrow which is constructed on the site of the pyre is filled with treasure, the same treasure that was recovered from the dragon's hoard (lines 3164–5) having been placed in another barrow by the Last Survivor [...] There is also strong reminiscence of Scyld's funeral at sea, both in a minor way in that, before Beowulf's cremation, the dragon is disposed of by being pushed off the cliff into the waves (lines 3129–31), and in a major way in that Beowulf's funeral takes place by the sea [...] Scyld's departing ship was pictured as if from the eyes of the bereaved retainers on shore, disappearing into the unknown. In a reversal of the view, Beowulf's barrow brings sea travellers safely to shore.[68] □

It would be hard to find a better discussion of the complexity of the poem's structure, and the poet's use of parallelisms.

The final point to note here about Owen-Crocker's analysis of *Beowulf* is what she says about the hero's behaviour during his last fight. As we know, many critics see the ending of the poem as problematic, and it has even been suggested that by acting out of pride in his battle with the dragon Beowulf jeopardizes the future of his people. Owen-Crocker, however, takes a more sympathetic view of the hero's final actions:

■ The third section [of *Beowulf*] explores the nature of courage, a quality which has been taken for granted, at least in the principal characters, earlier in the poem. It takes a different kind of bravery to face a monster when your age tells you that death is inevitably near, from the valour when you are young and have every hope of a long life ahead if successful in the immediate fight.[69] □

Rather than seeing Beowulf's battle with the dragon as being arrogant and foolhardy, Owen-Crocker, in 'a reversal of the view', sees it as being perhaps the most noble and brave act he performed in all of his life.

THE POSTMODERN *BEOWULF*

No assessment of recent *Beowulf* criticism would be complete without some mention of *The Postmodern 'Beowulf'* (2006), edited by Eileen A. Joy and Mary K. Ramsey. Joy acknowledges in her Preface 'that the reception of theory in Old English studies has been less than welcoming'.[70] As a consequence, many felt a great need for a volume like *The Postmodern 'Beowulf'*:

■ The attempt to restore historical complexity to our understanding of the past and its cultural forms, and to also show [sic.] how Old English studies both practice and reformulate theory, suffices as a description of the project of *The Postmodern 'Beowulf'*, which was initially born out of a desire to provide for students an anthology of 'the best of' contemporary critical approaches to the poem and then later developed into a casebook that we hope more than amply demonstrates the ways in which Old English scholarship has debated, elucidated, practised, historicized, and even developed theory in relation to the critical analysis of *Beowulf*.[71] □

The essays in the volume have been divided into different headings: History/Historicism; Ethnography/Psychoanalysis; Gender/Identity; Text/Textuality; Philology and Postcolonialism. Under the first heading we find writings by scholars by now familiar to readers of this guide – Nicholas Howe, Allen J. Frantzen, and John D. Niles. And we meet James W. Earl and Janet Thormann again in the section on Ethnography/Psychoanalysis. Gender/Identity are served by essays such as Mary Dockray-Miller's '*Beowulf*'s Tears of Fatherhood' and Shari Horner's 'Voices from the Margins: Women and Textual Enclosure in *Beowulf*'. Under Text/Textuality, Seth Lerer, in 'Hrothgar's Hilt and the Reader in *Beowulf*', continues to explore some of the issues raised in 'Grendel's Glove' (discussed above). In 'Hrothgar's Hilt and the Reader in *Beowulf*' Lerer also provides an excellent summary of the history of *Beowulf* criticism. For the purposes of this guide it seems appropriate to quote him here in full:

■ Throughout the nearly three centuries of *Beowulf*'s reception, that need for critical interpretation has been focused on a set of issues dealing primarily, though not exclusively, with dating, history, and Christian content. Traditionally, the relationship between the poet and his material has been seen in terms of these three issues and as questions in the varying degrees of knowledge he and his sources, or he and his characters, share. The poet and his audience, for example, 'know' about God and Creation in ways that Beowulf and his companions do not; or, from a different angle, the poem's allusive fragments of Swedish history testify to a knowledge of events that the poet does not share with his imagined characters or their historical forebears. The critical adjudication of problems of this nature depends on many, often tacit, assumptions about the poem's date and mode of composition, the constitution of his audience, and the circumstances of its transcription. The myriad confusions that surround the *Beowulf* manuscript itself, and the interpretations silently enshrined in printed editions that use modern punctuation and capitalization, only add to any insecurities attending a reader of the poem.[72] □

Lerer addresses here the history of *Beowulf* criticism, but what of its future? Volumes like *The Postmodern 'Beowulf'* have taken the study of the poem in new directions. Other important recent studies that come to mind are Andy Orchard's *A Critical Companion to Beowulf* (2003) and Chris Jones' *Strange Likeness: The Use of Old English in Twentieth-Century Poetry* (already mentioned in Chapter One of this guide). Jones' argument, a forceful one indeed, is that 'without Old English, twentieth-century English poetry would have developed in different ways.'[73] It should be clear as we near the end of this guide that without *Beowulf* the work of literary critics of the past three hundred years would have been significantly diminished. This scholarly journey will, no doubt, continue well into the future for, to quote Natalia Breizmann again, 'With the ending of Beowulf's adventure the quest of the reader begins'[74] and it begins anew. No anecdote speaks to this more eloquently than the one told by James W. Earl in 'Reading *Beowulf* with Original Eyes':

■ at a cocktail party on Martha's Vineyard, I met a judge who had managed one of JFK's [John F. Kennedy, 1917–63; President of the United States from 1961 to 1963] early campaigns. When I told him that I was a *Beowulf* scholar, he told me the following story. One day he went to the Capitol to meet Kennedy for lunch, but the Senate was still in session; so he went up to the gallery to wait, and looking down into the Senate chamber, he saw Kennedy, feet up on his desk reading a book. Later he asked him what the book was, and Kennedy held up a copy of *Beowulf*. Now the judge asked me: 'Why *Beowulf* ?' To me it seemed obvious. I said, 'This is the man who wrote *Profiles in Courage* [1956], the hero of PT 109. He was studying to be a hero and a leader. *Beowulf*'s a classic on the subject.'

Little in this narrative of mine is really 'subjective.' [...] On reflection, many of the crisscrossing cathexes in my mind are really only the traces of the external world passing through me. Now when I lecture on *Beowulf*, nearly every episode in the poem evokes strings of associations like these, moments when I registered the sharp impacts of the world – even world-historical events.[75] □

The above account of *Beowulf*'s political relevance is fascinating, and it implies that President Kennedy read the poem as a type of Mirror for Princes. Earl's anecdote also illustrates just how diverse *Beowulf*'s audience is, and the unexpected uses to which it has been put. That this continues to be the case will become clear as we move to the final chapter of this guide, which deals with *Beowulf* in other media.

CHAPTER EIGHT

Beowulf in Popular Culture

M ichael Livingston and John William Sutton have remarked upon the large number of adaptations of the poem in other media:

■ Since the publication of J.R.R. Tolkien's seminal essay '*Beowulf*: The Monsters and the Critics' (1936), if we are to select an arbitrary cut-off date, there have been two plays, six musical or symphonic productions, more than a dozen novel-length retellings, at least fifteen children's books, five comic books or series, numerous poems, parodies, short stories, computer games, films, an episode of *Star Trek: Voyager*, and even Mardi Gras tokens that have direct connections to the poem.[1] □

Of course, an examination of all of these genres is far beyond the scope of this guide. What will be offered here, then, is a brief survey of some of the novels, films, animations, musical pieces, retellings for children, comic books and graphic novels based (faithfully or otherwise) on *Beowulf*.

NOVELS

JOHN GARDNER'S GRENDEL

It is perhaps no surprise that John Gardner (1933–1982) turned his hand to *Beowulf*; being a novelist as well as an Anglo-Saxonist made him doubly equipped to take on the Old English epic. Since its publication in 1971, Gardner's *Grendel* has been seen as a 'marked turning point in Beowulfiana'[2] and the following quotation reveals exactly why this is so:

■ [Gardner] turns the original story upside down and inside out, retelling it from the perspective of the monster. Gardner humanizes Grendel, transforming him from an animalistic creature into a sentient being with human emotions. His Grendel is also a deeply introspective character, one who struggles to find his place in a world he does not understand. Grendel remains the adversary of human culture, but through his eyes we see a human culture that is ugly and flawed [...] Gardner presents a decidedly unfavourable view of Germanic warrior culture, which is epitomized by a cruel, inscrutable, anti-heroic Beowulf. As such, *Grendel* strongly resists that familiar but too easy distinction of 'good hero' and 'evil monster.' [...] It was as if Gardner had opened the doors to reading *Beowulf* in new and exciting ways. Of course, certainly not all *Beowulf* narratives of the past three-and-a-half decades have based their interpretations on Gardner's work, but his subversive Grendel has provided many other creative minds with an ingenious vehicle for social commentary.[3] □

This final point will be clear from our examination of Julie Taymor's opera *Grendel* and the various film versions of *Beowulf* discussed below.

Of course, Gardner was not the first person to see a human side to Grendel. This aspect of the creature was, as we have seen throughout the course of this guide, also identified by scholars working on the Old English poem. Gardner also shares with some literary critics a particular type of reading of *Beowulf* – a post-colonial one. In Gardner's novel, Grendel is, in effect, a symbol of the indigenous population uprooted and displaced by the colonizing tendencies of Hrothgar and his people. The following quotation perfectly illustrates this point:

■ In the beginning there were various groups of them: ragged little bands that roamed the forest on foot or horseback, crafty-witted killers that worked in teams, hunting through the summer, shivering in caves or little huts in the winter, occasionally wandering out into the snow to plow through it slowly, clumsily, after more meat [...] As the bands grew larger, they would seize and clear a hill and, with the trees they'd cut, would set up shacks, and on the crown of the hill a large, shaggy house with a steeply pitched roof and a wide stone hearth, where they'd all go at night for protection from other bands of men.[4] □

Grendel effectively, then, becomes the Other. As one critic has noted:

■ Although in calling him a son of Cain [as in *Beowulf*] they implicitly know him as kin, they cast him out and call him Other. Beowulf and his men are 'quick as wolves [...] mechanical, terrible' (152), and Beowulf himself knows that Grendel is his brother, and that the hero must, paradoxically, kill the monster to demonstrate that link; Beowulf becomes Cain when he kills Grendel.[5] □

As Gardner's novel is told from Grendel's point of view, it is obvious that language is central to the novel's message. Unlike the mute 'monster' found in *Beowulf*, therefore, Gardner's Grendel is extremely articulate; much more so, in fact, than the barbaric humans who populate

Hrothgar's kingdom. Grendel's mother, however, does not share her son's eloquence. Her son observes her thus:

■ Behind my back, at the world's end, my pale slightly glowing fat mother sleeps on, sick at heart, in our dingy underground room. Life-bloated, baffled, long-suffering hag. Guilty, she imagines, of some unremembered crime. (She must have some human in her.) Not that she thinks. Not that she dissects and ponders the dusty mechanical bits of her miserable life's curse. She clutches at me in her sleep as if to crush me. I break away.[6] □

Despite his ability to speak well, Gardner's Grendel shares many things in common with the figure of the same name in *Beowulf*. Both are fatherless exiles and descendants of Cain who are maddened by the sound of harps. The character in the novel, however, also has a certain amount of awe and respect for the *scop* (or 'Shaper', to use Gardner's word) whom he overhears performing in Hrothgar's hall:

■ The harper sang [...] I listened, felt myself swept up. I knew very well that what he said was ridiculous, not light for their darkness but flattery, illusion, a vortex pulling them from sunlight to heat, a kind of midsummer burgeoning, waltz to the sickle. Yet I was swept up.[7] □

Other dissimilarities between *Beowulf* and *Grendel* have also been noted:

■ As the dragon's presence in Act 1 suggests, Gardner's *Grendel* is not quite the 'retelling' of *Beowulf* from the monster's point of view so often alleged. The dragon does not appear in *Beowulf* until the hero is an old man (2312), and Grendel's consciousness disappears from the poem at line 835. At that point Beowulf has met the monster, ripped off his arm, and nailed Grendel's huge claw under the roof of Heorot (835–36). After Grendel's mother is killed by Beowulf (1567), Grendel himself is beheaded (1591) and his head dragged before Hrothgar, where it lies as Beowulf recounts his triumph over the monster's mother (1647–76). By introducing the dragon to a youthful Grendel, Gardner perhaps wanted to parallel Beowulf's reflections as an old man on the ways of youth (2425–2509). This is one of many points when the novel silently plays off of an assumed knowledge of *Beowulf*. The dragon supplies an ancient consciousness, provides cynical advice, and, not incidentally, casts a spell that protects Grendel from weapons. Gardner's dragon is sour but also magnificent. 'Ah, Grendel!,' he said. 'You've come [...] we've been expecting you' (58). Gardner describes the dragon as having a 'vast, red-golden, huge tail coiled, [with] limbs sprawled over his treasure-hoard.' Even his teeth are grand: 'razorsharp tusks, [they] gleamed and glinted as if they too, like the mountain beneath him, were formed of precious stones and metals (57)'.[8] □

MICHAEL CRICHTON'S EATERS OF THE DEAD

Gardner's *Grendel* is not, of course, the only novel to play off, 'silently' or otherwise, 'an assumed knowledge of *Beowulf*'. The same could be said of *The Eaters of the Dead* (1976) by Michael Crichton (1942–2008). *The Eaters of the Dead* is perhaps Crichton's least-read novel and must be counted as 'one of his more eccentric efforts'.[9] It is also one of his most interesting. The novel begins with an introduction which states that the text is a translation of a German version of 'the Ibn Fahdlan manuscript',[10] namely the *Risala*, a work originally written in Arabic. As Livingston and Sutton explain, Crichton's introduction and opening chapters are written 'in an academic way: he includes historical background to Fahdlan's journeys, a detailed account of the manuscript's provenance, and even a large number of footnotes – items that all seem to guarantee credibility.'[11]

A closer examination of Crichton's bibliography at the end of the novel, however, reveals names such as 'Fraus-Dolus', two words which can be translated as 'fraud'. Also, the final item in the bibliography is *The Necronomicon*, the name of a famously non-existent work invented by the horror writer H.P. Lovecraft (1890–1937). On one level, the reference to Lovecraft is a nod to a fellow author who also crafted ingenious faux-academic works; however, there is more to it and it demonstrates just how much thought went in to Crichton's novel. Lovecraft was also an admirer of *Beowulf*. He made reference to it in his study, *Supernatural Horror in Literature* (1927) and argued that the poem was one of the first horror stories, and one 'full of eldritch weirdness'.[12] Livingston and Sutton also think that these hoax references have a serious purpose. For them, Crichton uses the poem to investigate contemporary sociological phenomena. In particular, his focus is on our media-driven world and our willingness to accept misinformation as reality: 'As a society we have been taught to trust the printed word, and Crichton's book is an entertaining lesson about the dangers of trusting without examination and judgment.'[13]

This is not to say, though, that some of the novel is not based on fact: there *was* an Arabic traveller named Ibn Fahdlan, he did write the *Risala*, and *Eaters of the Dead* is a translation of that text – but only for the first two chapters. Crichton takes the historical meeting of Fahdlan with the Rus as a means to introduce the story of *Beowulf*.[14] Although 'the factual register [...] is convincingly imitated throughout,'[15] from this point onwards the novel's narrative parallels that of the poem. Fahdlan is forced to travel north with a Viking leader named Buliwyf (Beowulf) in order to assist him in fighting the mysterious Wendol (a race, revealed to be cave-dwelling and mother-worshiping Neanderthals, who stand in for Grendel). There is also a king named Rothgar, a queen named Weilew and a prince named Wiglif.

The novel primarily focuses on the first part of the poem, which deals with Buliwyf/Beowulf's exploits in Denmark, and it includes bloody battles with the Wendol in the mead-hall and in their cave-dwelling, where Buliwyf defeats their matriarch. In addition, the novel also incorporates key elements from the second part of the poem. In Crichton's version, Buliwyf is mortally wounded by the Mother of the Wendol and his funeral is one of the last recounted acts in the novel (it is based on the evocative real-life account of a Viking funeral in Fahdlan's manuscript). The dragon is also incorporated. Magennis notes that the Northmen 'in the novel believe in the existence of a fire-dragon. This dragon turns out, however, in accordance with Crichton's rationalist approach, which seeks always to "explain" the marvelous in logical terms, not to be a dragon at all'.[16] This process of demystification also extends to the Wendol, who are shown to be a tribe of remnant Neanderthals, and not monsters or creatures in possession of supernatural powers. Crichton's approach of providing a rational explanation to many of the poem's more mysterious aspects:

■ offers a way of rationalizing that which is unknown and psychologically disturbing, but it does so at the cost of transforming the source of the poem's powerful sense of evil into just another dangerous obstacle which humankind can overcome in the conquest of nature [...] The heroes have to confront a dangerous external threat in *Eaters of the Dead*, but not evil. Crichton captures the excitement of *Beowulf* in his de-mystifying adaptation, and his Wendol are certainly scary, but there is no psychological depth to the threat they pose.[17] □

Fahdlan is the mediator between the reader and the Northmen, who at first seem barbaric. The reader is repelled by their manners, habits and some of their actions, and rather identifies with the Arab's view of what is civilized. The reader can also 'sympathize with his responses as an unheroic outsider on a heroic expedition. He is one of us, and so when he is able to rise to the challenge we appreciate his bravery at a more human level'.[18] And, like Fahdlan, the reader also grows to respect the Northmen, their (slowly vanishing) way of life and their sense of honour. No such understanding is extended to the even more ancient culture of the Wendol, however. If Fahdlan ultimately discovers a kinship and commonality with the Northmen, the Wendol are shown as wholly barbaric and the death of their way of life is not mourned in the slightest.

MUSIC AND LIVE PERFORMANCE

GRENDEL THE OPERA

Lisi Oliver has observed that the 'meteoric rise of Seamus Heaney's translation of *Beowulf* to the bestseller lists in 2000 apparently inspired a further burst of enthusiasm for *Beowulf* stage adaptations.'[19] She notes several new dramatic and musical productions, including three in the 2005–6 season alone, and that is *not* including *Grendel*, the recent opera based on Gardner's novel. The work of the multi-award-winning team of director Julie Taymor (born 1952) (who also co-wrote the libretto with the poet J.D. McClatchy, born 1945) and composer Eliot Goldenthal (Taymor's husband, born 1954), it is fair to say that this opera was 'One of the most widely anticipated, discussed and dissected productions of the 2006 theatre season'.[20] Understandably so, as new operas are a rare enough phenomenon and Taymor's productions come with the promise of lavish spectacle and visual invention. Sadly, the opera generally did not live up to expectations and it opened to very mixed reviews, with many reviewers 'decrying to greater or lesser degrees the qualities of the libretto and score'.[21] Goldenthal's music demonstrated moments of power and invention, particularly the brief use of the Anglo-Saxon harp; however for the most part, the score never quite rose above the level of incidental film music.

The libretto was also disappointing despite interesting sections. For example, one critic pointed out that *Grendel* may have been the first opera to incorporate passages of Old English into the libretto and this alone was 'reason enough for Anglo-Saxonists to take an interest in the work'.[22] The same critic notes, however, that the opera is an all too 'slavish homage to Gardner's work' which fails to take adequate account of the novel's source and proceeds 'without so much as looking *Beowulf* in the eye'.[23] Frantzen also rightly bemoans other sections of the libretto, such as the confrontation in Grendel's lair between Unferth and the eponymous monster. Unferth sings of what it means to be a hero and Grendel undercuts it by turning to the audience and singing, 'This whole shit-ass scene was his idea, not mine'. As Frantzen notes, this moment received 'Big laughs! "Shit-ass" at the opera! Again and again, such trivialization derails what might have been an impressive and memorable work.'[24]

The one aspect that was unanimously praised, at least, was the design of the production. Those expecting another lavish (and expensive) spectacle from Taymor were not disappointed. There was an enormous revolving set, a dragon which filled the entire stage and an inventive use of puppets during the fight scenes, which made a marionette Grendel appear gigantic alongside his hand-puppet human victims. As impressive as these sets and costumes were, though, one could not help but get the impression of style over substance. Taymor is a flashy director, and consequently at times it seemed as if these visual effects were supposed to distract from the rather poor nature of the opera itself. Finally, as Oliver notes, *Grendel* 'seems unlikely [...] to become a standard item in the modern repertory'.[25] The production's primary virtue, its visual design, would be prohibitively expensive for most companies to recreate. This leaves the music and the libretto, the essential ingredients which determine whether or not an opera will last, and these are simply not strong enough to justify repeated productions of *Grendel* in the future.

HOWARD HANSON'S 'LAMENT FOR BEOWULF'

In addition, the poem has inspired one piece of modern music which has entered the repertoire – the choral work, 'Lament for Beowulf' (1925), by Howard Hanson (1896–1981). One of the leading American composers of the twentieth century, he was the son of Scandinavian immigrants and spent much of his youth studying in Europe. B.C. Tuthill has argued that this duality between the Nordic and the American is central to Hanson's work, as is the 'conflict between cult and secular music, between the essentially religious or spiritual in musical expression and the perhaps pagan striving for sensuous color'.[26] It is hardly surprising then that Hanson would be attracted to *Beowulf*, which shares this duality in its Nordic and Anglo-Saxon roots and its pagan and Christian elements. As Hanson himself explains:

■ It is quite understandable that the sagas of the northland should have been of great interest to me. They are the epics of my forebears. For years I read carefully a mass of this material. Then while on a visit to England I found a translation of the *Beowulf* epic by William Morris and A.J. Wyatt. It attracted me immensely and from this I chose one episode which is the text for my composition. Carrying my prize with me I went to Scotland for a short stay and there, in an environment rugged, swept with mist, and wholly appropriate to the scene of my story, I began my sketches of the music [...] My intention has been to realize in the music the austerity and stoicism and the heroic atmosphere of the poem. This is true Anglo-Saxon poetry and may well serve as a base for music composed by an American. The music follows closely the text and the text presents with Nordic epic vigour and terse eloquence the scene of Beowulf's burial.[27] □

By Hanson's own admission, the lament is a distinctly choral work and the text is derived verbatim from the final 46 lines of the Morris and Wyatt translation (which is discussed more fully in Chapter One of this guide). These lines make up Section XLIII of the burial of Beowulf of Morris and Wyatt's rendering and they read as follows:

■ For him then they geared, the folk of the Geats,
A pile on the earth all unweaklike that was,
With war-helms behung, and with boards of the battle,
And bright byrnies, e'en after the boon that he bade.
Laid down then amidmost their king mighty-famous
The warriors lamenting, the lief lord of them.
Began on the burg of bale-fires the biggest
The warriors to waken: the wood-reek went up
Swart over the smoky glow, sound of the flame
Bewound with the weeping (the wind-blending stilled),
Until it at last the bone-house had broken
Hot at the heart. All unglad of mind
With mood-care they mourned their own liege lord's quelling.
Likewise a sad lay the wife of aforetime
For Beowulf the king, with her hair all up-bounden,
Sang sorrow-careful; said oft and over
That harm-days for herself in hard wise she dreaded,
The slaughter-falls many, much fear of the warrior,
The shaming and bondage. Heaven swallow'd the reek.
Wrought there and fashion'd the folk of the Weders
A howe on the lithe, that high was and broad,
Unto the wave-farers wide to be seen:
Then it they betimber'd in time of ten days,
The battle-strong's beacon; the brands' very leavings
They bewrought with a wall in the worthiest of ways,
That men of all wisdom might find how to work.
Into burg then they did the rings and bright sun-gems,
And all such adornments as in the hoard there
The war-minded men had taken e'en now;
The earls' treasures let they the earth to be holding,
Gold in the grit, wherein yet it liveth,
As useless to men-folk as ever it erst was.
Then round the howe rode the deer of the battle,
The bairns of the athelings, twelve were they in all.
Their care would they mourn, and bemoan them their king,
The word-lay would they utter and over the man speak:
They accounted his earlship and mighty deeds done,
And doughtily deem'd them; as due as it is
That each one his friend-lord with words should belaud,
And love in his heart, whenas forth shall he
Away from the body be fleeting at last.
In such wise they grieved, the folk of the Geats,
For the fall of their lord, e'en they his hearth-fellows;

Quoth they that he was a world-king forsooth,
The mildest of all men, unto men kindest,
To his folk the most gentlest, most yearning of fame.[28] □

A brief two-part orchestral introduction sets the tone for the piece, with
'horns and 'trumpets ris[ing] above one another to crashing climaxes'[29]
in a manner typical of Hanson's work. The prominence of the horns
seems to have an added significance here, however. In the first part, the
horns evoke the sound of Viking blowing-horns. In the second part the
horns have a resonance that is altogether more modern and American
in that they recall 'Taps', the American Army bugle call which signals
the end of the day (lights out), but is also poignantly played at military
funerals. For Tuthill, 'Lament for Beowulf' is 'a work of compelling
effectiveness and gloom' in which 'the cold, dark gray of the north
continues almost unrelieved throughout [its] 18 minutes'.[30] In addition,
it is also a moving work which reflects Hanson's view of the poem as
one full of 'passion and its nostalgia [...] big, heroic, and yet tender'.[31]
Indeed, it is important to remember that the translation Hanson uses
ends with a heartfelt tribute to Beowulf from his people, who recall his
kindness as well as his heroism as seen in the lines quoted above.

BENJAMIN BAGBY

Perhaps the most notable live performer of the poem today is Benjamin
Bagby (born 1951), an academic and musician whom Leo Treitler has
called 'one of the great singers of medieval music'.[32] For Bagby performance and scholarly study are interrelated, and he and Barbara
Thornton (1950–98), who co-founded the early music ensemble
Sequentia in 1977, have long 'promoted performance as part of a heur-
istic [a speculative formulation] process involved in understanding
medieval music'.[33] The culmination of this practice is Bagby's one-
man show of *Beowulf* (first performed 1990), which takes the form of a
dramatic reconstruction of the poem, where he adopts the role of the
Anglo-Saxon *scop* and performs the first third of the text (lines 1–1062)
in Old English to the accompaniment of a six string harp. Bagby strives
to give what he calls a 'historically informed performance', recon-
structing the lost oral tradition of storytelling as authentically as possible. In addition, he argues that this must nevertheless involve a certain
amount of conjecture, as all historically informed performance:

■ thrives on the conviction that today's performers can find knowledge
and instruction in the documentation that has survived from past musical
practices [...] unfortunately, all of this documentation, which we performers

assiduously track down and study, is still missing the one crucial element of musical performance that we would most need and desire to possess: the actual sound, the presence of a living master [...] Deprived of this essential face-to-face musical experience, we are forever doomed to confront our own past musical cultures 'through a glass darkly'.[34] □

For Bagby 'the situation becomes much more complex and clouded when we seek to perform the musical arts of early medieval cultures which were largely pre-literate, which knew neither notation nor treatises, and from which we possess only a few descriptions of performance or surviving fragments of instruments.'

Bagby's own harp, as his programme notes state, is 'based on the remains of an instrument excavated from a seventh-century Alemannic nobleman's grave in Oberflacht (south of Stuttgart)'. Furthermore, in relation to a live performance of *Beowulf*, Bagby's notes relate that:

■ The performance – which, for the whole epic, might last between five and six hours – would never be exactly the same twice, as the 'singer of tales' subtly varied the use of poetic formulae to shape his unique version of the story.

The central dilemma in any attempt to revocalize a medieval text as living art is based on the fact that a written source can only represent one version (and possibly not the best version) of that text from a fluid oral tradition. The driving force behind the present performance has come from many directions: from the power of those bardic traditions, mostly non-European, which survive intact; from the work of instrument makers who have made thoughtful renderings of seventh-century Germanic harps; and from those scholars who have shown an active interest in the problems of turning written words back into an oral poetry meant to be absorbed through the ear/spirit rather than the eye/brain. But the principal impetus comes from the language of the poem itself, which has a chilling, magical power that no modern translation can approximate.[35] □

Bagby also believes that the music, whilst, again, partly improvised and never played the same way twice, has an integral part in the *scop*'s performance, becoming fused with his voice. In relation to this, he notes that:

■ The Anglo-Saxon ear was finely tuned to this web of sounds and syllable lengths which was always experienced as an aural event, inextricably bound up with the story being told. The lyre is a relatively quiet instrument, but in the ear of the bard it rings with an endless variation of gestures, melodic cells and repetitive figurations which give inspiration to the vocalization: in the course of the story the bard may move imperceptibly or radically between true speech, heightened speech, speech-like song and true song. The instrument acts as a constant point of reference, a friend and fellow-performer, a symbol of the *scop* and his almost magical role in the community of listeners.[36]

Writing of a performance of the poem from the late 1980s, Joseph McLellan of *The Washington Post* argues that Bagby offered 'a vivid demonstration of what has been lost in the process of becoming modern' and argues that 'His performances should be recorded and made required listening.'[37] Subsequently, one of Bagby's extended performances of the first third of the poem, in Helsingborg, Sweden, was filmed by the Swedish director Stellan Olsson and released on DVD in 2007. In an article on teaching the Middle Ages on film, Martha Driver claims that that the recording of Bagby's performance is 'the best of the modern *Beowulf* texts (because it is the *Beowulf* text)'.[38] However, the film fails to replicate either the atmosphere or the experience of the live performance. The former deficiency is perhaps unavoidable, as viewing a film is quite another experience from watching a live performance. The film's major fault, though, largely derives from some poor choices on the part of Olsson. Firstly there is the decision to cut away from Bagby's *scop* to shots of the Swedish landscape. These scenes were clearly intended to 'open out' the drama and lend some variation to the film's visuals, but the postcard views of rock formations, sunsets and waves crashing on the beach seem rather half-hearted attempts to do this and these inserts are an unnecessary distraction.

Furthermore, there is a problem with the filming of Bagby's recital itself. Bagby, perhaps rightly, does not alter his usual performance style for the filmed versions. Olsson, however, films him predominantly in medium shots and close-ups, which makes his performance seem altogether too broad and sometimes loses sight of Bagby's use of his entire body as an instrument. Interestingly, this is decidedly not the case when viewed from a distance during a live performance (the equivalent of a cinematic extreme long shot). This, of course, is one of the key faults with many filmed records of theatrical performances. Stage acting relies on large, broad gestures and voice projection to compensate for the distance between the actor and his or her audience. The film camera however, magnifies each gesture and expression and amplifies the voice; therefore, an altogether more restrained style of performance is required. Despite these flaws, the filmed version of Bagby's *Beowulf* remains an invaluable record of a performance which perhaps comes closer than any other to showing what a recital by an Anglo-Saxon *scop* might have been like.

BEOWULF ON FILM

Considering the number of films based on ancient and mediaeval legends, and the vivid depiction of battles between heroes and monsters in *Beowulf*, it is perhaps surprising that the poem has not been translated directly to the screen more often. Indeed, there are countless films based on the life of Joan or Arc and derived from aspects of the Arthurian legends which date back to the earliest days of cinema, but there are only a handful of Beowulf films, and all of these have been released relatively recently.

Despite this fact, critics such as Hugh Magennis and Joseph Andriano have rightly pointed out that variations on the *Beowulf* story have been a mainstay of commercial cinema. As Magennis notes:

> ■ As it relates to myth and heroism, in one sense *Beowulf* has always been at the movies. The story of *Beowulf* dramatizes in stark form the archetypal themes of the testing of the hero and the struggle of the hero against a monster, themes that have provided and continue to provide staple elements of popular cinema. The details of some scenes in *Beowulf* are strikingly paralleled in Hollywood productions, the result, presumably, not of borrowing but of shared underlying patterns.[39] □

For example, Magennis sees a clear similarity between *Beowulf* and the climax of *The Silence of the Lambs* (1991) where the hero, 'here a female, ventures alone into the underground lair of a beast which possesses superhuman powers (night vision), and overcomes it in mortal combat'.[40] Similarly, he finds many of the heroic themes in *Beowulf* are also 'particularly evident [...] in the classic Western'.[41] In many ways such parallels can be drawn because the poem's protagonist is an archetypal hero; Grendel, his dam and the dragon are archetypal (although sometimes sympathetic) monsters and the narrative of the poem itself is a standard plot for numerous films across several genres.

Indeed, variations on the *Beowulf* story can be found not only in Westerns and fantasy films, but also in the horror film, where the confrontation between humans and monsters is a central trope. Kim Newman, in his review of *The 13th Warrior* (1999) (an adaptation of Crichton's *The Eaters of the Dead*, and a *Beowulf* film in all but name), argues that the genre which the film 'comes closest to is the horror movie'[42] and he is not the first to note a strong element of horror in the *Beowulf* story. For example, H.P. Lovecraft argued that:

> ■ As may naturally be expected of a form so closely connected with primal emotion, the horror-tale is as old as human thought and speech themselves. Cosmic terror appears as an ingredient of the earliest folklore of all races, and is crystallised in the most archaic ballads, chronicles, and sacred writings.[43] □

As mentioned earlier, for Lovecraft *Beowulf* was one of the first horror stories. Perhaps unsurprisingly then, variations on the three monsters in *Beowulf* have found their way into numerous horror films. Andriano has seen the eponymous beast in *The Creature from the Black Lagoon* (1954) as a possible 'reincarnation of [...] Grendel'.[44] Like Grendel, the creature attacks because he feels his home and his land have been invaded and, again like Grendel, he too loses an arm (or in this case a claw). Moreover, the black lagoon where he lives:

■ is the same mythical locus as Grendel's mere. Both signify the darkest pool – either an abyss of water among mountains and caves, or a pond becoming swamp leading to marsh and fen. [...] Grendel's mere is a water/land border where boundaries are unstable, where quagmires threaten to swallow us, and where monsters have lurked since humans had imaginations to conjure them.[45] □

Another horror/science fiction hybrid, *Predator* (1987), goes even further in its borrowings from the poem and several critics have noted 'some specifically *Beowulf*ian moments'[46] in the film.

PREDATOR *AND* THE 13TH WARRIOR

Predator, which stars Arnold Schwarzenegger (born 1947), indeed contains many similarities with the first third of *Beowulf*. In the film Schwarzenegger's character, Dutch, leads a small squad of elite mercenaries into the South American jungle on a hostage rescue mission. This assignment is soon successfully completed, but during their evacuation Dutch's men are brutally killed by an invisible foe, the Predator of the title, and the film's Grendel figure. This alien leaves the skinned corpses of his victims hanging from trees and displays heads as trophies and, in an interesting inversion, severs the arm of one of Dutch's men. However, Dutch eventually discerns that this Predator also has a sense of honour as it does not kill an unarmed woman. Finally, as in Beowulf's meeting with Grendel, Dutch throws away his weapons and strips himself to face the creature as an equal. They fight, and Dutch narrowly defeats the monster, which resigns itself to death.

Critics have perhaps been keen to pick up on the *Beowulf* parallels in *Predator* because its director, John McTiernan (born 1951), also made *The 13th Warrior* with Vladimir Kulich (born 1956) as Buliwyf. The latter film had a troubled production history and was one of the more notorious box-office failures of the 1990s. Several scholars, however, have written favourably about it, and despite its complicated origins it is in many ways the most successful film adaptation of *Beowulf*. Although McTiernan finished the film in 1997, it did not perform well at initial test screenings and Crichton himself came in to rewrite and reshoot several sequences. The film was radically reedited and a new score was added before it was officially released in 1999. The released version clearly 'bears the battle scars of having been through the preview process, losing a few subplots and character explanations along the way'.[47] Indeed, Diane Venora (born 1952) is second-billed as Rothgar's wife, Weilew, despite the fact that she only appears in a handful of scenes. The rest of her performance was presumably left on the cutting-room floor. Similarly, with the exception of Antonio Banderas (born 1960) as Fahdlan and Dennis Storhøi (born 1960) as Herger (the film's best performance) many of the 13 warriors of the title are given too little screen time to make an individual impression and it is not even obvious when some of them are killed. Ironically, this even (partly) applies to Vladimir Kulich's Buliwyf.

One of the key alterations made to *The Eaters of the Dead* in the film is the extent to which Fahdlan actively participates in the action. In the novel he is almost entirely passive during the many battles and Kim Newman argues that this inactivity partly carries over to the film. He sees Fahdlan as being almost subversively unheroic for a mainstream 'summer movie', adding that he is 'in effect an observer who leaves all the heavy lifting to the Vikings'.[48] While this may in part be true, Hugh Magennis rightly points out that 'the role was made more macho than in the novel [...] Fahdlan gets a chance to show off his skills as a horseman and swordsman and is fierce in battle; he even rescues a child from the Wendol at one point.'[49]

Interestingly, and perhaps bravely for a Hollywood film released in the late 1990s, *The 13th Warrior* asks the audience to identify most closely with an Arab character (albeit one played by Banderas, a Spanish actor). Amongst the rather uncouth Northmen, Fahdlan clearly stands out as a more modern, civilized figure. He is 'literate, fastidiously clean [and] reluctantly violent'[50] and the viewer shares Fahdlan's 'revolted reaction' to the 'unsanitary morning ablutions of the Norsemen'.[51] Finally, the Arab character has much more in common with the contemporary Western viewer than our more direct Norse ancestors. Furthermore, through the presence of (and the viewer's identification with) this civilized and 'appropriately aristocratic' Saracen other, the film undermines orientalist notions of Eastern inferiority and usefully examines 'the relation of heroism to advanced and refined civilization'.[52]

By introducing the monotheistic Fahdlan amongst the polytheistic, pagan Northmen, the film is also able to address the issues of faith and the changing nature of an ancient culture that are so central to the poem. Interestingly, when Fahdlan is asked by Buliwyf to recite something before the latter's coronation, he declaims: 'In the beginning the earth was without form and void.' This, of course, is the opening of the Hebrew Bible, not the Qur'an. It could be argued, however, that this is not merely a concession to a Western audience, but rather that this substitution of one holy text for another serves to show the similarities between the Jewish, Christian and Islamic creation stories. It also stresses the fact that it is Fahdlan's belief in one god, not many, that is important.

Perhaps as a result of this decision to make Fahdlan more of a hero and the audience's primary point of identification, both Buliwyf and his deeds are somewhat marginalized. Strangely, the most extended one-on-one combat in the film is not between Buliwyf and the Mother of the Wendol, nor does it involve Fahdlan. Rather, it is between Herger and Angus, the retainer of Wigliff, Hrothgar's devious, plotting son. Grindley has also noted that mediaeval heroes are often associated with a weapon, one which is commonly imbued with mystical powers. Excalibur is perhaps the most famous of such weapons, but Hrunting plays an important role in *Beowulf*. In *The Eaters of the Dead*, Crichton includes the sword, but 'instead casts the sword as Beowulf's own ancestral weapon'[53] whilst also renaming it 'Runding'. However, Runding is written out of *The 13th Warrior*, and the principal weapon in the film is not Buliwyf's sword but rather Fahdlan's. For Grindley, this is because 'Fahdlan has so supplanted Buliwyf as the film's hero, that he has to be identified by a particular object, and Buliwyf's sword must vanish.'[54] Fahdlan receives his weapon when they land at Venden, Rothgar's kingdom. Herger throws him one of the broadswords the Northmen carry and the Arab replies that the weapon is too heavy for him to lift, a clear reference back to Runding in the novel, which is described as being 'so large and heavy that even Buliwyf grunted at the carrying of it'.[55] Later in the film Fahdlan refashions the weapon to make it unique and instantly identifiable as his; he uses a blacksmith's tools to cut the sword down to the approximate size and shape of a scimitar. It is perhaps ironic that the most iconic weapon in the film is no longer larger than life, like Runding, but rather small and light. The Northmen even make fun of it, asking Fahdlan 'when you die, can I give that to my daughter?' Grindley argues that this teasing is indicative of the fact that 'at some level, the film shows discomfort with the idea of Fahdlan achieving centrality [over Buliwyf] and the script almost rebels.'[56]

In effect, then, the film has two heroes. Whilst this is slightly unusual, even eccentric, for a mainstream film, it is (perhaps unwittingly) in keeping with the notion of bifurcation, the dividing of a narrative between two heroes which is not uncommon in mediaeval literature. The first of the film's heroes, Fahdlan, despite being far more active than in the novel, 'remains an ineffective warrior, by far the least able of his compatriots'.[57] The second, despite in essence being Beowulf, 'is always at two removes, even when taking command and improving himself by learning to write and Vladimir Kulich's quiet reading of the role is never given enough screen weight to suggest the foundation of a legend which will last for a thousand years'.[58]

If the attempt to make Fahdlan more heroic has the effect of drawing attention away from its Beowulf surrogate, another important change made to the novel ironically brings *The 13th Warrior* closer to the tone of the original poem than any other film version. Unlike *The Eaters of the Dead*, where the Northmen 'don't think twice about engaging in public sex at every opportunity',[59] and subsequent *Beowulf* films, *The 13th Warrior* almost entirely avoids any mention of sex and features no 'romantic interest beyond a little wound-tending'.[60] This is one of the other ways Newman sees the film as going against the trends of the summer event movie as it also avoids the temptation to appeal to a modern audience by bringing women into the centre of the action even in a non-sexual way. Rather, *The 13th Warrior* remains a deeply male-dominated film and prefers to concentrate on the bloody battles with Wendol and the homo-social bonding between the warriors, especially Fahdlan and Herger. As a result of this Sutton has argued that the film superbly illustrates the *comitatus*, the 'early medieval Germanic fellowship of an aristocratic lord and his band of loyal retainers'.[61]

Many critics have rightly pointed to the film *Seven Samurai* (1953) by the Japanese filmmaker Akira Kurosawa (1910–1998) as a key influence on the battle scenes in *The 13th Warrior*. This is particularly true of the night-time clash with the Wendol, which is lit only by fires and torches, and the final battle in the rain, both of which draw clear inspiration from Kurosawa's film. Conversely, the first encounter with the Wendol (which takes place in the film's equivalent of Heorot) and the fight in the Wendol's cave derive directly from the poem. Martha Driver also believes that they 'underscore the loneliness and isolation of Anglo-Saxon warriors as documented in Old English poems such as *The Battle of Maldon* and *The Wanderer*'[62] as well as *Beowulf*.

Despite the numerous cuts made to the film and the rather sketchy nature of many supporting characters, the narrative of *The 13th Warrior* is far from disjointed. On the contrary, the film contains many of the primary characteristics of an epic. While the released version of the film does not open with an evocation of a muse, an earlier draft from 1991 did, beginning with the words, 'Praise be to God, the Merciful, the Compassionate'.[63] In the final version, these words are transferred to the end when we see Fahdlan writing his story. However, the released version begins *in medias res* (in the midst of the action), with Fahdlan and the Northmen fighting a storm in their longboat. Fahdlan, in voiceover, tells the audience his name and says 'it was not always like this', and a flashback begins to tell us his story. The film involves several journeys and covers a wide geographical area, from Arabia to

Scandinavia (in cinematic terms maps and techniques such as fades and dissolves are used to condense the great journey north to around ten minutes of screen-time). Furthermore, at the end of the film, Fahdlan begins his *nostoi*, the journey homeward that is another characteristic of the epic.

Also, regardless of any dispute over who the true 'hero' of the film is, Buliwyf unquestionably remains the film's hero in the epic sense. Like his model, Beowulf, he personifies the cultural values and beliefs of his people and it is on his success or failure in defeating the Wendol that the fate of all the Northmen rests. In an earlier draft of the screenplay, the mortally wounded Buliwyf emerges to fight the final battle with two ravens on his shoulder. On one level, this reference to Odin makes explicit the hero's imminent death, in that he will soon join Odin in Valhalla. On another level, however, this image makes Buliwyf and Odin one and the same and Buliwyf's death becomes symbolically linked with the old manner of living which will soon give way to the world of literate, monotheistic men like Fahdlan. Although this scene is not in the finished film, references to the changing nature of the Northmen's culture and world are still present from the outset. For example, in the opening reel there is a 'funeral scene drawn from Ibn Fahdlan's chronicle and based on actual Norse practice'.[64] Fahdlan is dumbfounded, especially as the young girl walks willingly onto the funeral pyre. At this point, Herger, speaking through a translator, tell the Arab that 'this is the old way. You will not see this again'. Not long after this, when the Northmen are about to land in Rothgar's kingdom, their longboat moves through a dense fog. One of Buliwyf's men shoots flaming arrows into the fog as his leader stands on the bough calling out to Odin. This sequence foreshadows Buliwyf's death (his meeting with Odin) at the hands of the Wendol (who only attack in the fog).

The 13th Warrior, while unquestionably flawed, is never less than fascinating and, ironically, it is closer in spirit and tone to the original poem than either Crichton's novel or the subsequent film adaptations which will now be examined.

BEOWULF & GRENDEL *AND ROBERT ZEMECKIS'S* BEOWULF

Alongside *The 13th Warrior* there have been four other feature film adaptations of the poem since 1999. Although they are all rather loose renderings, three of them claim direct kinship with the poem in their title. *Beowulf* directed by Graham Baker (1999) is a straight-to-video science-fiction reimagining, which transposes the poem's narrative to a post-apocalyptic future and stars Christopher Lambert (born 1957) as the eponymous hero. *Beowulf & Grendel* (2005), directed by Sturla Gunnarsson (born 1951), is an interesting if flawed low-budget adaptation which was unfairly but understandably overshadowed by the star-studded, multi-million dollar *Beowulf* (2007), directed by Robert Zemeckis (born 1952) using 'performance capture' technology, which fuses live action with digital animation. More recently, there has been another version, *Outlander* (2008), directed by Howard McCain, which again features science-fiction trappings, although here they are combined with a period setting, characters named Rothgar and Unferth, and passages of dialogue in Old Norse.

For the purposes of this guide, I will largely limit myself to an examination of Gunnarsson's *Beowulf & Grendel* and Zemeckis's version, as these are the most widely available *Beowulf* films which are also set during the Middle Ages. Also, while no film is obliged to remain faithful to a literary source, and criticisms that focus on a film's departures from it can be rather limiting, it is perhaps necessary to concentrate on the radical changes and additions the filmmakers have made to the poem. Indeed, while these two films are in many ways very different, there are a number of uncanny similarities in the way their respective screenwriters viewed and approached their source material. Neil Gaiman (born 1960) and Roger Avary (born 1965), the screenwriters of Zemeckis's *Beowulf*, argue that the poem's 'odd two-act structure' made it 'difficult' to adapt as it is too fractured and 'in movie terms [...] a detriment'.[65] Instead, they have Beowulf stay in Denmark and inherit Hrothgar's kingdom and queen. It is here, rather than in Geatland, that he has his final battle with the dragon. Andrew Rai Berzins, the writer of *Beowulf & Grendel*, seems implicitly to agree with this, as his film ends with Beowulf sailing back to Geatland after the battles with Grendel and his mother. Also, the fight with the dragon is only alluded to when a new character, a witch, says that she knows how Beowulf dies.

Another problem Berzins encountered was the poem's lack of conventional dialogue. As he notes in his blog on the film's official website: 'with very few exceptions [such as the Unferth/Beowulf friction at supper], it's substantially a series of monologues by various characters. It is absolutely unwieldy in any conventional sense of film dialogue.'[66] As a result, Berzins and Gaiman and Avary have had to come up with suitable dialogue to replace these extended and 'unwieldy' monologues. Berzins does not try to make his dialogue sound authentically of the period; rather, he has the characters speak contemporary English with some Nordic and Scots idioms added for good measure. On one level, this allows the dialogue to avoid the common pitfall of films set in the Middle Ages, namely lapsing into unintentionally amusing *faux* 'olde English'. As John Aberth notes in *A Knight at the Movies: Medieval*

History on Film, 'who can resist ridiculing [...] *The Black Shield of Falworth* (1954) in which Tony Curtis [born 1925], summoning up his best medieval Bronx accent, utters the immortal line, "Yonda lies the castle of my fodda"?'.[67] Berzins's frequent use of 'Anglo-Saxon' expletives, however, gives the dialogue a rather anachronistic feel that is similarly amusing. The example most cited by reviewers of *Beowulf & Grendel* is the line 'this troll [Grendel] must be one tough prick.' Whether this dialogue is intentionally amusing is a matter of debate. Todd McCarthy, reviewing the film for *Variety*, argued that the line is 'one of the script's more comical attempts to give a contempo[rary] ring to the ancient story'.[68] Bill Gallo in *The Village Voice*, on the other hand, agrees that the film plays 'fast and loose with history' but he thinks that the dialogue is all part of the film's 'bawdy, sly humor', which has strong echoes of *Monty Python*.[69]

Gaiman and Avary's *Beowulf* features similarly problematic dialogue and delivery. For example, Ray Winstone's Beowulf repeatedly says, 'I've come about your monster,' in a very thick cockney accent. As Wally Hammond notes, lines such as this and 'Bollocks! Give me a gobble, then!' are just one of 'the many miscalculations' made in the film. He adds that 'It's evident from the script [...] that it wasn't the power and beauty of the language [of the poem] that attracted the filmmakers.'[70] Although some Old English can be heard in the film (Grendel's broken dialogue and a *scop* reciting line 809–19 are notable examples), in his introduction to the published screenplay Avary says little about the language but rather declares that his 'intention [was] to remain true to the letter of the epic, but [to] read between the lines and find greater truths than had been explored before'.[71] By 'reading between the lines', Avary is referring to a series of questions that he thought the poem raised but did not answer. These initial questions would form the basis of his first treatment of the story:

■ If Grendel is half-man, half-demon [...] then who is his father?
   Why does Grendel never attack Hrothgar, the king?
   How does Beowulf hold his breath for days on end during the fight with Grendel's Mother? Maybe he wasn't fighting her? Or maybe he isn't human?
   When Beowulf goes into the cave to kill Grendel's Mother, why does he emerge with Grendel's head instead of hers? Where's the proof that the mother was killed?[72] □

For Avary, this:

■ all seemed to add up to rather nefarious conclusions. [...] Though it's not in the poem, clearly, Grendel was Hrorhgar's bastard son. He had sired the child in exchange for worldly wealth and fame. [...] And what of Beowulf? Surely he wasn't telling his thanes the full truth. Had he given in to the siren-witch and accepted her offer of gold and glory for his seed, which she needed in order to procreate?[73] □

Based on these conclusions, Avary declared his intention to 'write Beowulf into an epic'.[74] Gaiman further suggested that if Grendel is Hrothgar's son, then the dragon must logically be Beowulf's son, come to back to haunt the hero. Avary has jokingly called this Gaiman's 'Beowulf Unified Field Theory' adding more seriously that it solved 'a problem that has plagued frustrated filmmakers for decades'.[75] The original two-part structure is one of the key characteristics of Beowulf that makes it an epic poem (though some critics, as we have seen, argue that Beowulf is a poem of three parts). The hero's return to his Geatland is an example of nostoi, the story of a 'return home' that was central to classical epics and, by extension, Beowulf. Ironically then, despite his intentions, Avary's attempt to unify the action of the film actually makes it less epic than the poem.

Despite this contradiction, there are critics who have applauded the screenwriters' alterations to the text. For example, in his review in The Guardian, Peter Bradshaw writes that he found Gaiman and Avary's inventions 'witty and sometimes rather brilliant'. He also thought that the film brought together the three battles with Grendel, Grendel's mother and the dragon 'in a tight new storyline that puts desire, betrayal and lifelong guilt at the centre of Beowulf's psychological makeup and gives the dragon's battle with Beowulf a mighty new Freudian significance'.[76]

Whilst one might think that the battle scenes in Beowulf provide more than enough interest and action for one feature film, if not two, both these adaptations of the poem greatly embellish the role of women and add a strong element of sex to the story. On one level this is an attempt to update an unquestionably male-dominated text for a modern audience raised with notions of gender equality. For Berzins, the lack of women in the poem should not be taken 'as any sort of accurate depiction of the relations between men and women in that culture', and he sees Denmark as a land largely populated by unfortunate women who have been 'widowed before their time' by Grendel.[77] More cynically, however, such additions are also a concession to demographics, as producers are reluctant to finance a film which may be seen as only appealing to men (thus excluding half a film's potential audience), which a faithful adaptation of Beowulf perhaps would.

Undoubtedly, the sheer amount of sex Gaiman and Avary inject into their adaptation must stand as their most significant alteration to the poem. The re-imaging of Grendel's mother as a shape-shifter who morphs into a *femme fatale* succubus (played by Angelina Jolie, born 1975) is merely the most discussed of many such additions and alterations. The film is populated by dozens of large-breasted wenches who do little but dispense mead and make bawdy comments. Hrothgar is first seen half naked, carried out of an orgy with two young women and the older Beowulf is given a young mistress named Ursula. Then, of course, there is Wealtheow, whose role is greatly expanded here. The dignity and deportment she demonstrates in the poem and her function as a 'peace-weaver' are greatly in evidence, even if the nuances of the performance of Robin Wright-Penn (born 1966) are somewhat buried under the motion capture technology. Gaiman and Avary's Heorot is a very dirty and earthy place, but their Wealtheow seems to rise above it in an appropriately regal way.

Beowulf & Grendel similarly expands the role of Wealtheow and again makes her a strong queen. However, she still remains at the periphery of the action while a new character, a witch named Selma, who can see men's deaths and shares her bed with both Beowulf and Grendel, takes a more central role. This character is certainly the film's weakest link. The role is underwritten (in addition to providing a love interest, she is essentially there to speak sympathetically to Beowulf about Grendel) and given some embarrassingly silly (and vulgar) dialogue to speak. Furthermore, as played by Sarah Polley (born 1979), complete with Ontario accent, she is far too modern and anachronistic a creation to have existed in the intended period. For Manohla Dargis of *The New York Times*, the character is also a distraction and 'Polley [...] has to bat her lashes at two opponents better suited to batting each [other]'; indeed, he finds that Selma detracts so much from the central conflict that a 'more accurate title [...] might be *Beowulf & the Vixen*'.[78]

What, however, is one to make of all this added sex? Richard North, a London-based mediaevalist who reviewed the film for *Time Out*, suggests that it is perhaps a necessary evil and argues that if a 'movie can make *Beowulf* more widely known, any sex is welcome'.[79] Bradshaw agrees, writing that 'Zemeckis's quixotic and enjoyable gallop back into the misty literary past will get people signing up [to Medieval literature courses] after all.'[80] These comments typify another trend in reviews of the film which argue that it may have the effect of drawing more readers back to the original. There is also an obvious danger to this, though, to which Andrew Osmond alludes in his piece in *Sight and Sound*. Osmond agrees that Avary and Gaiman present a 'clever spin' on the poem; but he wonders if it might seem so natural that 'viewers new to *Beowulf* may assume that it was always told that way.'[81] Indeed, new readers may be enticed to the poem by the film; however, they may also be confused or even disappointed by the comparatively uncomplicated narrative and character relationships and the total absence of sex.

Interestingly, these two films do not merely add more prominent female characters to the poem's male-dominated narrative of kingship, battle and the *comitatus*; they also seek to make their male heroes distinctly flawed. This is particularly the case with Hrothgar. It seems that the presence of a stronger Wealtheow requires a weakening of Hrothgar as a counterbalance. The difference between Hrothgar in the poem and the character as played by Anthony Hopkins (born 1937) in *Beowulf* is like that of night and day. The published first draft of the screenplay offers a depiction of Hrothgar much closer to the poem's, saying that he 'is a man past the prime of his years, but still a mighty warrior and a charismatic leader of men'.[82] However, by the final draft (and in the finished film) he is 'as fat a king as you're ever likely to see', who is prone to letting 'loose RIP ROARING FART[S]'.[83] This Hrothgar is vulgar, undignified, drunken and finally suicidal. As a consequence, he is a far cry from the character in the poem who tells Beowulf of his responsibilities to stay focused and alive for the good of his people. *Beowulf & Grendel*'s Hrothgar, as played by Stellan Skarsgård (born 1951), is by no means a caricature but an altogether more human and sympathetic figure than Hopkins's incarnation. This Hrothgar is still, however, a drunkard who, in the words of Todd McCarthy, 'oozes remorse and boozy breath' and is 'distinctly unregal'.[84] Skarsgård and Gunnarsson agreed on their conception of the character. The director argues that Hrothgar 'was a great warrior and now he's getting old and he's cranky, he's drinking and he's facing his mortality and he doesn't like it. He's haunted by one action in his past that's brought his entire kingdom to ruin.'[85]

The 'one action' Gunnarsson is referring to is the (rather unmotivated) killing of Grendel's father by Hrothgar in the film's invented prologue. It is this event that establishes the blood feud between Grendel and the Danes. However, in the resulting clashes, Grendel always leaves Hrothgar alive, leading the king to drink out of despair and guilt. The addition of flaws that do not appear in the original poem can be seen as attempts to add moral and psychological complexity to characters that may seem 'two-dimensional'[86] to a modern audience.

This raises another of the 'problems' screenwriters have seen in the poem that discourages attempts to adapt it: the characterization and depiction of Beowulf himself. In his blog Berzins argues that Beowulf 'is one of the most straightforward and uncomplicated characters in literature'[87] and both films, in different ways and with varying levels of success, attempt to humanize the myth of Beowulf and add depth and complexity to the figure. Gunnarsson cast the physically imposing Scottish actor Gerard Butler (born 1969) in the role, and North sees him as bringing a 'soulful'[88] quality to Beowulf. In this version the hero travels to Denmark with the intent of killing an evil monster for glory and fame. He does not find an evil monster, however, but a misunderstood and marginalized figure and as Beowulf learns more about Grendel he grows ever more reluctant to fight him. This version of *Beowulf*, and Butler's sensitive playing of the role, actually makes the audience question whether or not Beowulf will actually go through with his pledge to fight Grendel. And, in a way, he does not. The fight between Beowulf and Grendel only happens because of the foolish actions of one of Beowulf's men, who desecrates Grendel's cave-dwelling, and both Beowulf and the monster seem to enter into their confrontation unwillingly, as if fulfilling a historical destiny neither of them wanted. The fight is abrupt and Beowulf manages to fit a noose around Grendel's arm as the latter tries to escape from the roof of Heorot. Hanging by his arm as a shocked Beowulf looks on, Grendel severs his own broken limb to ensure that he is not captured and runs to the sea to die with his mother. The film thus deprives Beowulf of the glory of defeating the monster and taking his arm as he does in the poem.

In addition, the next day at Heorot, Beowulf is made physically uncomfortable by the sight of Grendel's arm pegged to the rafters. This is not the first time in the film that Beowulf is unsettled by the publication of his deeds. Earlier in the film Beowulf finds Thorkel entertaining a group of Geat children with a story about Beowulf defeating Grendel *before* it has actually happened. He sends the children away and tells Thorkel not to 'feed them lies'. Interestingly, Gunnarsson and Berzins implicitly align Thorkel with the *Beowulf* poet in this scene, by having him call Beowulf 'God's awful arm' before invoking the name of Jesus Christ. This clearly foreshadows his later conversion to Christianity. Berzins writes that the story the *Beowulf* poet eventually composed would indeed have been based on exaggerations and cultural additions that accumulated over centuries of oral storytelling, in a manner akin to the children's game 'telephone'.[89] Here then, the film is drawing an important distinction between Beowulf's own 'epic boasting', which is culturally acceptable and backed up by his actual heroic feats, and the exaggerations of Thorkel (and by extension the *scop* and *Beowulf* poet), who is prone to embellish and present the legend, not the facts.

Like the heroes of many revisionist Westerns and mediaeval equivalents such as *Robin and Marian* (1976), directed by Richard Lester (born 1932), Butler plays Beowulf as a man who finds it difficult to accept and live up to the mythical status his society has attached to him. Nevertheless, he is still a hero who never exaggerates his own deeds and is seen to perform acts of bravery, such as his venture into the mere to defeat Grendel's mother (the film's climax). However, the portrayal of the character by Ray Winstone (born 1957) in Zemeckis's *Beowulf* is rather different. Firstly, due to the 'performance capture' technology,

Winstone's is an almost superhuman figure, an eight-foot-tall Aryan superman. Yet despite this physical superiority to Butler's incarnation, Winstone's Beowulf is an altogether more flawed and perhaps less heroic character. Firstly, Gaiman and Avary have added the seemingly complex, but ultimately underdeveloped, web of guilt over the hero's sexual transgression with Grendel's mother, which leads to the conception of the dragon and the near ruin of his kingdom. Additionally, and perhaps ruinously, Avary and Gaiman make their Beowulf a liar and a braggart. When confronted by Unferth about his swimming race with Brecca, Beowulf claims to have killed nine sea monsters, as he does in the poem. However, the film undermines this claim with a cut to Wiglaf, who whispers to a fellow Geat, 'it was four last time.' This scene alone makes it is impossible to take this Beowulf for the honourable hero of the Old English epic. And the killing of Grendel takes this sense even further. After he has slammed the door of Heorot on Grendel's arm and causes the monster to scream in pain, Beowulf hisses threats that he is Grendel's doom, everything Grendel had believed himself to be, and his voice rises to a crescendo as he triumphantly shouts his name.[90]

Unquestionably, the film is offering a radically different conception of the hero than that found in the poem. The original Beowulf's interest in performing heroic deeds and achieving fame is here distorted into a lust for power and bloodshed. What is more, Beowulf here not only compares himself to Grendel, he even goes as far as to say that he is the more monstrous; he is all the things Grendel only believed himself to be. This parallel between Beowulf and Grendel is continued at the end of the film as Beowulf's death directly mirrors his killing of Grendel for he must sever his own arm to reach the dragon's heart and slay it. Perhaps the most obvious justification for these changes comes from a desire to give Beowulf's final sacrifice a redemptive quality.

Andrew Osmond argues, however, that for all the script's invention it is lacking in resonant characterizations, and thus becomes a 'high tragedy without anyone to really engage with [it]'.[91]

Michael Morpurgo (born 1943), who has written his own adaptation of the poem for children, goes further and simply suggests that 'The film changes the very nature of its hero. He becomes vulnerable and flawed, and he loses much of his nobility [...] the minute he starts lying, he becomes less interesting.'[92] What is also surprising is that Gaiman, who admits that his first exposure to the poem was in the form of the DC Comic *Beowulf: Dragon Slayer*,[93] chose not to see Beowulf as a literary forebear of modern comic-book superheroes and depict him as such in the film (the comic-book style storyboards included in the screenplay show that the connection was certainly not lost on Gaiman and Avary, but rather rejected). Perhaps they thought that the hero's story would not only be more redemptive, but also more human, if they resisted this path. However, even if the nature of the protagonist is not changed and Beowulf remains a super-heroic character, the poem still provides ample instances of human frailties and flaws. In fact, *Beowulf* is at once one of the great tales of youthful bravado and heroism *and* one of the great examinations of old age and the inevitability of death. For all his superhuman powers, Beowulf cannot stop time and the decay of age, and in the poem's second half Hrothgar's warning to Beowulf takes on its full poignancy as the ageing hero faces the dragon.

In the light of the changes deemed to be 'necessary' in order to film *Beowulf*, it seems unlikely that a faithful film adaptation of the poem is ever likely to be made, or indeed even possible in mainstream cinema. To date there has been only one faithful film version of the poem and it falls distinctly outside the mainstream. This little known amateur *Beowulf* film was made in 1973 for a pittance by members of the BBC drama department and directed by the award-winning film editor, Don Fairservice. This version sticks closely to the modern verse translation by Kevin Crossley-Holland (born 1941) and offers an instructive point of comparison with the later films. Indeed, while watching Fairservice's *Beowulf* one perhaps begins to see several other reasons why it took filmmakers so long to make any version of the poem, let alone a faithful one.

The first reason is a practical one that relates to technology and finance. Fairservice's film is a textbook example of how to make a movie with extremely limited resources. Locations in the Lake District effectively stand in for Denmark and Geatland and moody black and white photography helps lend an atmosphere of menace. Perhaps unsurprisingly, the budget did not extend to special effects and none of the three monsters is ever seen. Rather, sound effects and point-of-view tracking shots give the impression of Grendel approaching Heorot. Beowulf's battle with Grendel is again filmed from Grendel's point-of-view and is intercut with scenes of a much older Beowulf remembering and reliving his deeds. The older Beowulf grabs a large branch on a tree and twists it off, the breaking bough cleverly standing in for Grendel's severed arm. Such ingenuity is laudable in an amateur film; however, one would expect more direct representations of the monsters and the battles in a professionally made studio picture. And it is perhaps for this very reason that filmmakers have only recently begun adapting *Beowulf* to the screen. While a director's initial conception of the three monsters is limited only by the bounds of the human imagination, the actual visualizing of them on screen is greatly constrained by the resources at his or her disposal and the limitations of modern special effects.

The British director, John Boorman (born 1933), whose work includes the Arthurian epic *Excalibur* (1981), spent three years in the early 1970s working on a film version of Tolkien's *Lord of the Rings* trilogy, which draws a great deal from *Beowulf*. Ultimately, Boorman's film never reached the shooting stage and he recalls the great difficulties he had in trying to adapt the texts. Quite apart from the problems of condensing the three-volume work, in the pre-computer era the special effects needed to depict magical events, miniaturize the hobbits and create Tolkien's monsters presented almost insuperable problems. By the time the script was produced the costs were too prohibitive for the company to undertake.[94]

Boorman also remembers that Tolkien wrote to him about his plans, and was greatly relieved to hear Boorman did not intend to make an animated film, a prospect that Tolkien dreaded.[95] (In fact, an animated version of *The Lord of the Rings* was released shortly after Tolkien's death.) Similarly, until recently it would seem that *Beowulf*, with its three monsters and larger-than-life hero, was deemed to be a subject better suited to animation, where the imagination is not limited by what modern special effects can achieve. However, by the end of the 1990s technology and computer-generated imagery had advanced to the point that film companies and directors felt that they could successfully adapt and visualize texts such as Tolkien's trilogy and *Beowulf* without having to compromise their vision – or hide their monsters.

This is unquestionably the case with Zemeckis's *Beowulf*. In his introduction to the published screenplay, Avary discusses the impact 'performance capture' technology had on the final film and notes how it enabled Gaiman and him radically to rewrite their initial script, which was to have been shot as a conventional live-action film. According to Avary, Zemeckis excitedly told the writers to 'go hog wild'[96] because:

> ■ With Performance Capture everything costs the same. Whether you're showing someone sitting in a chair or a dragon burning up a village – it all costs the same. So don't [...] let your imaginations be restrained by the limits of traditional 2-D filmmaking. Write whatever you ever wanted to write but didn't think you could.[97] □

The appearance of both Grendel and the dragon are unquestionably well realized. The former, thanks to the new technology, is made utterly grotesque, with blood and pus oozing from the sores that cover his deformed body. Furthermore, this Grendel is very large. His hand is roughly the same size as Hrothgar. While the appearance of the monster is 'impressive',[98] the performance of Crispin Glover (born 1964) as Grendel is less so. Unrestrained and mumbling in Old English (while his mother speaks Modern English to him), his portrayal of Grendel utterly eschews the pathos and complexity John Gardner brought to the character. Glover rather plays Grendel as 'a brain-damaged child in perpetual tantrum [...] like the next degeneration of Gollum in *The Lord of the Rings*'.[99]

The performance capture technique is well suited to action sequences and creating the film's monsters. It shows its limitations, however, in the dialogue and character-driven scenes. Here, the technology, which merely has to replicate human forms and mannerisms, has the effect of distancing the audience from the drama and the characters as they are more cartoon-like than human. As Osmond says, with this technique there is 'a chronic shot-to-shot inconsistency between characters we accept as human and the "same" characters looking artificial and soulless [...] Audiences have long accepted cartoon characters as human, and human actors as cartoons, but the *Beowulf* characters' shifting state corrodes their film's reality.'[100]

Finally, Zemeckis's *Beowulf* is commonly and correctly seen as a rather trivial film and this view is all-too-easily born out by the handling of the fight between Beowulf and Grendel. Inexplicably, Zemeckis decided to have Beowulf fight Grendel completely naked, though his genitals are obscured in each successive shot by a different object – a candlestick, a table leg, the hilt of a sword and so on. Morpurgo found it 'just ridiculous'.[101] Worse than that, however, it is utterly distracting. Indeed, Morpurgo admits that he was unable to keep his mind on the fight between the hero and the monster, saying that he 'was sitting there in my 3D glasses, and I kept wondering, if I just leaned a little bit to the left [...]'.[102] The fight between Beowulf and Grendel is perhaps the most pivotal, famous episode in the poem and should be considered one of the central sequences in any film adaptation of *Beowulf*. But here it is robbed of any possible seriousness and drama by a very puerile joke. Wally Hammond, also writing for *Time Out*, found the entire film 'puerile' and argued that 'even as a mere convenient launchpad for some vertiginous, 3D-assisted, man-on-beast heroics located in the eternally-adolescent gothic/fantasy/horror comic-book tradition, it seems an irrelevance.'[103]

Beowulf & Grendel, which was made on a far lower budget than Zemeckis's film, solves the problem of how to visualize the monsters in a simple way. As stated above, the film's narrative ends with Beowulf leaving Geatland for Denmark, and therefore does not include the dragon. It also makes Grendel and his mother recognizably human descendants of Cain. Indeed, the filmmakers prided themselves on the fact that their movie contained no computer-generated imagery (CGI), but rather used more old-fashioned *trompe l'oeil* effects to make the actor playing Grendel, Ingvar Sigurdsson (born 1963), appear around eight feet tall. As the film's title implies, Grendel plays a significant role in this version. The conception of the monster in the film is, ultimately, far from monstrous and bears the influence of Gardner's novel. As a result, this Grendel is far easier to identify with than the one in Zemeckis's film and for all of his size and strength he is also clearly a man. He cries when his father is killed. He shows a sense of honour by not attacking Beowulf and his men until provoked (here his feud is with Hrothgar and the Geats, not with the foreign Danes). He also has a sense of humour and several of his scenes, such as his urinating on the door of Heorot as the Geats wait for him inside and his taunting and throwing stones at a confused Beowulf, are genuinely amusing.

Some critics, such as Dargis, have seen Grendel's humanity as a failing in the film, arguing that 'this Grendel is not a mythic force with a direct line back to Cain, but akin to a persecuted, disappointingly human (if hairy) ethnic minority.'[104] For Dargis the film also loses much of its mythic mystery and resonance by trying too hard to find contemporary relevance. Therefore, he expresses dismay with the fact that this Grendel is too easily explained and granted psychological motivation for his actions. He kills simply for revenge, 'not because he is a demon, the necessary embodiment of all that humans fear'.[105] This is not to say that the film does not have its champions. North, for example, sees the portrayals of the antagonistic title characters as among the film's key strengths. He especially praises the film's depiction of Grendel as a sympathetic Neanderthal who slowly forces the hero to question his role and argues that Beowulf & Grendel 'is the finest of all Beowulf films'.[106] However, one must put this comment into context, as Gunnarsson's film is only the best of a very small and rather poor bunch. As North notes, 'however you read it, Beowulf is a complex poem'; he suggests that the Swedish director Ingmar Bergman (1918–2007) or the Russian director Andrei Tarkovsky (1932–86) could have 'filmed it closely'.[107] It is safe to say that we are still waiting for a great, let alone definitive, Beowulf film.

ANIMATION

Perhaps the most notable animated versions of the Beowulf story are Grendel, Grendel, Grendel (Alexander Stitt, 1981), an adaptation of Gardner's novel, and a rather faithful version of Beowulf made for British, Russian and American television by Yuri Kulakov in 1998. The former is a rather eccentric affair. It is animated in a 'limited' style, which is self-consciously crude and child-like. Grendel and the dragon are sympathetically voiced by Peter Ustinov (1921–2004), whilst the Danes have working-class Australian accents. Beowulf, enigmatically enough, says nothing. It also features an array of songs, with titles such as 'Your Mother Loves You', which help to tell the story in the style of a troubadour or *scop*. The animated *Beowulf*, which first aired on the BBC as part of its 'Animated Epics' series, sticks close to the original poem and ambitiously tries to tell the whole story in just under 30 minutes. It is largely successful and often very well animated. The film's one failing, however, is the slightly abstract depictions of the fights with the three monsters. In each, Beowulf is seen to 'enter' the monster, and defeat it from within, rather than in straightforward combat as in the poem. As a result, the fights are not as visceral, as exciting or as long as they perhaps should be. This is more than compensated for by the excellent narration of the English-language version by Derek Jacobi (born 1938), and the fine readings by Joseph Fiennes (born 1970), Timothy West (born 1934) and other British film and stage actors as the major characters.

BEOWULF FOR CHILDREN

There have been more than a few retellings of *Beowulf* for children, many of which denude the original tale of its tragic and problematic elements. On such version is *Beowulf: Dragonslayer* (1961) by Rosemary Sutcliff (1920–1992). As can be seen from the following extract, Sutcliff's rendering of the ending of *Beowulf* is devoid of the bleak vision presented in many other versions:

■ Then they [Wiglaf and seven retainers] set the four slow yoke of oxen straining up the steep slope to the headland, where the pyre stood waiting against the sky. They laid the body of Beowulf on the stacked brushwood and thrust in the torches, and presently all men far and wide saw the red fire on the Whale's Ness, and knew that Beowulf had gone to join his kindred.

All night long the fire burned, and when it sank at dawn they piled about the ashes the precious things of the dragon's hoard, and upreared the golden banner over all. Then they set themselves to raise the barrow as the old King had bidden them. For ten days they laboured, building it high and strong for the love that they had borne him, and on the tenth day the great howe of piled stones stood finished, notching the sky for all time on the uttermost height of the Whale's Ness, where the cliffs plunged sheer to the sea.

The 12 chieftains of his bodyguard rode sunwise about it, singing the death song that the harpers [poets] had made for him. And when the song was sung, all men went away, and left Beowulf's barrow alone with the sea wind and the wheeling gulls and the distant ships that passed on the Sail-Road.[108] □

Sam Rahim and Toby Clements remark that 'Beowulf is an ideal children's story. Fearsome monsters, powerful heroes and gruesome murders should be enough to keep the most bloodthirsty young reader satisfied.' However, whilst several more recent efforts do not sanitize or deproblematize the work as Sutcliff did, they 'seem intent on cluttering it with modern concerns'.[109] One such example is *The Geat: the Story of Beowulf and Grendel* (2007), which is adapted by John Harris, who has been performing a live version of the story for school children for over a decade. The comically grotesque and gory illustrations by Tom Morgan-Jones recall the work of Quentin Blake (born 1932) with Roald Dahl (1916–1990). Perhaps taking his cue from John Gardner, Harris gives 'Grendel a sympathetic backstory: before his attack on Hrothgar's castle, he remembers "wanting to be friends with some children when he too was very young", but not having the courage to approach them. So he kills and eats Hrothgar's warriors – the jocks of the Anglo-Saxon world.'[110]

Perhaps the most successful of the recent children's versions of the poem is that of the former British Children's Laureate, Michael Morpurgo (2007), whose retelling of the poem was selected as one of *The Daily Telegraph's* Top 100 Children's Books in 2008. Rather than alter the content of the poem to make it relevant to modern readers, Morpurgo begins his version with a variation on the opening of the original poem, which states quite clearly why *Beowulf* is still meaningful today:

■ Hear, and listen well, my friends, and I will tell you a tale that has been told for a thousand years and more. It may be an old story, yet, as you will discover, it troubles and terrifies us now as much as it did our ancestors, for we still fear the evil that stalks out there in the darkness and beyond. We know that each of us in our own time, in our own way, must confront our fears and grapple with this monster of the night, who, given a chance, would invade our homes, even our hearts, if he could.

So roll back now the years, back to the fifth century after the birth of Christ and come with me over the sea to the Norse lands we now know as Sweden and Norway and Denmark, to the ancient Viking lands of the Danes and the Geats the Angles and the Jutes. This will be our here and now as this tale of courage and cruelty unfolds, as brave Beowulf battles with the forces of darkness, first with that foul fiend Grendel, then with his sea-hag of a mother, and last of all, with the death-dragon of the deep.[111] □

As Charles McGrath notes, Morpurgo 'preserves much of the oddness and complexity of the original, and, though his text is in prose, even some of the poetry'.[112] As can be seen from the above quotation, Morpurgo uses alliteration to good effect, describing Grendel as a 'foul fiend' and the 'death-dragon of the deep'. He also manages to give Grendel a clear motivation for his actions without altering the character's origins or trying to make him sympathetic:

■ But there was another listener. Outside the walls of Heorot in the dim and the dark, there stalked an enemy from hell itself, the monster Grendel, sworn enemy of God and men alike, a beast born of evil and shame. He heard that wondrous story of God's creation, and because it was good it was hateful to his ears. He heard the sweet music of the harp and afterward the joyous laughter echoing through the hall as the mead-horn was passed around. Nothing has ever so enraged this beast as night after night he had to listen to all this happiness and harmony. It was more than his evil heart could bear.[113] □

These few examples give us a good idea of the various ways in which *Beowulf* has been successfully adapted for children, bloodthirsty or otherwise.

COMIC BOOKS AND GRAPHIC NOVELS

Although there have been surprisingly few film versions of *Beowulf*, there have been numerous comic book versions of the poem, including several full-length graphic novel retellings, a short-lived series from DC Comics called *Beowulf: Dragon Slayer*, a contemporary manga (Japanese comic style) series by David Hutchison, which locates the action in a post-apocalyptic future, and the series of *Grendel* comics by Matt Wagner (born 1961), which are loosely based on the poem and aspects of John Gardner's novel. While an exhaustive study of this phenomenon is outside the scope of this guide, a brief survey of some of the most significant *Beowulf* comics will be offered here.

The number and variety of *Beowulf* inspired comics is perhaps unsurprising. The story and the characters provide ample material for comic book scriptwriters and artists alike. Gareth Hinds, author and illustrator of one of the finest *Beowulf* comics (first published in 1999), speaks for many fellow adaptors when he writes that '*Beowulf* gave me the chance to explore one of the traditional comic book genres – the superhero story – in a more timeless way, without the skin-tight suits and some of the other wacky conventions of that genre. I want to show people how cool this story really is.'[114] It is easy to see what Hinds means; Beowulf is indeed a kind of proto-superhero, a direct forebear of characters such as Thor or Conan the Barbarian. Also, Hinds's enthusiasm for the poem and his wish to introduce it to a wider audience is typical of the attitude of many comic book adaptors. As a consequence, it is safe to say that these comic book retellings play a significant part in establishing a young readership for *Beowulf*.

In a note in the first issue of *Beowulf: Dragon Slayer*, the author, Michael Uslan, states that 'When DC [Comics] first announced its interest in developing some new titles, we searched for a subject that would not only be a fast-paced comics-magazine but would also have specific educational value. For the field of education is the place that comics can do the most good in the years to come. And so came *Beowulf*.'[115] He stresses, however, that his primary purpose in adapting the poem is to show how 'exciting' it is, lest anyone think that 'action will be sacrificed for 'educational value'. He also adds that the original is 'unbelievably gory' and it was in fact necessary for it to be 'toned down'.[116]

In addition, Uslan argues that his intention is to 'produce a book that you'll be proud to bring into your classroom and show to your teacher'. And yet, he includes a disclaimer:

■ While we'll be doing what we can to capture the flavour and spirit of the poem (including the use of alliteration, internal rhyme and the kenning), we caution you not to try writing those book reports after reading the comic book version. We'll be diverging enough from the original so that you'll have a hard time telling what is straight from the poem and what is not.[117] □

For those acquainted with the poem, though, the divergences are amusingly apparent on the initial page of the first volume, which depicts a red-haired Beowulf wearing only a metal vest of armour, a loin-cloth and a Viking helmet with 'horns so wide that he would have to take off his headgear to go through a door'.[118] On this full-page 'splash panel', the hero is depicted doing battle with a giant fire-breathing monster, while a virtually naked female warrior, named Nan-Zee, looks on in the foreground.

It is worth noting that the reasons and justifications Uslan gives for these changes and additions are remarkably close to those offered by the writers of the *Beowulf* films discussed above. In his note to the second issue, Uslan states that Nan-Zee, was 'a necessity of 1975' as the poem's 'general disdain for women' was seen as 'outmoded for today's audience'.[119] Furthermore he also argues that the poem 'left many unanswered questions' about the story and the appearance of the central characters. In this last regard, comic book adaptations have a great advantage over film versions in that the visual depiction of the monsters is limited only by the confines of the artist's imagination. Here, Uslan and illustrator Ricardo Villamonte conceive of Grendel as a 'shadow-walker'. Their Grendel is Satan's spawn, but it is unclear if he is 'man or beast [...] dragon or God of death'.[120] His colouring, red, orange and yellow, effectively reflects the flames of Hell. If this conception is effective, their depiction of Beowulf is less so. They view him not as the son of a hero, but rather a 'heroic missing link' between ape and man.[121]

Beowulf: Dragon Slayer ultimately had a very short run and only six issues were published between 1975 and 1976. Despite such liberties, the comic *did* have the desired effect and prompted some young readers to seek out the original. For example, Neil Gaiman remembers the comics as his first introduction to *Beowulf*. He recalls that 'The story – which made Beowulf into a sort of bargain basement Conan – still made enough impression on me to make we want to read the original and find out what the real story was. Nobody told me it was a classic; I just thought it was something they'd based a comic on.'[122]

A 2007 graphic novel version of the poem by Stefan Petrucha (born 1957) and Kody Chamberlain (born 1972) features the caption 'the world's first – and greatest – hero' on the cover. It is distinctly possible that this is a paraphrase of the banner printed on the last four issues of *Beowulf: Dragon Slayer*, which reads: 'Beowulf – first and greatest hero of them all!'. Even if it is not, however, the recurrence of this statement clearly demonstrates the appeal of Beowulf as an archetypal hero and the timeless nature of the story. Petrucha and Chamberlain's graphic novel is just one of many comic book versions published in the first decade of the twenty-first century. Unlike the film versions, however, many of the comics are remarkably faithful to the poem. This is perhaps indicative of the perceived need for more 'positive' heroes. Indeed, at a time when most heroes in popular culture are depicted as either flawed, brooding or cynical, *Beowulf* appealingly harks back to a simpler time when heroes were uncomplicatedly heroic.

Petrucha and Chamberlain's version certainly bears this out. On the penultimate page, a very young Wiglaf berates his kinsmen who only return to their dying king's side after the dragon has been defeated. His scorn and the overall tone of this text is brilliantly encapsulated in his line, '*now* you return [...] I *pity* you all'.[123] This is followed by a depiction of Beowulf's funeral on the final page. In a departure from the poem, however, only Wiglaf is present at the hero-king's burial. We are told that 'dark times came to Geats after that', and the image of the solitary Wiglaf (whose name means 'remnant of the battle'), in silhouette next to the burning pyre, tells us why; rather than emulate their king and his bravery, as Wiglaf did, the other Geats have grown cowardly and overly dependant on Beowulf for protection. One could, of course, argue that there is something rather reactionary about this ending, in its celebration of the heroism of a few superior men. However, one cannot deny that it remains close to the spirit of the original.

Perhaps the best of the graphic novel versions of the poem is that of Gareth Hinds. Hinds uses A.J. Church's 1904 prose translation, but as Charles McGrath points out, 'great stretches of this *Beowulf* take place with no words at all,'[124] and the success of this version derives largely from the author's ability eloquently to tell stories through images. The fight scenes are particularly vivid and he choreographs them 'like a kung-fu master and then draws them from a variety of vantage points, with close-ups, wide angles and aerial views'.[125] However, it is also a visually sophisticated adaptation, which is designed as a kind of triptych. Each of the poem's three sections (the battles with the individual monsters) is drawn with a distinct colour palette. The first part, ending with the death of Grendel, is drawn with ink pen but drained of most of its colour, giving it the feel of a sepia photograph. As a result, other colours (the blacks of Grendel and a few primaries) that do appear seem to jump off the page, and splashes of ink very evocatively stand in for the gore of the battles. The second section, depicting the fight with Grendel's mother, is drawn and painted onto wood panels and it has the effect of a series of wood cuts. The palette is again subdued but this time brings in a series of subtle blues and greens while under water, and reds and oranges in the mere. The final section, involving the fight with the dragon, finds a visual equivalent of Beowulf's old age in a stark palate of greys, blacks and whites, which are drawn using various shades of charcoal. For McGrath, the final result is 'as visceral as the Old English, which was consciously onomatopoeic, and by changing his palette for each of the poem's three sections he evokes its darkening rhythm'.[126]

Hinds also manages to bring out Beowulf's superhuman strength *and* humanity in his drawing. Before the main text begins Hinds includes a wordless splash panel depicting the old Beowulf standing bare-chested, holding his sword. The image is of a man of great strength; his arms are like tree trunks, his muscles bulge and the sword he holds looks too big for any normal man to carry. At the same time, it is also an image of great human frailty. Beowulf is clearly very old. His head is bald, his beard long and grey, the chiselled muscles on his arm and his abdomen are covered in liver-spots and everywhere there are wrinkles, not least under his very tired and sunken eyes.

David Hutchison's *Beowulf* (renamed *Biowulf* for the collected edition), was a short series published by Antarctic Press (2006 to the present) which transports the story to a post-apocalyptic future, where a feudal society once again faces the wrath of Grendel, a cybernetic creature, once human, but now transformed into the personification of evil. This cyberpunk re-working of the story is told in a style very much influenced by manga. The idea of a futuristic feudal society providing the setting for the conflict was perhaps influenced by Matt

Wagner's *Grendel*, the longest-running and most commercially successful version of the Beowulf story in comics.

Matt Wagner's *Grendel* first appeared in 1982, in a series of comics published by the independent company Comico ('independent'
meaning it was not one of the big American publishers – Marvel or
DC Comics). At around the same time as Wagner created *Grendel* he
was also producing *Mage*, a story in which King Arthur is reborn in
modern America (with a baseball bat replacing Excalibur!). *Mage* and
Grendel were quite similar in some respects, dealing with personifica-
tions of ancient characters, one a hero, the other a villain. The fact that
Wagner's mother was an English teacher is evident, as he clearly had
a profound interest in literature from a young age, and his work continually shows the integration of these influences into the superhero
milieu. *Grendel* was also clearly influenced by Gardner's novel of the
same name.

Grendel introduced Hunter Rose, a gifted but twisted young genius,
who, after losing his lover, is consumed by grief and, in true Batman
style, dons a costume to punish criminals. Acting as an assassin and
taking the name 'Grendel', Hunter, known to the world as a social-
ite and celebrated novelist, eventually positions himself at the heart of
a criminal empire, gaining a reputation as a cold-blooded killer, yet
finding no one who is his equal. His costume is simple – black with
a distinctive mask, with two large white eyes, somewhat like Spider-
man's, but with a scar through each eye. His weapon is a double-bladed
spear. In the course of the story Hunter finds himself drawn into conflict with the mysterious and seemingly immortal werewolf Argent,
who is trying to control his bloodlust and regain his humanity. Argent
stands in for Beowulf, working with the police to restore order, fighting the chaos that Grendel has created. In the end the two battle, leaving Hunter dead and the beast wounded. These early stories were later
reworked as *Devil by the Deed,* a graphic novel published in 1986, which
Wagner has described as his *Le Morte d'Arthur.*[127]

The various comic versions of the Beowulf story are strikingly
different, demonstrating the flexibility of the story, but also showing
that the mythic power of this early superhero transcends time, culture,
genre and medium.

Conclusion

This guide has taken the reader on a very long journey through the history of *Beowulf* criticism. The introduction attempted to establish some important facts about *Beowulf*: that it is enigmatic, incites contentious debate and is endlessly interpreted. When all is said and done, it is a poem of 'uncertainties' whose body of criticism seems to grow daily. It is ultimately hoped that this guide has defined the exact nature and extent of these uncertainties through an examination of essential criticism of *Beowulf*. The guide's chronological approach is further intended to assist the reader in an understanding of the history of this criticism and how various scholars have influenced one another. The impact of Tolkien's 'The Monsters and the Critics', on the work of *Beowulf* critics after 1936, for example, cannot be overestimated.

But what does the future of *Beowulf* criticism hold? No crystal ball can tell us for sure, of course, but some educated guesses can be made. Post-modern and post-colonial readings of the poem are still largely in their infancy, so there is obviously still much to do here. Feminist and masculinity studies will also no doubt continue to assert their influence on the field. There is room as well for more translations of the poem, as Seamus Heaney's will not be considered 'definitive' forever. Perhaps another established poet will take on the challenge of rendering *Beowulf* into modern English soon? In addition, more work on the indebtedness of later writers to a text like *Beowulf* is needed. Chris Jones' *Strange Likeness: The Use of Old English in Twentieth-Century Poetry* has paved the way for scholarship of this nature.

If our discussion of *Beowulf* and popular culture is anything to go by, it is accurate to assert that novelists (graphic and otherwise), film makers and composers will continue to interpret the text – faithfully or otherwise. The question of the poem's influence on other media leads, of course, to the subject of *Beowulf* and technology. It is Andy Orchard's opinion that in the future (near and distant) *Beowulf* studies will be transformed beyond our wildest dreams as a consequence of continuing technological advancements. He confidently states in Chapter Nine, enigmatically titled 'Afterword: Looking Forward', of *A Critical Companion to Beowulf* that:

■ A hundred years from now, a reader of *Beowulf*, should such an exotic creature still exist, will have access to a vast array of material unimaginable today. And much of that access will be instant. Even now, at the turn of the twentieth century, a well-equipped (which is to say well-funded) scholar can easily travel the world carrying not only the entire surviving corpus of Old English, but also vast bibliographies, together with books and articles complete and in progress, large numbers of downloaded dissertations, and a range of high quality manuscript-facsimiles, all collected together on a laptop computer that can be plugged into the internet to gain relatively speedy access not merely to friends and colleagues for questioning, commiseration, and companionship, but to a splendid array of library-catalogues, bibliographies, and other multimedia resources. In the future (and the not-so-distant future, if we are to believe the cyber-prophets who have virtually predicted it already), almost every would-be reader of *Beowulf* will have access to much more information than anyone today, in a much more compact form, and all at the click of a button, or (since doubtless buttons will seem quite quaint by then) at least in the wink of an eye.[1] □

Ultimately, Orchard's view of *Beowulf*'s future is an optimistic and exhilarating one:

■ A hundred years from now, for all the new data and analyses and hypotheses about *Beowulf* that will doubtless arise, at the heart of it all will still remain the poem itself, still read so many centuries after it was first composed, a poem the meaning of which will even then continue to excite debate and admiration because, like all great works, *Beowulf* still retains enormous power, across the centuries, to move. And if a hundred years from now someone not yet born can perhaps, even 'in a place far from libraries', still take pleasure reading *Beowulf,* then surely it seems a future worth looking forward to after all.[2] □

Beowulf will, indeed, continue to 'excite debate' in years to come. The search for its meaning is, after all, never-ending if the history of *Beowulf* criticism is anything to go by. As Natalia Breizmann has remarked, 'with the ending of Beowulf's adventure the quest of the reader begins – the quest for reading and understanding the poem's [...] message.'[3] Each new generation of readers must, therefore, embark on its own journey to find out what *Beowulf*, one of our most enigmatic of poems, is about.

Notes

Introduction: Hwæt!

1 James W. Earl, *Thinking about Beowulf* (Stanford: Stanford University Press, 1994), p. 11.
2 R.D. Fulk and Christopher M. Cain, *A History of Old English Literature* (Oxford: Blackwell, 2003), p. 194.
3 Bertha S. Philpotts, 'Wyrd and Providence in Anglo-Saxon Thought', in Caroline F.E. Spurgeon (ed.) *Essays and Studies by Members of the English Association Vol. 13* (Oxford: Clarendon Press, 1928), pp. 7–8.
4 Fulk and Cain (2003), p. 191.
5 William Witherle Lawrence, *Beowulf and Epic Tradition* (London: Harvard University Press, 1928), p. 282.
6 Seamus Heaney, *Beowulf: A Verse Translation* (London: Faber, 2007), p. xi.
7 J.R.R. Tolkien, '*Beowulf*: The Monsters and the Critics', in Christopher Tolkien (ed.), *The Monsters and the Critics and Other Essays* (London: Harper Collins, 2006), p. 31.
8 Tolkien (2006), p. 8.
9 Ibid. (2006), pp. 8–9, citing Tolkien's '*Beowulf*: The Monsters and the Critics', p. 106.
10 S.A.J. Bradley, *Anglo-Saxon Poetry: An Anthology of Old English Poems* (London: Dent, 1982), p. xiv.
11 Signe Carlson, 'The Monsters of *Beowulf*: Creations of Literary Scholars', *The Journal of American Folklore*, 80:318 (October–December 1967), p. 358.
12 Andrew Prescott, 'Beowulf Manuscript', in *The Electronic Beowulf Project*, http://penelope.uchicago.edu/~grout/encyclopaedia_romana/britannia/anglo-saxon/beowulf/vitellius.html.
13 Karl Brunner, 'Why was *Beowulf* Preserved?', *Études Anglaises,* 7 (1954), pp. 3–4.
14 John D. Niles, 'Locating *Beowulf* in Literary History', *Exemplaria*, 5 (March 1993), pp. 79–81.
15 John Hermann, quoted in Niles (1993).
16 Niles (1993), pp. 79–81.
17 Chris Jones, *Strange Likeness: The Use of Old English in Twentieth-Century Poetry* (Oxford: Oxford University Press, 2006), p. 15.
18 William Benzie, *Dr. F.J. Furnivall, Victorian Scholar Adventurer* (Norman, Okla: Pilgrim Books, 1983), p. 3.
19 John Churton Collins, *The Study of English Literature: A Plea for its Recognition and Organization at the Universities* (London: Macmillan, 1891), p. 22.

One   'Rude Beginning': 1705–1899

1 Sharon Turner, *The History of the Manners, Landed Property, Government, Laws, Poetry, Literature, Religion, and Language, of the Anglo-Saxons* (London: Longman, Hunt, Rees, and Orme, 1805), p. 374.
2 Signe Carlson, 'The Monsters of *Beowulf*: Creations of Literary Scholars', *The Journal of American Folklore*, 80:318 (October–December 1967), p. 358.
3 Douglas Short, *Beowulf Scholarship: An Annotated Bibliography* (New York: Garland, 1980), p. 7.

4 John Earle, *The Deeds of Beowulf: An English Epic of the Eighth Century Done Into Modern Prose* (Oxford: Clarendon, 1892), p. x.

5 Ibid., p. xii.

6 Ibid., p. xii.

7 Frank Cooley, 'Early Danish Criticism of *Beowulf*', *ELH: A Journal of English Literary History*, 7:1 (March 1940), p. 45.

8 Earle (1892), p. xi.

9 Stopford A. Brooke, *The History of Early English Literature, being the History of English Poetry from its Beginnings to the Accession of King Ælfred* (London: Macmillan, 1892), p. 25.

10 Brooke (1892), p. 29.

11 Marijane Osborn, 'Translations, Versions, Illustrations', in Robert E. Bjork and John D. Niles (eds), *A Beowulf Handbook* (Exeter: Exeter University Press, 1997), p. 347.

12 Chris Jones, *Strange Likeness: The Use of Old English in Twentieth-Century Poetry* (Oxford: Oxford University Press, 2006), p. 230.

13 Conor McCarthy, 'Language and History in Seamus Heaney's *Beowulf*', *English*, 50:197 (Summer 2001), p. 149.

14 R.D. Fulk and Christopher M. Cain, *A History of Old English Literature* (Oxford: Blackwell, 2003), p. 204.

15 Robert E. Bjork and John D. Niles (eds), *A Beowulf Handbook* (Exeter: Exeter University Press, 1997), p. 11.

16 J.R.R. Tolkien, '*Beowulf*: The Monsters and the Critics', in Christopher Tolkien (ed.), *The Monsters and the Critics and Other Essays* (London: Harper Collins, 2006), p. 52.

17 Turner (1805), p. 120.

18 Ibid., pp. 398–9.

19 Ibid., p. 408.

20 Knut Stjerna, *Essays On Questions Connected with the Old English Poem of Beowulf* (Coventry: Curtis & Beamish, 1912), p. 197.

21 William Morris and A.J. Wyatt, *The Tale of Beowulf* (London: Kelmscott Press, 1895), pp. 273–4.

22 Thomas Arnold, *Beowulf: A Heroic Poem of the Eighth Century* (London: Longmans, Green and Co., 1876), p. xvii.

23 Ibid., p. xxxiii.

24 Ibid., p. xxxiii.

25 Francis Adelbert Blackburn, 'The Christian Coloring in the *Beowulf*', *PMLA*, 12 (1897), p. 205.

26 Blackburn (1897), p. 225.

27 Osborn (1997), pp. 346–7.

28 Fiona McCarthy, *William Morris: A Life for Our Times* (London: Faber, 1994), pp. 648–9.

29 Jones (2006), pp. 20–1.

30 Ibid., p. 21.

31 William Morris and A.J. Wyatt, *The Tale of Beowulf* (London: Kelmscott Press, 1895), p. xvii.

32 Earle (1892), p. 11.

33 Bjork and Niles (1997), p. 1.

Two   'Conflicting Babel': 1900–1931

1 J.R.R. Tolkien, '*Beowulf*: The Monsters and the Critics', in Christopher Tolkien (ed.), *The Monsters and the Critics and Other Essays* (London: Harper Collins, 2006), p. 106.

2 Tom Burns Haber, *A Comparative Study of the Beowulf and the Aeneid* (Princeton: Princeton University Press, 1931), p. 1.

3 W.P. Ker, *The Dark Ages* (New York: Mentor Books, 1958), p. 163.

4 R.B. Onians, 'Review of *A Comparative Study of the Beowulf and the Aeneid* by Tom Burns Haber', *The Classical Review,* 47:5 (November 1933), p. 200.

5 Onians (1933), p. 200.

6 Haber (1931), p. 4.

7 Ibid., p. 19.

8 Ibid., p. 18.

9 William Morris and A.J. Wyatt, *The Tale of Beowulf* (London: Kelmscott Press, 1895), p. xviii.

10 Albert S. Cook 'The Possible Begetter of the Old English *Beowulf* and *Widsith*', *The Transactions of the Connecticut Academy of Arts and Sciences,* 25 (April, 1922), p. 339.

11 Kemp Malone, 'Hildeburg and Hengest', *Journal of English Literary History,* 10:4 (December 1943), p. 271.

12 Jane Chance. 'The Structural Unity of *Beowulf*: the Problem of Grendel's Mother', in Helen Damico and Alexandra Hennessey (eds), *New Readings on Women in Old English Literature* (Bloomington: Indiana University Press, 1990), p. 257.

13 Margaret Schlauch, *English Medieval Literature and its Social Foundations* (London: Oxford University Press, 1956), p. 44.

14 Ibid., p. 44.

15 Ibid., p. 45.

16 Michael Swanton, *English Literature before Chaucer* (London: Longman, 1987), p. 106.

17 Ibid., p. 56.

18 Edward.B. Irving Jr., *A Reading of Beowulf* (New Haven: Yale University Press, 1968), p. 83.

19 Friedrich Klaeber, 'The Christian Elements in *Beowulf*', *Subsidia,* 24 (1996), p. 62.

20 Carleton Brown, '*Beowulf* and the *Blickling Homilies* and Some Textual Notes', *PMLA,* 53:4 (December 1938), p. 905.

21 Raymond Wilson Chambers, *Beowulf* (Cambridge: Cambridge University Press, 1921), pp. 100–1.

22 Raymond Wilson Chambers, '*Beowulf* and the Heroic Age', Archibald Strong (trans.), *Beowulf: Translated into Modern English Rhyming Verse* (London: Constable, 1925), p. 12.

23 Ibid., p. xii.

24 Ibid., p. xxvi.

25 Ibid., p. xxvi.

26 Ibid., pp. xxviii–xxix.

27 Ibid., p. xxix.

28 Ibid., p. xiii.

29 Ibid., p. xxii.

30 Bertha S. Philpotts, 'Wyrd and Providence in Anglo-Saxon Thought', in Caroline F.E. Spurgeon (ed.) *Essays and Studies by Members of the English Association Vol. 13* (Oxford: Clarendon Press, 1928), p. 16.

31 Philpotts (1928), pp. 19–20.

32 Ibid., p. 27.

33 Ibid., p. 23.

Three   The Monsters Meet the Critics: the 1930s and 1940s

1 W.P. Ker, *The Dark Ages* (New York: Mentor Books, 1958), pp. 251–4.

2 Christopher Tolkien (ed.) *The Monsters and the Critics and Other Essays* (London: Harper Collins, 2006), p. 11.

3 Claire A. Lees, 'Men and *Beowulf*', in Claire Lees (ed.), *Medieval Masculinities: Regarding Men in the Middle Ages* (Minneapolis: University of Minnesota Press, 2006), p. 131.

4 Ibid., p. 131.

5 J.A. Cuddon, The *Penguin Dictionary of Literary Terms and Literary Theory* (London: Penguin, 1999), p. 544.

6 R.D. Fulk and Christopher M. Cain, *A History of Old English Literature* (Oxford: Blackwell, 2003), p. 204.

7 Ibid., p. 204.

8 Tolkien (2006), p. 11.

9 Andy Orchard, *Pride and Prodigies: Studies in the Monsters of the Beowulf Manuscript* (Cambridge: D.S. Brewer, 1995), p. 1.

10 Ibid., p. vii.

11 T.M. Gang, 'Approaches to *Beowulf*', *The Review of English Studies*, 3:9 (January 1952), p. 1.

12 Tolkien (2006), p. 28.

13 Seamus Heaney, *Beowulf: A Verse Translation* (London: Faber, 2007), p. xiv.

14 Tolkien (2006), pp. 26–7.

15 Ibid., p. 31.

16 E.M.W. Tillyard, *The English Epic and its Background* (London: Chatto and Windus, 1954), p. 122.

17 Lees (2006), pp. 134–5.

18 Tolkien (2006), p. 33.

19 Robert E. Bjork and John D. Niles (eds), *A Beowulf Handbook* (Exeter: Exeter University Press, 1997), p. 5.

20 Tolkien (2006), p. 2.

21 Ritchie Girvan, *Beowulf and the Seventh Century: Language and Content* (London: Methuen, 1935), p. 57.

22 Ibid., p. 31.

23 Ibid., p. 50.

24 Frederick R. Rebsamen, *Beowulf Is My Name: And Selected Translations of other Old English Poems* (San Francisco: Rinehart, 1971), p. x.

25 Tillyard (1954), p. 122.

26 Henry Bosley Woolf, 'On the Characterisation of Beowulf', *Journal of English Literary History*, 15:2 (June 1948), p. 85.

27 Ibid., p. 86.

28 Ibid., p. 87.

29 Ibid., p. 85.

30 Ibid., p. 92.

31 Adrien Bonjour, *Twelve Beowulf Papers, 1940–1960* (Geneva: Librarie E. Droz, 1962), p. 14.

32 Ibid., pp. 15–18.

33 Ibid., pp. 29–30.

34 Ibid., p. 30.

35 Ibid., p. 35.

36 Ibid., p. 36.

37 Ibid., p. 42.

38 Ibid., p. 45.

39 Harold Bloom, *Modern Critical Interpretations, Beowulf* (New York: Chelsea House, 1987), p. 4.

40 Joan Blomfield, 'The Style and Structure of *Beowulf*', *The Review of English Studies,* 14 (1938), p. 397.

41 Ibid., p. 398.

42 Ibid., p. 398.

43 Ibid., pp. 402–3.

Four   The Debates Continue: the 1950s and 1960s

1 C.L. Wrenn (ed.), *Beowulf with the Finnesburg Fragment* (London: Harrap, 1953), p. 45.
2 Ibid., p. 45.
3 Peter S. Baker (ed.), *The Beowulf Reader* (New York: Garland, 2000), p. 52.
4 Douglas Short, *Beowulf Scholarship: An Annotated Bibliography* (New York: Garland, 1980), p. 82.
5 Robert L. Chapman, 'Alas, Poor Grendel', *College English*, 17 (1956), p. 334.
6 Ibid., p. 334.
7 Ibid., p. 337.
8 Short (1980), p. 92.
9 Nora Chadwick, 'The Monsters and Beowulf', in Peter Clemoes (ed.), *The Anglo-Saxons: Studies in Some Aspects of the History and Culture Presented to Bruce Dickins.* (London: Bowes, 1959), p. 171.
10 Ibid., p. 172.
11 Ibid., pp. 172–3.
12 Ibid., pp. 202–3.
13 Signe Carlson, 'The Monsters of *Beowulf*: Creations of Literary Scholars', *The Journal of American Folklore*, 80:318 (October–December 1967), p. 357.
14 Ibid., p. 358.
15 Ibid., p. 362.
16 Ibid., p. 363.
17 Larry Benson, 'The Pagan Coloring of *Beowulf*', in R.P. Creed (ed.), *Old English Poetry: Fifteen Essays* (Providence, R.I.: Brown University Press, 1967), pp. 206–7.
18 Adrien Bonjour, 'Jottings on *Beowulf* and the Aesthetic Approach', in R.P. Creed (ed.), *Old English Poetry: Fifteen Essays* (Providence, R.I.: Brown University Press, 1967), p. 179.
19 Ibid., p. 179.
20 Ibid., p. 180.
21 Ibid., p. 191.
22 Ibid., p. 191.
23 Dorothy Whitelock, *The Audience of Beowulf* (Oxford: Clarendon Press, 1951), p. 2.
24 Ibid., p. 3.
25 Ibid., p. 3.
26 Ibid., p. 70.
27 Ibid., p. 71.
28 Ibid., p. 105.
29 Ibid., p. 99.
30 Kenneth Sisam, *The Structure of Beowulf* (Oxford: Clarendon Press, 1965), p. 1.
31 Ibid., p. 2.
32 Ibid., p. 3.
33 Ibid., p. 5.
34 Ibid., p. 78.
35 Edward B. Irving Jr., 'Ealuscerwen: Wild Party at Heorot', *Tennessee Studies in Literature*, 12 (1967), p. 164.
36 Ibid., p. 164.
37 Edward.B. Irving Jr., *A Reading of Beowulf* (New Haven: Yale University Press, 1968), p. 18.
38 Ibid., p. 21.
39 Ibid., p. 43.
40 Ibid., p. 44.

Five   Stock-taking: the 1970s

1 Dorothy Whitelock, *The Audience of Beowulf* (Oxford: Clarendon Press, 1951), p. 1.
2 Marijane Osborn, 'The Great Feud: Scriptural History and Strife in *Beowulf*', *PMLA*, 93 (1978), p. 973.
3 Stanley B. Greenfield, 'The Authenticating Voice in *Beowulf*', in Peter Clemoes (ed.), *Anglo-Saxon England 5* (Cambridge: Cambridge University Press, 1976), p. 51.
4 Ibid., p. 53.
5 Ibid., p. 61.
6 Margaret E. Goldsmith, *The Mode and Meaning of 'Beowulf'* (London: The Athlone Press, 1970), p. 1.
7 Ibid., p. 5.
8 Ibid., p. 5.
9 Ibid., p. 267.
10 Ibid., p. 6.
11 Ethelbert Talbot Donaldson, *Beowulf* (New York: Norton, 1966), p. 53.
12 Goldsmith (1970), p. 241.
13 Ibid., p. 211.
14 Alvin A. Lee, *The Guest-Hall of Eden: Four Essays on the Design of Old English Poetry* (New Haven: Yale University Press, 1972), p. 172.
15 Goldsmith (1970), p. 211.
16 Ibid., p. 226.
17 Andreas Haarder, *Beowulf: The Appeal of a Poem* (Viborg: Akademisk Forlag, 1975), p. 13.
18 Ibid., pp. 171–2.
19 Ibid., p. 172.
20 Ibid., p. 171.
21 Ibid., pp. 209–10.
22 Ibid., p. 211.
23 Ibid., p. 211.
24 Lee (1972), p. 173.
25 Ibid., p. 171.
26 Ibid., p. 195.
27 Kathryn Hume,' The Concept of the Hall in Old English Poetry', *ASE* 3 (1974), p. 73.
28 Ibid., p. 62.
29 Ibid., p. 64.
30 C.L. Wrenn, 'Sutton Hoo and Beowulf', in Lewis E. Nicholson (ed.), *An Anthology of Beowulf Criticism* (Notre Dame: Notre Dame University Press, 1963), p. 311.
31 Ibid., pp. 314–16.
32 Ibid., pp. 325–6.
33 Bernice Kliman, 'Women in Early English Literature, *Beowulf* to the "Ancrene Wisse"', *Nottingham Medieval Studies*, 21 (1977), p. 33.
34 Ibid., p. 33.
35 Paul Acker, 'Horror and the Maternal in *Beowulf*', *PMLA*, 121:3 (2006), p. 702.
36 Ibid., p. 702.
37 Ibid., p. 703.
38 Ibid., p. 708.
39 Ibid., p. 704.
40 Ibid., p. 705.
41 Ibid., p. 706.
42 Ibid., p. 709.

43 Thomas Cable, *The Meter and Melody of Beowulf* (Chicago: University of Illinois Press, 1974), p. 4.
44 Ibid., p. 4.
45 Ibid., p. 108.
46 Jeff Opland, '*Beowulf* on the Poet', *Medieval Studies*, 38 (1976), p. 442.
47 Ibid., p. 443.
48 Ibid., p. 444.
49 Ibid., p. 444.
50 Ibid., p. 445.
51 Ibid., p. 447.
52 Ibid., p. 452.
53 Ibid., p. 453.
54 Ibid., p. 466.

Six   Critics on the Crest of a Wave: the 1980s

1 J.D.A Ogilvy and Donald C. Baker, *Reading Beowulf* (Norman: University of Oklahoma Press, 1993), p. xi.
2 Seth Lerer, '*Beowulf* and Contemporary Critical Theory', in Robert E. Bjork and John D. Niles (eds), *A Beowulf Handbook* (Exeter: Exeter University Press, 1997), p. 325.
3 Jeffrey Helterman, '*Beowulf*: The Archetype Enters History', *ELH*, 35:1 (March 1968), p. 2.
4 Ibid., p. 1.
5 Ibid., p. 2.
6 Ibid., p. 3.
7 Ibid., p. 3.
8 Ibid., p. 10.
9 Ibid., p. 11.
10 Ibid., p. 13.
11 Ibid., p. 13.
12 Ibid., p. 13.
13 Ibid., p. 14.
14 Ibid., p. 20.
15 Ibid., p. 20.
16 Alexandra Hennessy Olsen, 'Gender Roles', in Bjork and Niles (eds), *A Beowulf Handbook* (1997), pp. 312–13.
17 Ibid., 314.
18 Ibid., 317.
19 Ogilvy and Baker (1993), pp. 159–60.
20 Ibid., p. 165.
21 Ibid., p. 12.
22 Ibid., p. 41.
23 Ibid., p. 23.
24 Ibid., p. 45.
25 Ibid., p. 95.
26 Ibid., pp. 11–12.
27 Ibid., p. 27.
28 Ibid., pp. 72–3.
29 Ibid., p. 19.
30 Ibid., p. 22.
31 Ibid., p. 22.
32 Ibid., pp. 180–1.

33 Fred C. Robinson, 'Teaching the Backgrounds: History, Religion, Culture', in J.B. Bessinger and R.F. Yeager (eds), *Approaches to Teaching Beowulf* (New York: Modern Language Association, 1984), p. 118.

34 Robinson (1984), p. 122.

35 Bernard Huppé, *The Hero in the Earthly City* (Binghamton: SUNY Binghamton Press, 1984), p. ix.

36 Ibid., p. ix.

37 Ibid., p. 89.

38 Ibid., p. 96.

39 Ibid., p. 25.

40 Ibid., p. 25.

41 Ibid., p. 97.

42 Fred C. Robinson, *Beowulf and the Appositive Style* (Konxville: University of Tennessee Press, 1987), p. 3.

43 Ibid., p. 22.

44 Ibid., p. 24.

45 Ibid., pp. 72–3.

46 Ibid., p. 11.

47 Ibid., p. 82.

48 Linda Georgianna, 'King Hrethel's Sorrow and the Limits of Heroic Action in *Beowulf*', *Speculum*, 62 (1987), pp. 829–30.

49 Ibid., p. 850.

50 Ibid., p. 848.

51 Stanley B. Greenfield, *Hero and Exile: The Art of Old English Poetry* (London: Hambledon, 1989), p. 89.

52 Ibid., p. 4.

53 Ibid., p. 17.

54 Ibid., p. 17.

Seven   An Embarrassment of Critical Riches: the 1990s to the present

1 Natalia Breizmann, '*Beowulf* as Romance: Literary Interpretation as Quest', *MLN*, 113:5 (December 1998), p. 1030.

2 Nicholas Howe, *Migration and Mythmaking in Anglo-Saxon England* (Notre Dame: University of Notre Dame Press, 1989), pp. xi–xii.

3 Ibid., p. 145.

4 Ibid., p. 176.

5 Ibid., pp. 176–7.

6 Ibid., p. 177.

7 Ibid., p. 179.

8 Ibid., p. 180.

9 Ibid., p. 162.

10 Ibid., p. 147.

11 Ibid., p. 162.

12 Ibid., p. 174.

13 Ibid., p. 164.

14 Gillian R. Overing and Marijane Osborn, *Landscape of Desire: Partial Stories of the Medieval Scandinavian World* (London: University of Minnesota Press, 1994), p. xv.

15 Ibid., p. 4.

16 Ibid., p. 2.

17 Ibid., p. 35.

18 Jonathan Wilcox (ed.) *Humour in Anglo-Saxon Literature* (Cambridge: D.S. Brewer, 2000), p. 7.

19 Raymond P. Tripp Jr., 'Humour, Wordplay, and Semantic Resonance in *Beowulf*', in Jonathan Wilcox (ed.), *Humour in Anglo-Saxon Literature* (Cambridge: D.S. Brewer, 2000), p. 55.

20 Ibid., p. 60.

21 Ibid., p. 67.

22 Allen J. Frantzen, *Before the Closet: Same-sex Love from Beowulf to Angels in America* (London: University of Chicago Press, 1998), p. 7.

23 Ibid., p. 1.

24 Ibid., p. 3.

25 Ibid., pp. 92–3.

26 Ibid., p. 95.

27 Ibid., p. 98.

28 Thelma Fenster, 'Why Men?', in Claire Lees (ed.), *Medieval Masculinities: Regarding Men in the Middle Ages* (Minneapolis: University of Minnesota Press, 2006), p. ix.

29 Fenster (2006), p. x.

30 Claire Lees (ed.), *Medieval Masculinities: Regarding Men in the Middle Ages* (Minneapolis: University of Minnesota Press, 2006), p. xv.

31 Ibid., p. 129.

32 Jane Chance, 'The Structural Unity of *Beowulf*: The Problem of Grendel's Mother', in Helen Damico and Alexandra Hennessey (eds), *New Readings on Women in Old English Literature* (Bloomington: Indiana University Press, 1990), p. 249.

33 Ibid., p. 255.

34 Ibid., pp. 257–8.

35 Gillian R. Overing, 'Gender and Interpretation in *Beowulf*', in Peter S. Baker (ed.), *The Beowulf Reader* (New York: Garland Publishing, 2000), p. 220.

36 Ibid., p. 220.

37 Ibid., p. 226.

38 Ibid., p. 222.

39 Fred C. Robinson, 'Teaching the Backgrounds: History, Religion, Culture', in J.B. Bessinger and R.F. Yeager (eds), *Approaches to Teaching Beowulf* (New York: Modern Language Association, 1984), pp. 218–19.

40 Henrietta Leyser, *Medieval Women: A Social History of Women in England, 450–1500* (London: Phoenix Press, 2002), p. 55.

41 Ibid., p. 56.

42 Ibid., p. 57.

43 James W. Earl, *Thinking about Beowulf* (Stanford: Stanford University Press, 1994), p. viii.

44 Ibid., p. viii.

45 Ibid., p. 47.

46 Ibid., p. 121.

47 Ibid., p. 50.

48 Ibid., p. 131.

49 Mary Clayton, 'Constructing Identities: Angles, Angels and English', an inaugural lecture delivered at Trinity College Dublin (April 2002), p. 14.

50 Breizmann (1998), p. 1022.

51 Ibid., p. 1022.

52 G.T. Shepherd, '*Beowulf*: An Epic Fairy-Tale', in Boris Ford (ed.), *The New Pelican Guide to English Literature, Vol. 1: Medieval Literature* (London: Penguin, 1984), p. 92.

53 Breizmann (1998), p. 1022.

54 Ibid., p. 1022.

55 Ibid., pp. 1022–3.

56 James W. Earl, '*Beowulf* and the Origins of Civilization', in Allen J. Frantzen (ed.), *Speaking Two Languages: Traditional Disciplines and Contemporary Theory on Medieval Studies* (Albany: SUNY Press, 1991), p. 68.

57 Breizmann (1998), p. 1024.

58 Ibid., p. 1029.

59 Ibid., p. 1033.

60 Seth Lerer, 'Grendel's Glove', *ELH*, 61:4 (winter, 1994), p. 723.

61 Breizmann (1998), p. 1027.

62 Lerer (1994), p. 721.

63 Ibid., p. 735.

64 Ibid., pp. 721; 742–3.

65 Gale R. Owen-Crocker, *The Four Funerals in Beowulf* (Manchester: Manchester University Press, 2000), p. 1.

66 Ibid., p. 1.

67 Ibid., p. 218.

68 Ibid., p. 227.

69 Ibid., p. 226.

70 Eileen A. Joy and Mary K. Ramsey (eds), *The Postmodern Beowulf* (Morgantown: West Virginia University Press, 2006), p. xiv.

71 Ibid., p. xv.

72 Seth Lerer, 'Hrothgar's Hilt and the Reader in *Beowulf*', in Ramsey and Joy (2006), p. 589.

73 Chris Jones, *Strange Likeness: The Use of Old English in Twentieth-Century Poetry* (Oxford: Oxford University Press, 2006), p. 3.

74 Breizmann (1998), p. 1033.

75 James W. Earl, 'Reading *Beowulf* with Original Eyes', in Mary K. Ramsey and Eileen A. Joy (eds), *The Post-Modern Beowulf* (Morgantown: West Virginia University Press, 2006), pp. 691–2.

Eight   *Beowulf* in Popular Culture

1 Michael Livingston and John William Sutton, 'Reinventing the Hero: Gardner's Grendel and the Shifting Face of Beowulf in Popular Culture', *Studies in Popular Culture,* 29 (2006), pp. 1–2.

2 Ibid., p. 2.

3 Ibid., pp. 3–4.

4 John Gardner, *Grendel* (New York: Knopf, 1971), p. 31.

5 Joseph D. Andriano, *Immortal Monster: The Mythological Evolution of the Fantastic Beast in Modern Fiction and Film* (Westfield, Con.: Greenwood Press, 1999), p. 121.

6 Gardner (1971), p. 31.

7 Ibid., p. 48.

8 Allen J. Frantzen, ' "Hrothgar Built Roads": Grendel's Ride in LA', *Old English Newsletter*, 39 (2006), pp. 29–30.

9 Kim Newman, '*The 13th Warrior*', *Sight and Sound*, 9 (1999), p. 57.

10 Michael Crichton, *The Eaters of the Dead* (New York: Knopf, 1976), p. 1.

11 Livingston and Sutton (2006), pp. 4–5.

12 H.P. Lovecraft, *Supernatural Horror in Literature* (New York, NY: Dover Publications, 1973), p. 11.

13 Livingston and Sutton (2006), pp. 4–5.

14 Ibid., p. 5.

15 Hugh Magennis, 'Michael Crichton, Ibn Fahdlan, Fantasy Cinema: Beowulf at the Movies', *Old English Newsletter*, 35:1 (2001), p. 35.

16 Ibid., p. 34.

17 Ibid., p. 35.

18 Ibid., p. 35.

19 Lisi Oliver, 'Banner Year for Beowulf on the Boards', *Old English Newsletter*, 39:3 (2006), p. 22.

20 Ibid., p. 22.

21 Ibid., p. 22.

22 Frantzen (2006), p. 27.

23 Ibid., p. 27.

24 Ibid., p. 31.

25 Oliver (2006), p. 26.

26 Burnett C. Tuthill, 'Howard Hanson', *The Musical Quarterly*, 22:2 (1936), p. 147.

27 Howard Hanson, 'Lament for Beowulf'in Robert Stephen Hines (ed.), *The Composer's Point of View: Essays on Twentieth-century Choral Music by Those Who Wrote it* (Santa Barbara: Greenwood, 1980), p. 15.

28 William Morris and A.J. Wyatt, *The Tale of Beowulf* (London: Kelmscott Press, 1895), pp. 273–4.

29 Tuthill (1936), 143.

30 Ibid., 144.

31 Hanson (1980), p. 16.

32 Leo Treitler, *With Voice and Pen: Coming to Know Medieval Song and How it was Made* (Oxford: Oxford University Press, 2003), p. xii.

33 Sam Barrett, 'Performing Medieval Music', *Journal of the Royal Musical Association*, 130:1 (2005), p. 123.

34 Benjamin Bagby, '*Beowulf,* the *Edda* and the Performance of Medieval Epic: Notes from the Workshop of a Reconstructed "Singer of Tales"', in Evelyn Birge Vitz, Nancy Freeman Regalado, and Marilyn Lawrence (eds), *Performing Medieval Narrative* (Cambridge: D.S. Brewer, 2005), pp. 181–92.

35 Benjamin Bagby, 'Programme Notes', presented by the Edinburgh Festival Society (2007), unnumbered.

36 Ibid.

37 Joseph McLellan, 'Sequentia's Medieval Magic', *The Washington Post* (5 October 1987), p. B10.

38 Martha Driver, 'Teaching the Middle Ages on Film: Visual Narrative and the Historical Record', *History Compass*, 5:1 (2007), p. 167.

39 Magennis (2001), p. 34.

40 Ibid., p. 34.

41 Ibid., p. 34.

42 Newman (1999), p. 57.

43 Lovecraft (1973), pp. 6–7.

44 Andriano (1999), p. 111.

45 Ibid., p. 111.

46 Magennis (2001), p. 34.

47 Newman (1999), p. 57.

48 Ibid., p. 57.

49 Magennis (2001), p. 36.

50 Newman (1999), p. 57.

51 Martha Driver, '"Stond and Delyver": Teaching the Medieval Movie', in Martha Driver and Sid Ray (eds) *The Medieval Hero on Screen: From Beowulf to Buffy* (London: McFarland, 2004), p. 211.

52 John M. Ganim, 'The Hero in the Classroom', in Driver and Ray (2004), p. 243.

53 Carl James Grindley, 'The Hagiography of Steel: The Hero's Weapon and its Place in Pop Culture', in Driver and Ray (2004), p. 160.

54 Ibid., p. 161.

55 Crichton (1976), p. 61.

56 Grindley (2004), p. 161.

57 Ibid., p. 161.

58 Newman (1999), p. 57.

59 Magennis (2001), p. 35.

60 Newman (1999), p. 57.

61 William Sutton, *Beowulfiana: Modern Adaptations of* Beowulf, *http://www.library.rochester. edu/camelot/BeowulfBooklet.htm#4.6.*

62 Driver (2004), p. 211.

63 William Wisher and Warren Lewis, *The Eaters of the Dead*, Revised Draft (March 1991). http://eaters.ifrance.com/screenplay.htm.

64 Driver (2004), p. 211.

65 Neil Gaiman and Roger Avary, *Beowulf: The Script Book* (London: Harper, 2007), p. 10.

66 Andrew R. Berzins, 'The Challenge of an Adaptation' (August 2004), http://www. beowulfandgrendel.com/site/pages.html.

67 John Aberth, *A Knight and the Movies: Medieval History on Film* (New York: Routledge, 2003), p. vii.

68 Todd McCarthy, 'Beowulf and Grendel', *Variety* (17–23 October 2005), p. 48.

69 Bill Gallo, 'The Blood of a Poem: Icelandic Director Gives *Beowulf* the Monty Python treatment', *The Village Voice* (27 June 2006), http://www.villagevoice.com/2006-06-27/ film/the-blood-of-a-poem/.

70 Wally Hammond, 'Beowulf', *Time Out* (14 Nov 2007), p. 72.

71 Gaiman and Avary (2007), p. 6.

72 Ibid., p. 5.

73 Ibid., pp. 5–6.

74 Ibid., p. 6.

75 Ibid., p. 10.

76 Peter Bradshaw, ' "Oi, dragon. Over 'ere!": Ray Winstone is buff, sleek and totally unrec-ognisable as Beowulf in this wildly silly CGI epic', *Guardian* (16 November 2007), p. 9.

77 Berzins (2004).

78 Manhola Dargis, 'Beowulf and Grendel', *The New York Times* (7 July 2006), p. 16.

79 Richard North, 'Poetry in Motion?', *Time Out* (14 November 2007), p. 70.

80 Bradshaw (2007), p. 9.

81 Andrew Osmond, 'Beowulf', *Sight and Sound*, 1 (2008), p. 61.

82 Gaiman and Avary (2007), p. 1.

83 Ibid., pp. 6–8.

84 McCarthy (2005), p. 48.

85 Sturla Gunnarsson, 'Production Notes' (2005), http://www.beowulfandgrendel.com/ site/pages.html.

86 Ibid.

87 Berzins (2004).

88 North (2007), p. 70.

89 Berzins (2004).

90 Gaiman and Avary (2007), pp. 55–6.

91 Osmond (2008), p. 61.

92 Michael Morpurgo, 'Children's Author Michael Morpurgo on *Beowulf*', *Guardian* (20 November 2007a), p. 29.

93 Mark Cotta Vaz and Steve Starkey, *The Art of Beowulf* (New York: Pocket Books, 2007), p. 9.

94 John Boorman, *Adventures of a Suburban Boy* (London: Faber, 2003), p. 179.

95 Ibid., p. 179.

96 Gaiman and Avary (2007), p. 139.

97 Ibid., p. 139.

98 Osmond (2008), p. 61.

99 Ibid., p. 61.

100 Ibid., p. 61.
101 Morpurgo (2007a), p. 29.
102 Ibid., p. 29.
103 Hammond (2007), p. 72.
104 Dargis (2006), p. 16.
105 Ibid., p. 16.
106 North (2007), p. 70.
107 Ibid., p. 70.
108 Rosemary Sutcliff, *Beowulf: Dragonslayer* (London: Bodley Head, 1961), p. 93.
109 Sameer Rahim and Toby Clements, 'Younger Readers and Upwards', *The Daily Telegraph* (5 January 2008), p. 32.
110 Rahim and Clements (2008), p. 32.
111 Michael Morpurgo, *Beowulf* (London: Walker Books, 2007b), pp. 7–8.
112 Charles McGrath, 'Untitled', *The New York Times* (17 June 2007), p. 17.
113 Morpurgo (2007b), p. 10.
114 Gareth Hinds, *Beowulf* (Somerville, Mass.: Candlewick Press, 2007), unnumbered.
115 Michael Uslan, *Beowulf: Dragon Slayer*, DC Comics, issue 1 (1975), unnumbered.
116 Ibid.
117 Ibid.
118 Vaz and Starkey (2007), p. 9.
119 Uslan, issue 1 (1975), unnumbered.
120 Ibid.
121 Michael Uslan, *Beowulf: Dragon Slayer*, DC Comics, issue 2 (1975), unnumbered.
122 Vaz and Starkey (2007), p. 9.
123 Stefan Petrucha and Kody Chamberlain, *Beowulf* (London: Harper Trophy, 2007), p. 95.
124 McGrath (2007), p. 17.
125 Ibid., p. 17.
126 Ibid., p. 17.
127 Comixology, 'Episode 6: Grendel with Matt Wagner' (19 November 2007), http://www.comixology.com/podcasts/7/Grendel-with-Matt-Wagner.

Conclusion

1 Andy Orchard, *A Critical Companion to Beowulf* (Cambridge: D.S. Brewer, 2003), p. 265.
2 Ibid., p. 267.
3 Natalia Breizmann, '*Beowulf* as Romance: Literary Interpretation as Quest', *MLN*, 113:5 (December 1998), p. 1033.

Select Bibliography

EDITIONS

Chickering, Howell D. *Beowulf: Parallel Text*. New York: Doubleday and Co., 1975. An indispensable parallel text edition for readers of *Beowulf* who know little, or no, Old English.

Dobbie, Elliot van Kirk. *Beowulf and Judith*. The Anglo-Saxon Poetic Records, no. 4. New York: Columbia University Press. Along with Klaeber, this edition is considered to be of major scholarly importance.

Jack, George. *Beowulf: A Student Edition*. Oxford: Oxford University Press, 1994. Student-friendly edition with excellent side glosses and glossary which may eventually supersede Klaeber.

Klaeber, Friedrich. *Beowulf and The Fight at Finnsburg*. Boston: Heath, 1922. Has long been considered by scholars to be the definitive edition of the poem.

Swanton, Michael. *Beowulf*. Manchester: Manchester University Press, 1997. Contains a wide range of explanatory notes and a prose translation facing the text.

TRANSLATIONS

Alexander, Michael. *Beowulf: A Verse Translation*. London: Penguin Classics, 2003. This now classic translation is ambitious and faithful to the original in equal measure.

Crossley-Holland, Kevin. *Beowulf* (Oxford World's Classics). London: Oxford Paperbacks, 1999. This highly acclaimed translation is accompanied by a critical introduction and a comprehensive editorial apparatus.

Donaldson, Ethelbert Talbot. *Beowulf*. New York: Norton, 1966. An accurate, faithful to the original and very readable prose translation which is widely available.

Heaney, Seamus. *Beowulf: Verse Translation*. London: Faber, 2007. Highly acclaimed since its original publication in 1999. One of the best of the available verse translations of *Beowulf*.

Morgan, Edwin. *Beowulf: A Verse Translation into Modern English*. Manchester: Carcanet, 2002. Originally done in the 1940s, this remains one of the best and most interesting verse translations of the Old English epic.

WORKS BASED ON *BEOWULF*

Crichton, Michael. *The Eaters of the Dead*. New York: Knopf, 1976.

Gardner, John. *Grendel*. New York: Knopf, 1971.

Harris, John. *The Geat: The Story of Beowulf and Grendel*. Chelmsford: notreallybooks, 2007.

Hinds, Gareth. *Beowulf*. Somerville, Mass.: Candlewick Press, 2007.

Hutchison, David. *Biowulf*. San Antonio: Antarctic Press, 2007.

Morpurgo, Michael. *Beowulf*. London: Walker Books, 2007.

Petrucha, Stefan and Chamberlain, Kody. *Beowulf*. London: Harper Trophy, 2007.

Sutcliff, Rosemary. *Beowulf: Dragonslayer*. London: The Bodley Head, 1961, p. 93.

Uslan, Michael. *Beowulf: Dragon Slayer*. DC Comics. Issues 1–6, 1975–6.

Wagner, Matt. *Grendel*. Milwaukie, OR: Dark Horse: 2007.

Wagner, Matt. *Grendel: Devil by the Deed*. Milwaukie, Oreg.: Dark Horse, 2007.

ESSAYS AND ARTICLES

Acker, Paul. 'Horror and the Maternal in *Beowulf*'. *PMLA*, 121:3 (2006), pp. 702–16.

Barrett, Sam. 'Performing Medieval Music'. *Journal of the Royal Musical Association*, 130:1 (2005), pp. 119–35.

Bennett, Helen. 'The Female Mourner at Beowulf's Funeral: Filling in the Blanks/Hearing the Spaces'. *Exemplaria*, 4 (1992), pp. 35–50.

Blackburn, Francis Adelbert. 'The Christian Coloring in the *Beowulf*'. *PMLA*, 12 (1897). pp. 205–25.

Blomfield, Joan. 'The Style and Structure of *Beowulf*'. *The Review of English Studies*, 14 (1938), pp. 396–403.

Bloomfield, Morton W. 'Beowulf and Christian Allegory: An Interpretation of Unferth'. *Traditio*, 7 (1949–51), pp. 410–15.

Bonjour, Adrien. 'The Use of Anticipation in *Beowulf*'. *The Review of English Studies*, 14:63 (1940), pp. 290–9.

Bonjour, Adrien. 'Grendel's Dam and the Composition of *Beowulf*'. *English Studies*, 30 (1949), pp. 113–24.

Bonjour, Adrien. 'Beowulf and the Beasts of Battle'. *PMLA*, 72:4 (September 1957), pp. 563–73.

Bradshaw, Peter. '"Oi, dragon. Over 'ere!": Ray Winstone is buff, sleek and totally unrecognisable as Beowulf in this wildly silly CGI epic'. *The Guardian* (16 November 2007), p. 9.

Breizmann, Natalia. '*Beowulf* as Romance: Literary Interpretation as Quest'. *MLN*, 113:5 (December 1998), pp. 1022–35.

Brown, Carleton. '*Beowulf* and the *Blickling Homilies* and Some Textual Notes'. *PMLA*, 53:4 (December 1938), pp. 905–16.

Brunner, Karl 'Why Was *Beowulf* Preserved?'. *Études Anglaises*, 7 (1954), pp. 1–5.

Carlson, Signe. 'The Monsters of *Beowulf*: Creations of Literary Scholars'. *The Journal of American Folklore*, 80:318 (October–December 1967), pp. 357–64.

Chapman, Robert L. 'Alas, Poor Grendel'. *College English*, 17 (1956), pp. 334–7.

Clover, Carol J. 'Regardless of Sex: Men, Women and Power in Early Northern Europe'. *Speculum*, 68:2 (1993), pp. 363–87.

Cohen, Henning. '*Beowulf*, 86–92'. *Explicator*, 16 (1958), Item 40.

Cook, Albert S. 'The Possible Begetter of the Old English *Beowulf* and *Widsith*'. *The Transactions of the Connecticut Academy of Arts and Sciences*, 25 (April, 1922), pp. 281–346.

Cooley, Frank. 'Early Danish Criticism of *Beowulf*'. *ELH: A Journal of English Literary History*, 7:1 (March 1940), pp. 45–67.

Dargis, Manhola. 'Beowulf and Grendel'. *The New York Times* (7 July 2006), p. 16.

Driver, Martha. 'Teaching the Middle Ages on Film: Visual Narrative and the Historical Record'. *History Compass*, 5: 1 (2007) pp. 159–74.

Earl, James W. 'The Role of the Men's Hall in the Development of the Anglo-Saxon Superego'. *Psychiatry*, 46 (May, 1983), pp. 139–60.

Emerson, Oliver. 'Legends of Cain, Especially in Old and Middle English'. *PMLA*, 21 (1906) pp. 831–929.

Frantzen, Allen J. '"Hrothgar Built Roads": Grendel's Ride in LA'. *Old English Newsletter*, 39 (2006), pp. 29–30.

Gang, T.M. 'Approaches to *Beowulf*'. *The Review of English Studies*, 3:9 (January 1952), pp. 1–12.

Georgianna, Linda. 'King Hrethel's Sorrow and the Limits of Heroic Action in *Beowulf*'. *Speculum*, 62 (1987), pp. 829–50.

Hagen, Sivert N. 'Classical Names and Stories in *Beowulf*'. *Modern Language Notes*, 19:3/4 (March–April, 1904), pp. 65–74.

Hammond, Wally. 'Beowulf'. *Time Out* (14 Nov 2007), p. 72.

Haruta, Setsuko. 'The Women in *Beowulf*'. *Poetica*, 23 (1986), 1–15.

Helterman, Jeffrey. '*Beowulf*: The Archetype Enters History'. *ELH*, 35:1 (March 1968), 1–20.

Hume, Kathryn. 'The Concept of the Hall in Old English Poetry'. *ASE*, 3 (1974), pp. 62–74.

Irving, Edward B. Jr. 'Ealuscerwen: Wild Party at Heorot'. *Tennessee Studies in Literature*, 12 (1967), pp. 161–8.

Kiessling, Nicolas K. 'Grendel: A New Aspect'. *Modern Philology*, 65:3 (February 1968), pp. 191–201.

Klaeber, Friedrich. 'The Christian Elements in *Beowulf*'. *Subsidia*, 24 (1996), pp. 1–89.

Kliman, Bernice. 'Women in Early English Literature, *Beowulf* to the "Ancrene Wisse"'. *Nottingham Medieval Studies*, 21 (1977), pp. 32–49.

Lawrence, W.W. 'Some Disputed Questions in *Beowulf* Criticism'. *PMLA*, 24 (1909), pp. 220–73.

Lawrence, W.W. 'The Haunted Mere in *Beowulf*'. *PMLA*, 27 (1912), pp. 208–45.

Lerer. Seth. 'Grendel's Glove'. *ELH*, 61:4 (winter, 1994), pp. 721–51.

Leyerle, J. 'Beowulf the Hero and the King'. *Medium Aevum*, 34 (1965), pp. 89–102.

Livingston, Michael and Sutton, John William. 'Reinventing the Hero: Gardner's *Grendel* and the Shifting Face of Beowulf in Popular Culture'. *Studies in Popular Culture*, 29 (2006), pp. 1–16.

Lindqvist, Sune. 'Sutton Hoo and Beowulf'. *Antiquity*, 22:87 (1948), pp. 131–40.

McCarthy, Conor. 'Language and History in Seamus Heaney's *Beowulf*'. *English*, 50:197 (summer 2001), p. 149.

McCarthy, Todd. 'Beowulf and Grendel'. *Variety* (17–23 October 2005), p. 48.

McGrath, Charles. 'Untitled'. *New York Times* (17 June 2007). p. 17.

McLellan, Joseph. 'Sequentia's Medieval Magic'. *The Washington Post* (5 October 1987), p. B10.

Magennis, Hugh. 'Michael Crichton, Ibn Fadlan, Fantasy Cinema: Beowulf at the Movies'. *Old English Newsletter*, 35:1 (2001), pp. 34–8.

Malone, Kemp. 'Hygd'. *Modern Language Notes*, 56:5 (May 1941), pp. 356–8.

Malone, Kemp. 'Freawaru'. *Journal of English Literary History*, 7:1 (March 1943), pp. 39–44.

Malone, Kemp. 'Hildeburg and Hengest'. *Journal of English Literary History*, 10:4 (December 1943), pp. 257–84.

Morpurgo, Michael. 'Children's Author Michael Morpurgo on *Beowulf*'. *Guardian* (20 November 2007), p. 29.

Mustanoja, Tauno F. 'The Unnamed Woman's Song of Mourning over Beowulf and the Tradition of Ritual Lamentation'. *Neuphilologische Mitteilungen*, 48:1 (1967), pp. 1–27.

Newman, Kim. '*The 13th Warrior*'. *Sight and Sound*, 9 (1999), p. 57.

Niles, John D. 'Locating *Beowulf* in Literary History'. *Exemplaria*, 5 (March 1993), pp. 79–109.

Niles, John D. 'Understanding *Beowulf*: Oral Poetry Acts'. *The Journal of American Folklore*, 106:420 (spring, 1993), pp. 131–55.

North, Richard. 'Poetry in Motion?' *Time Out* (14 November 2007), p. 70.

Oliver, Lisi. 'Banner Year for Beowulf on the Boards'. *Old English Newsletter*, 39:3 (2006), pp. 22–6.

Onians, R.B. 'Review of *A Comparative Study of the Beowulf and the Aeneid* by Tom Burns Haber'. *The Classical Review*, 47:5 (November 1933), pp. 200–1.

Opland, Jeff. '*Beowulf* on the Poet'. *Medieval Studies*. 38 (1976), pp. 442–67.

Osborn, Marijane. 'The Great Feud: Scriptural History and Strife in *Beowulf*'. *PMLA*, 93 (1978), pp. 973–81.

Osmond, Andrew. 'Beowulf'. *Sight and Sound*, 1 (2008), p. 61.

Philpotts, Bertha S. 'Wyrd and Providence in Anglo-Saxon Thought'. *Essays and Studies by Members of the English Association*, 13 (1928), Caroline F.E. Spurgeon (ed). Oxford, Clarendon Press, pp. 7–27.

Prescott, Andrew. 'The Electronic *Beowulf* and Digital Restoration'. *Literary and Linguistic Computing* 12 (1997), pp. 185–95.

Rahim, Sameer and Clements, Toby. 'Younger Readers and Upwards'. *The Daily Telegraph* (5 January 2008), p. 32.

Robinson, Fred C. 'Is Wealhþeow a Prince's Daughter?'. *ES*, 45 (1964), pp. 36–9.

Thormann, Janet. '*Beowulf and* the Enjoyment of Violence'. *Literature and Psychology*, 43:1–2 (1997), pp. 65–76.

Tuthill, Burnett C. 'Howard Hanson'. *The Musical Quarterly*, 22:2 (1936), pp. 140–53.

Van Meurs, J.C. '*Beowulf* and Literary Criticism'. *Neophilologus*, 39 (1955), pp. 114–30.

Woolf, Henry Bosley. 'On the Characterisation of Beowulf'. *Journal of English Literary History*, 15:2 (June 1948), pp. 85–92.

CHAPTERS IN BOOKS

Bagby, Benjamin. '*Beowulf,* the *Edda* and the Performance of Medieval Epic: Notes from the Workshop of a Reconstructed "Singer of Tales" '. Evelyn Birge Vitz, Nancy Freeman Regalado, and Marilyn Lawrence (eds), *Performing Medieval Narrative*. Cambridge: D.S. Brewer, 2005. pp. 181–92.

Baum, Paul F. 'The *Beowulf* Poet'. Lewis E. Nicholson (ed.) *An Anthology of Beowulf Criticism*. Notre Dame: Notre Dame University Press, 1963. pp. 353–65.

Benson, Larry D. 'The Pagan Coloring of *Beowulf*'. R.P. Creed (ed.) *Old English Poetry: Fifteen Essays*. Providence, R.I.: Brown University Press, 1967. pp. 193–213.

Benson, Larry D. 'The Originality of *Beowulf*'. Morton W. Bloomfield (ed.) *The Interpretation of Narrative: Theory and Practice*. Cambridge: Harvard University Press, 1970. pp. 1–43.

Bonjour, Adrien. 'Jottings on *Beowulf* and the Aesthetic Approach'. R.P. Creed (ed.) *Old English Poetry: Fifteen Essays*. Providence, R.I.: Brown University Press, 1967. pp. 179–91.

Chadwick, Nora. 'The Monsters and Beowulf'. Peter Clemoes (ed.) *The Anglo-Saxons: Studies in Some Aspects of the History and Culture Presented to Bruce Dickins*. London: Bowes, 1959. pp. 171–203.

Chambers, Raymond Wilson. '*Beowulf* and the Heroic Age'. *Beowulf Translated into Modern English Rhyming Verse*. London: Constable, 1925. p. 12.

Chambers, Raymond Wilson. '*Beowulf* and the "Heroic Age" in England'. In R.W. Chambers, *Man's Unconquerable Mind*. London: Cape, 1939. pp. 53–69.

Chance, Jane. 'The Structural Unity of *Beowulf*: the Problem of Grendel's Mother'. Helen Damico and Alexandra Hennessey Olsen (eds) *New Readings on Women in Old English Literature*. Bloomington: Indiana University Press, 1990. pp. 248–61.

Dockray-Miller, Mary. 'Beowulf's Tears of Fatherhood'. Mary K. Ramsey and Eileen A. Joy (eds) *The Post-Modern Beowulf*. Morgantown: West Virginia University Press, 2006. pp. 439–66.

Donahue, Charles. 'Potlatch and Charity: Notes on the Heroic in *Beowulf*'. Lewis Nicholson and Dolores Warwick Frese (eds) *Anglo-Saxon Poetry: Essays in Appreciation*. Notre Dame: University of Notre Dame Press, 1975. pp. 23–40.

Driver, Martha. ' "Stond and Delyver": Teaching the Medieval Movie'. Martha Driver and Sid Ray (eds) *The Medieval Hero on Screen: From Beowulf to Buffy*. London: McFarland, 2004. pp. 211–16.

Earl, James W. '*Beowulf* and the Origins of Civilization'. Allen J. Frantzen (ed.) *Speaking Two Languages: Traditional Disciplines and Contemporary Theory on Medieval Studies*. Albany: SUNY Press, 1991. pp. 65–89.

Earl, James W. 'Reading *Beowulf* with Original Eyes'. Mary K. Ramsey and Eileen A. Joy (eds) *The Post-Modern Beowulf*. Morgantown: West Virginia University Press, 2006. pp. 587–704.

Fenster, Thelma. 'Why Men?' Claire Lees (ed.) *Medieval Masculinities: Regarding Men in the Middle Ages*. Minneapolis: University of Minnesota Press, 2006. pp. ix–xiv.

Ganim, John M. 'The Hero in the Classroom'. Martha Driver and Sid Ray (eds) *The Medieval Hero on Screen: From Beowulf to Buffy*. London: McFarland, 2004. pp. 237–50.

Gardner, John. 'Guilt and the World's Complexity: The Murder of Ongentheow and the Slaying of the Dragon'. Lewis Nicholson and Dolores Warwick Frese (eds) *Anglo-Saxon Poetry: Essays in Appreciation*. Notre Dame: University of Notre Dame Press, 1975. pp. 14–22.

Greenfield, Stanley B. 'The Authenticating Voice in *Beowulf*'. Peter Clemoes (ed.) *Anglo-Saxon England 5*. Cambridge: Cambridge University Press, 1976. pp. 51–62.

Grindley, Carl J. 'The Hagiography of Steel: The Hero's Weapon and its Place in Pop Culture'. Martha Driver and Sid Ray (eds) *The Medieval Hero on Screen: From Beowulf to Buffy*. London: McFarland.

Hanson, Howard. 'Lament for Beowulf'. Hines, Robert Stephen (ed.) *The Composer's Point of View: Essays on Twentieth-century Choral Music by Those Who Wrote it*. Santa Barbara: Greenwood, 1980. pp. 14–21.

Kaske, R.E. '*Sapientia et Fortitudo* as the Controlling Theme of *Beowulf*'. Lewis E. Nicholson (ed.) *An Anthology of Beowulf Criticism*. Notre Dame: Notre Dame University Press. 1963. pp. 269–310.

Kim, Susan M. 'As I Once Did With Grendel: Boasting and Nostalgia in *Beowulf*'. Mary K. Ramsey and Eileen A. Joy (eds) *The Post-Modern Beowulf*. Morgantown: West Virginia University Press, 2006. pp. 629–54.

Lees, Claire A. 'Men and *Beowulf*'. Claire Lees (ed.) *Medieval Masculinities: Regarding Men in the Middle Ages*. Minneapolis: University of Minnesota Press, 2006. pp. 129–48.

Lerer, Seth. '*Beowulf* and Contemporary Critical Theory'. Robert E. Bjork and John D. Niles (eds) *A Beowulf Handbook*. Exeter: Exeter University Press, 1997. pp. 325–39.

Lerer, Seth. 'Hrothgar's Hilt and the Reader in *Beowulf*'. Mary K. Ramsey and Eileen A. Joy (eds) *The Post-Modern Beowulf*. Morgantown: West Virginia University Press, 2006. pp. 587–628.

Luecke, Janemarie. '*Wulf and Eadwacer*. Hints for Reading from *Beowulf* and Anthropology'. Martin Green (ed.) *The Old English Elegies*. Rutherford: Fairleigh Dickinson University Press, 1983. pp. 190–203.

McNamee, M.B. '*Beowulf* – An Allegory of Salvation?'. Lewis E. Nicholson (ed.) *An Anthology of Beowulf Criticism*. Notre Dame: Notre Dame University Press, 1963. pp. 331–52.

Malone, Kemp. 'Beowulf'. Lewis E. Nicholson (ed.) *An Anthology of Beowulf Criticism*. Notre Dame: Notre Dame University Press, 1963. pp. 137–54.

Osborn, Marijane. 'Translations, Versions, Illustrations'. Robert E. Bjork and John D. Niles (eds) *A Beowulf Handbook*. Exeter: Exeter University Press, 1997. pp. 325–40.

Olsen, Alexandra Hennessy. 'Women in *Beowulf*'. Jess B. Bessinger, Jr. and Robert F. Yeager (eds) *Approaches to Teaching Beowulf*. New York: MLA, 1984. pp. 150–6.

Olsen, Alexander Hennessy. 'Gender Roles'. Robert E. Bjork and John D. Niles (eds) *A Beowulf Handbook*. Exeter: Exeter University Press, 1997. pp. 311–24.

Overing, Gillian R. 'Gender and Interpretation in *Beowulf*'. Peter S. Baker (ed.) *The Beowulf Reader*. New York: Garland Publishing, 2000. pp. 219–60.

Prescott, Andrew. '"Their present miserable state of cremation": the Restoration of the Cotton Library'. C.J. Wright (ed.) *Sir Robert Cotton as Collector: Essays on an Early Stuart Courtier and his Legacy*. London: The British Library, 1997. pp. 391–454.

Roberts, Jane. 'Understanding Hrothgar's Humiliation: *Beowulf* lines 144–74 in Context'. Alastair Minnis and Jane Roberts (eds) *Text, Image, Interpretation: Studies in Anglo-Saxon Literature and its Insular Context in Honour of Éamonn Ó Carragáin*. Turnhout: Brepols Publishers, 2007. pp. 355–67.

Robinson, Fred C. 'Teaching the Background: History, Religion, Culture'. J.B. Bessinger and R.F. Yeager (eds) *Approaches to Teaching Beowulf*. New York: Modern Language Association, 1984. pp. 103–22.

Robinson, Fred C. 'Elements of the Marvellous in the Characterisation of Beowulf: A Reconsideration of Textual Evidence'. In F.C. Robinson, *The Tomb of Beowulf and other Essays on Old English*. Oxford: Blackwell, 1993. pp. 20–35.

Robinson, Fred C. 'Ezra Pound and the Old English Tradition'. In F.C. Robinson, *The Tomb of Beowulf and Other Essays on Old English*. Oxford: Blackwell, 1993. pp. 259–74.

Robinson, Fred C. 'The Prescient Woman in Old English Literature'. In F.C. Robinson, *The Tomb of Beowulf and other Essays on Old English* Oxford: Blackwell, 1993. pp. 155–63.

Rogers, H.L. 'Beowulf's Three Great Fights'. Lewis E. Nicholson (ed.) *An Anthology of Beowulf Criticism*. Notre Dame: Notre Dame University Press, 1963. pp. 233–56.

Schücking, Levin L. 'The Ideal of Kinship in *Beowulf*'. Lewis E. Nicholson (ed.) *An Anthology of Beowulf Criticism*. Notre Dame: Notre Dame University Press, 1963. pp. 35–49.

Shepherd, G.T. '*Beowulf*: An Epic Fairy-Tale'. Boris Ford (ed.) *The New Pelican Guide to English Literature, Vol. 1: Medieval Literature*. London: Penguin, 1984. pp. 85–96.

Thormann, Janet. 'Enjoyment of Violence and Desire for History in *Beowulf*'. Mary K. Ramsey and Eileen A. Joy (eds) *The Post-Modern Beowulf*. Morgantown: West Virginia University Press, 2006. pp. 287–318.

Tolkien, J.R.R. '*Beowulf*: The Monsters and the Critics'. Christopher Tolkien (ed.) *The Monsters and the Critics and Other Essays*. London: Harper Collins, 2006. pp. 5–48.

Tolkien, J.R.R. 'On Translating *Beowulf*'. Christopher Tolkien (ed.) *The Monsters and the Critics and Other Essays*. London: Harper Collins, 2006. pp. 49–71.

Tripp, Raymond P., Jr. 'Humour, Wordplay, and Semantic Resonance in *Beowulf*'. Jonathan Wilcox (ed.) *Humour in Anglo-Saxon Literature*. Cambridge: D.S. Brewer, 2000. pp. 49–69.

Wrenn, C.L. 'Sutton Hoo and Beowulf'. Lewis E. Nicholson (ed.) *An Anthology of Beowulf Criticism*. Notre Dame: Notre Dame University Press, 1963. pp. 311–30.

BOOKS

Aberth, John. *A Knight at the Movies: Medieval History on Film*. New York: Routledge, 2003.

Andriano, Joseph D. *Immortal Monster: The Mythological Evolution of the Fantastic Beast in Modern Fiction and Film*. Westfield, Con.: Greenwood Press, 1999.

Arnold, Thomas. *Beowulf: A Heroic Poem of the Eighth Century*. London: Longmans, Green and Co., 1876.

Baker, Peter S. (ed.) *Beowulf: Basic Readings*. New York: Garland, 1995.

Baker, Peter S. (ed.) *The Beowulf Reader*. New York: Garland, 2000.

Benzie, William. *Dr. F.J. Furnivall, Victorian Scholar Adventurer*. Norman, Okla: Pilgrim Books, 1983.

Bjork, Robert E. and Niles, John D. (eds) *A Beowulf Handbook*. Exeter: Exeter University Press, 1997.

Bloom, Harold. *Modern Critical Interpretations, Beowulf*. New York: Chelsea House, 1987.

Bolton, W.F. *Alcuin and Beowulf: An Eighth-Century View*. London: Edward Arnold, 1979.

Bonjour, Adrien. *The Digressions in Beowulf*. Oxford: Blackwell, 1950.

Bonjour, Adrien. *Twelve Beowulf Papers, 1940–1960*. Geneva: Librarie E. Droz, 1962.

Boorman, John. *Adventures of a Suburban Boy*. London: Faber, 2003.

Bradley, S.A.J. *Anglo-Saxon Poetry: An Anthology of Old English Poems*. London: Dent, 1982.

Brooke, Stopford A. *The History of Early English Literature, being the History of English Poetry from its Beginnings to the Accession of King Ælfred*. London: Macmillan, 1892.

Cable, Thomas. *The Meter and Melody of Beowulf*. Chicago: University of Illinois Press, 1974.

Carroll, Robert and Prickett, Stephen (eds) *The Bible: Authorized King James Version*. Oxford: Oxford University Press, 1998.

Chadwick, H. Munro. *The Heroic Age*. Cambridge: Cambridge University Press, 1912.

Chambers, Raymond Wilson. *Beowulf*. Cambridge: Cambridge University Press, 1921.

Chance, Jane. *Woman as Hero in Old English Literature*. Syracuse: Syracuse University Press, 1986.

Collins, John Churton. *The Study of English Literature: A Plea for its Recognition and Organization at the Universities*. London: Macmillan, 1891.

Cuddon, J.A. *The Penguin Dictionary of Literary Terms and Literary Theory*. London: Penguin, 1999.

Damico, Helen and Olsen, Alexandra Hennessey (eds) *New Readings on Women in Old English Literature*. Bloomington: Indiana University Press, 1990.

Earl, James W. *Thinking about Beowulf*. Stanford: Stanford University Press, 1994.

Earle, John. *Anglo-Saxon Literature*. London: Society for Promoting Christian Knowledge, 1884.

Earle, John. *The Deeds of Beowulf: An English Epic of the Eighth Century Done Into Modern Prose*. Oxford, 1892.

Frantzen, Allen J. *Before the Closet: Same-sex Love from Beowulf to Angels in America*. London: University of Chicago Press, 1998.

Fry, Donald K. (ed.) *The Beowulf Poet: A Collection of Critical Essays*. Englewood Cliffs, N.J.: Prentice-Hall, 1968.

Fulk, R.D. (ed.) *Interpretations of Beowulf: A Critical Anthology*. Bloomington: Indiana University Press, 1991.

Fulk, R.D. and Cain, Christopher M. *A History of Old English Literature*. Oxford: Blackwell, 2003.

Gaiman, Neil and Avary, Roger. *Beowulf: The Script Book*. London: Harper, 2007.

Girvan, Ritchie. *Beowulf and the Seventh Century: Language and Content*. London: Methuen, 1935.

Goldsmith, Margaret E. *The Mode and Meaning of 'Beowulf'*. London: The Athlone Press, 1970.

Greenfield, Stanley B. *Hero and Exile: The Art of Old English Poetry*. London: Hambledon, 1989.

Haarder, Andreas. *Beowulf: The Appeal of a Poem*. Viborg: Akademisk Forlag, 1975.

Haber, Tom Burns. *A Comparative Study of the Beowulf and the Aeneid*. Princeton: Princeton University Press, 1931.

Hall, John R. Clark. *Beowulf and the Finnesburg Fragment, A Translation into Modern English Prose*. London: Swan Sonnenschein, 1911.

Heusler, Andreas. *Die altgermanische Dichtung*, 2nd edn., Potsdam: Akademische Verlagsgellschaft Athenaion, 1943.

Howe, Nicholas. *Migration and Mythmaking in Anglo-Saxon England*. Notre Dame: University of Notre Dame Press, 1989.

Huppé, Bernard. *The Hero in the Earthly City*. Binghamton: SUNY Binghamton Press, 1984.

Irving, Edward.B. Jr. *A Reading of Beowulf*. New Haven: Yale University Press, 1968.

Jones, Chris. *Strange Likeness: The Use of Old English in Twentieth-Century Poetry*. Oxford: Oxford University Press, 2006.

Joy, Eileen A. and Ramsey, Mary K. (eds) *The Postmodern Beowulf*. Morgantown: West Virginia University Press, 2006.

Kemble, John Mitchell. *The Anglo-Saxon Poem of Beowulf*. London: W. Pickering, 1833–7.

Ker, W.P. *The Dark Ages*. New York: Mentor Books, 1958.

Kiernan, Kevin S. *Beowulf and the Beowulf Manuscript*. 2nd Edition. New Brunswick: Rutgers University Press, 1984.

Kristeva, Julia. *Powers of Horror: An Essay on Abjection*. Editions du Seuil Pouvoirs de l'horreur, 1980. New York: Columbia University Press, 1982.

Lawrence, William Witherle. *Beowulf and Epic Tradition*. Cambridge, Mass.: Harvard University Press, 1928.

Lee, Alvin A. *The Guest-Hall of Eden: Four Essays on the Design of Old English Poetry*. New Haven: Yale University Press, 1972.

Leyser, Henrietta. *Medieval Women: A Social History of Women in England, 450–1500*. London: Phoenix Press, 2002.

Lovecraft, H.P. *Supernatural Horror in Literature*. New York: Dover, 1973.

MacCarthy, Fiona. *William Morris: A Life for Our Times*. London: Faber, 1994.

Minnis, Alastair and Roberts, Jane (eds) *Text, Image, Interpretation: Studies in Anglo-Saxon Literature and its Insular Context in Honour of Éamonn Ó Carragáin*. Turnhout: Brepols Publishers, 2007.

Morris, Richard. *The Blickling Homilies of the Tenth Century*. London: N. Trüber, Early English Text Society, 1880.

Morris, William and Wyatt, A.J. *The Tale of Beowulf*. London: Kelmscott Press, 1895.

Müllenhoff, Karl Victor. *Beowulf: Untersuchungen über das angelächsische Epos und die älteste Geschichte der germanischen Seevölker*. Berlin: 1889.

Nicholson, Lewis E. (ed.) *An Anthology of Beowulf Criticism*. Notre Dame: Notre Dame University Press, 1963.

Niles, John D. *Beowulf: The Poem and its Traditions*. Cambridge: Cambridge University Press, 1983.

Ogilvy, J.D.A and Baker, Donald C. *Reading Beowulf*. Norman: University of Oklahoma Press, 1993.

Orchard, Andy. *Pride and Prodigies: Studies in the Monsters of the Beowulf Manuscript*. Cambridge: D.S. Brewer, 1995.

Orchard, Andy. *A Critical Companion to Beowulf*. Cambridge: D.S. Brewer, 2003.

Overing, Gillian R. *Language, Sign and Gender in Beowulf*. Carbondale and Edwardsville: Southern Illinois University Press, 1990.

Overing, Gillian R. and Osborn Marijane. *Landscape of Desire: Partial Stories of the Medieval Scandinavian World*. London: University of Minnesota Press, 1994.

Owen-Crocker, Gale R. *The Four Funerals in Beowulf*. Manchester: Manchester University Press, 2000.

Rauer, Christine. *Beowulf and the Dragon: Parallels and Analogues*. Cambridge: D.S. Brewer, 2000.

Rebsamen, Frederick R. *Beowulf Is My Name: And Selected Translations of other Old English Poems*. San Francisco: Rinehart, 1971.

Robinson, Fred C. *Beowulf and the Appositive Style*. Knoxville: University of Tennessee Press, 1987.

Robinson, Fred C. *The Tomb of Beowulf and other Essays on Old English*. Oxford: Blackwell, 1993.

Schlauch, Margaret. *English Medieval Literature and its Social Foundations*. London: Oxford University Press, 1956.

Schrader, Richard J. *God's Handiwork: Images of Women in Early Germanic Literature*. Westport: Greenwood, 1983.

Short, Douglas. *Beowulf Scholarship: An Annotated Bibliography*. New York: Garland, 1980.

Sisam, Kenneth. *Studies in the History of Old English Literature*. Oxford: Clarendon Press, 1953.

Sisam, Kenneth. *The Structure of Beowulf*. Oxford: Clarendon Press, 1965.

Stanley, Eric Gerald. *In the Foreground: Beowulf*. Cambridge: D.S. Brewer, 1994.

Stjerna, Knut. *Essays On Questions Connected with the Old English Poem of Beowulf*. Coventry: Curtis & Beamish, 1912.

Swanton, Michael. *English Literature before Chaucer*. London: Longman, 1987.

Thorkelin, Grímur Jónsson. *De Danorum rebus secul. III and IV: poëma Danicum dialecto Anglo-Saxonica*. Havniae: Rangel, 1815.

Tillyard, E.M.W. *The English Epic and its Background*. London: Chatto and Windus, 1954.

Tolkien, Christopher (ed.) *The Monsters and the Critics and Other Essays*. London: Harper Collins, 2006.

Treitler, Leo. *With Voice and Pen: Coming to Know Medieval Song and How it was Made*. Oxford: Oxford University Press, 2003.

Turner, Sharon. *The History of The Manners, Landed Property, Government, Laws, Poetry, Literature, Religion, and Language, of the Anglo-Saxons*. London: Longman, Hunt, Rees, and Orme, 1805.

Vaz, Mark Cotta and Starkey, Steve. *The Art of Beowulf*. New York: Pocket Books, 2007.

Wanley, Humphrey. *Antiquae literaturae septentrionalis libri duo*. Oxford: Sheldonian, 1705.

White, Judy Anne. *Hero-Ego in Search of Self: A Jungian Reading of Beowulf*. New York: Lang: 2004.

Whitelock, Dorothy. *The Audience of Beowulf*. Oxford: Clarendon Press, 1951.

Wilcox, Jonathan (ed.) *Humour in Anglo-Saxon Literature*. Cambridge: D.S. Brewer, 2000.

Williams, David. *Cain and Beowulf; A Study in Secular Allegory*. London: University of Toronto Press, 1982.

Wrenn, C.L. (ed.) *Beowulf with the Finnesburg Fragment*. London: Harrap, 1953.

Wright, C.J. (ed.) *Sir Robert Cotton as Collector: Essays on an Early Stuart Courtier and his Legacy*. London: The British Library, 1997.

Wyatt, A.J. (ed.) *Beowulf: With the Finnsburg Fragment*. Cambridge: Cambridge University Press, 1914.

OTHERS

Bagby, Benjamin. 'Programme Notes'. Presented by the Edinburgh Festival Society (2007).

Clayton, Mary. 'Constructing Identities: Angles, Angels and English'. An inaugural lecture delivered at Trinity College Dublin (April 2002), p. 14.

INTERNET RESOURCES

Berzins, Andrew R. 'The Challenge of an Adaptation'. (August 2004), http://www. beowulfandgrendel.com/site/pages.html.

Comixology, 'Episode 6: Grendel with Matt Wagner'. (19 November 2007), http://www. comixology.com/podcasts/7/Grendel-with-Matt-Wagner.

Gallo, Bill.'The Blood of a Poem: Icelandic Director gives *Beowulf* the Monty Python Treatment'. *The Village Voice* (27 June 2006), http://www.villagevoice.com/2006-06-27/ film/the-blood-of-a-poem/.

Gunnarsson, Sturla. 'Production Notes'. (2005), http://www.beowulfandgrendel.com/site/ pages.html.

Prescott, Andrew. 'Beowulf Manuscript'. *The Electronic Beowulf Project*, http://penelope. uchicago.edu/~grout/encyclopaedia_romana/britannia/anglo-saxon/beowulf/vitellius. html.

Sutton, William. *Beowulfiana: Modern Adaptations of* Beowulf, http://www.library.rochester. edu/camelot/BeowulfBooklet.htm#4.6.

Wisher, William and Lewis, Warren. *The Eaters of the Dead*. Revised draft (March 1991), http://eaters.ifrance.com/screenplay.htm.

CD-ROM

Kiernan, Kevin (ed.) *Electronic Beowulf*, version 2. London: British Library Publications, 2003. In addition to interactive digital images of the *Beowulf* manuscript, this CD-ROM also includes early transcriptions of the manuscript, a glossarial index and an extensive bibliography.

FILMS

Beowulf (1973)
Production companies: Don Fairservice and The BFI Film Production Board.

Director: Don Fairservice.
Narrator: Richard Marquand.

Beowulf (animated version) (1998)
Production company: Christmas Films/Right Angle/SAC/BBC/HBO.
Director: Yuri Kulakov.
Screenplay: Murray Watts.
Principal voice cast: Derek Jacobi (Narrator); Joseph Fiennes (Beowulf); Timothy West (Hrothgar); Anna Calder-Marshall (Wealhtheow); Michael Sheen (Wiglaf).
Russia/UK/US, colour, 27 mins.

Beowulf (2007)
Production company: Image Movers/Shangri-La Entertainment.
Director: Robert Zemeckis.
Screenplay: Neil Gaiman and Roger Avary.
Principal cast: Ray Winstone (Beowulf); Anthony Hopkins (Hrothgar); John Malkovich (Unferth); Robin Wright-Penn (Wealhtheow); Brendon Gleeson (Wiglaf); Crispin Glover (Grendel); Angelina Jolie (Grendel's Mother).
US, colour, 114 mins.

Beowulf & Grendel (2005)
Production company: Movision/Darklight Films/Endgame Entertainment/Arclight Films/Beowulf Productions Limited/Film Works/Grendel Productions/Icelandic Film Corporation/Spice Factory/Téléfilm Canada/Union Station Media.
Director: Sturla Gunnarsson.
Screenplay: Andrew Rai Berzins.
Principal cast: Gerard Butler (Beowulf); Stellan Skarsgård (Hrothgar); Tony Curran (Hondscioh); Steinunn Ólína Thorsteinsdóttir (Weathlow); Sarah Polley (Selma); Ingvar E. Sigurdsson (Grendel).
Canada/UK/Iceland, colour, 103 mins.

The Creature from the Black Lagoon (1954)
Production company: Universal International Pictures.
Director: Jack Arnold.
Screenplay: Harry Essex, Arthur Ross, Maurice Zimm.
Principal Cast: Richard Carlson (Dr David Reed); Julia Adams (Kay Lawrence); Richard Denning (Dr Mark Williams); Antonio Moreno (Carl Maia).
US, black and white, 79 mins.

Grendel, Grendel, Grendel (1981)
Director: Alexander Stitt.
Screenplay: Alexander Stitt.
Principal cast: Peter Ustinov (Grendel).
Australia, colour, 88 Mins.

Predator (1987)
Director: John McTiernan.
Screenplay: Jim Thomas and John Thomas.
Principal cast: Arnold Schwarzenegger (Dutch); Carl Weathers (Dillon); Bill Duke (Mac); Jesse Ventura (Blain); Sonny Landham (Billy); Shane Black (Hawkins); Elpidia Carrillo (Anna); Kevin Peter Hall (The Predator).
US, colour, 107 mins.

The 13th Warrior (1999)
Director: John McTiernan (Michael Crichton, uncredited).

Screenplay: William Wisher Jr. and Warren Lewis.

Principal cast: Antonio Banderas (Ahmed Ibn Fahdlan); Vladmir Kulich (Buliwyf); Dennis Storhøi (Herger, the Joyous); Tony Curran (Weath, the Musician); Clive Russell (Helfdane, the Fat); Diana Venora (Queen Weilew); Sven Wollter (King Hrothgar); Omar Sharif (Melchisidek).

US, colour, 102 mins.

Index